YELLOW RAIN

YELLOW RAIN

A JOURNEY THROUGH THE TERROR OF CHEMICAL WARFARE

BY STERLING SEAGRAVE

M. EVANS AND COMPANY, INC.
NEW YORK

358.34
S

Excerpts from *The Third World War* reprinted with permission
of Macmillan Publishing Co., Inc. Copyright © 1978 by General
Sir John Hackett, Air Chief Marshal Sir John Barraclough, Sir
Bernard Burrow, Brigadier Kenneth Hunt, Vice-Admiral Sir Ian
McGeoch, Norman Macrae, and Major-General John Strawson

104650

Library of Congress Cataloging in Publication Data

Seagrave, Sterling.
  Yellow rain: a journey through the terror of chemical warfare.

  Bibliography: p.
  Includes index.
  1. Chemical warfare. 2. Biological warfare.
  I. Title.
  UG447.S37   358'34   81-12645

ISBN 0-87131-349-9   AACR2

M. Evans and Company, Inc.
216 East 49 Street
New York, New York 10017

Design by Diane Gedymin

Manufactured in the United States of America

9   8   7   6   5   4   3   2   1

To Jocelyn and Sean

Contents

1.

The "Bugs and Gas" Establishment

Denver's Stapleton International Airport is one of the busiest in America, with an endless queue of jets circling, landing, and taking off against the distant sawteeth of the Rocky Mountains. In the seat next to me as my plane made its landing approach in the autumn of 1980 was a five-year-old boy from New York City bound for a holiday exploring ancient Indian burial mounds in the southwestern deserts. He did not know, nor did his parents across the aisle, that at this moment we were practically flying over the most peculiar burial mound on earth, in the very suburbs of Denver. Just off the right wing tip, beginning at the exact edge of the airport and neatly demarcated by Interstate Highway 70 racing east-west and Interstate 80 pointing off to the northeast, was the place where the Pentagon keeps one of its most terrifying weapons secretly buried. This is Rocky Mountain Arsenal and, stacked like metal coffins or the eggs of warrior ants in sheds and neat rows over 250 acres of ground are 4.2 million pounds of deadly sarin-GB nerve gas contained in steel storage canisters, loaded bombs, rockets, land mines and artillery shells. Among them are 21,104 decrepit M-34 cluster bombs holding 163,000 gallons of sarin. Some of these rattle like sprung cuckoo clocks.

A few years earlier, working on a story for the magazine *Smithsonian,* I had flown through Denver unaware of the arsenal. If another passenger had drawn it to my attention, I would have had only the dimmest idea what he was talking about. Nerve gas was a familiar label, but I had no grasp of how it worked—it did something to your nervous system and you died, and there were various pesticides related to it. But beyond that, poison gas only evoked dim images of World War I trench warfare, and doughboys in Frisbee helmets wearing rat-faced gas masks. There had been a bit of a stink about nerve gas tests in the late 1960s that caused demonstrations in Washington, and a lot of sheep had died, but my recollections were mixed up with scenes of George C. Scott running around the Utah salt flats dying of some mysterious plague virus in a movie called *Outrage*.

There was really no reason why I should have known more. Life was settling into a quiet pattern. I was living in Alexandria, Virginia, across the Potomac from Washington, going sailing with my children on Chesapeake Bay, and working happily as a writer-editor for Time-Life Books. It was a welcome period of relative quiet after ten years in Asia as a correspondent. I carefully avoided getting caught up in any of the agonies or ecstasies sweeping through Washington, and saw only a few old friends from the Far East who were now posted in the Capital with the State Department or the Pentagon. I hardly expected that they would accidentally involve me in something so bizarre and harrowing that it would plunge me into four years of furious investigation and take me to the jungles of Laos, to the Russian-patrolled mountain wastes of northeastern Afghanistan, to the sullen deserts along the Red Sea—in search of elusive evidence of mass murder. I did not think the day would ever come when I would pore over the grisly autopsies of dead spies in search of clues to the exotic poisons that killed them, or pass through Denver knowing full well this time what lay below as the city slept late on a morning in autumn. But this time I was bound stubbornly for an island in the Pacific searching for a rare biotoxin, a superpoison of unbelievable potency secreted by something resembling a harmless sea anemone. It might explain the deaths of thousands of remote hill people who were being sprayed from the air by a deadly yellow rain. I had a hunch that I was at last on the verge of an explanation of what was really going on and who was behind it. It would come none too soon, because I was getting into very deep water. I recall somebody saying that the dragons are there all along in the darkness; we pretend that they do not exist because we have no choice, but every now and then we pass unwarily by a hole in the ground or a cave in a cliff and get scorched by a blast from the beast. Like some innocent tourist in Athens, Paris, or Berlin caught suddenly in the septic undercurrent of a spy novel plot, or a bystander at Lod airport or the Munich Olympics trapped in the midst of a terrorist attack, I had unwittingly let myself be drawn into a mystery that began as a simple riddle and grew and grew until I realized that I was holding the tail of the beast. The time had long past when it would do any good to call in a quavering voice for an exorcist.

Sometimes I would push it out of my mind, but it would come back. During the six years that I was based in Bangkok, I remember how the turf in the front yard of the bungalow cracked in the dry season, and the snakes that slithered out of the canals of the city stuck their heads up through the cracks in the turf like the periscopes of submarines. Everyone knew that they were always around; like everyone else I developed an automatic reflex of watching carefully where I put my feet, and worried when my son or daughter wanted to go outside to play. After a while I forgot that the snakes were there, until the next dry season. But once you know you can never really forget.

The breath of the beast now lay heavily over Denver. This time I knew exactly where it came from. I cast a last baleful eye over Rocky Mountain Arsenal as we touched down. That 4.2 million pounds of sarin was only a beginning. We do not do things halfway.

In addition to this ghoulish inventory of sarin, the arsenal also has great cairns of WETEYE bombs filled with the oily and even more potent nerve agent called VX. These by themselves would be enough to wipe out not only the entire population of Denver but of all Colorado and the adjacent states, along with most of the residents of Canada and Mexico. That would depend, of course, on how the nerve agent was spread—by freak accident or deliberately and methodically. One droplet of VX the size of a freckle on a man's arm is enough to kill him in minutes, in that spectacular way that nerve gas kills: suddenly jerking, slobbering, dancing, defecating, and collapsing in convulsions, as the muscles clench and cause paralysis and asphyxiation. Since VX does not evaporate quickly, but persists for weeks on end, a thousand gallons or so will suffice to do an extraordinary amount of killing.

As a precaution against leaks, the army customarily keeps cages of nervous rabbits among the rows upon rows of poison weapons and storage tanks, their pink noses twitching. They would not smell sarin or VX in any case, because the gases are odorless. They would simply begin to drool, stagger, jerk, and die. The guards would then sound the human alarms.

An accident could easily happen at Rocky Mountain Arsenal since it is on the north-south flight path for Stapleton International Airport. All that is necessary is for one of the big jumbo jets (or any aircraft, for that matter) to crash and demolish the contents of one of the arsenal's warehouses.

A severe storm or earthquake would do just as well. On August 19, 1972, for example, the U.S. Air Force had to hastily evacuate all personnel from its chemical warfare depot on Johnston Island south of Hawaii in the path of Hurricane Celeste, indicating that these stockpiles of war poisons are not very secure. And here in Denver, a place not normally inclined to have earthquakes, the secret disposal of poisonous waste from nerve gas production into a 12,045-foot deep well dug by the army beneath the city in the 1960s caused earthquakes of a magnitude up to four on the Richter scale. The army was obliged to pump the poisons back to the surface and find other means of disposal.

As it is, the WETEYE bombs are continually developing leaks. The Pentagon admits to 955 leaks since it got into the business of making nerve gas after World War II. That may be only the tip of the iceberg.

Some of the leaks occur because of decaying components or faulty hardware. Others are caused by human error. In 1968 at Dugway Proving Ground near Salt Lake City, Utah, an aircraft spraying VX nerve agent as part of ongoing tests and demonstrations had a valve that failed to close properly at the end of one run. A cloud of VX aerosol droplets was carried by the breeze across the hills and salt flats beyond Route 40 halfway to Salt Lake City. In its path, 6,300 sheep grazing in Skull Valley died in the snow-patched meadows among the cedar scrub, digging spastically with their hooves at the frozen ground. In the uproar that followed, Senator Frank Moss discovered that the army had sprayed precisely 320 gallons of VX from the aircraft the day the sheep began to die—but the army denied responsibility for more than a year, and then only grudgingly accepted blame. Residues of VX were found in the animals during autopsies, but that made no difference.

In 1966 at Fort Greely, Alaska, two hundred canisters of nerve gas stacked thoughtfully on the frozen surface of a lake sank through the ice and remained unnoticed on the lake bottom for three years, until a new base commander heard rumors of missing nerve gas and had the lake drained. Three years after that, in July 1972, fifty-three caribou died mysteriously near Fort Greely and wildlife experts ruled out natural causes; the army refused to investigate and denied that chemical agents might have been responsible.

As recently as 1976, fifty wild horses died under mysterious circumstances at Dugway Proving Ground. Despite army protests of innocence, the American Horse Protection Association found indications that the horses had died of a rare African disease unknown to the Utah salt flats.

As burial mounds go, Rocky Mountain Arsenal in the outskirts of this major American city is not absolutely unique. The U.S. nerve gas depot in Europe is in a suburb of booming Frankfurt, West Germany. History may record that only the American culture of the mid-twentieth century had the exotic trait of keeping its deadliest poisons practically in the heart of downtown—clearly a culture in some confusion about its priorities and its values.

If somebody at the Department of Defense had ordered all these nerve gas weapons and storage canisters brought to Denver, it might be possible to take him out and have him shot. But that was not the case. Nobody sent them here. This is a burial ground for the stillborn. These weapons and vats were all produced and filled here by the army on the assumption that they were going to be dispatched all over the earth to keep the world safe for democracy. It did not work out the way the army planned. Instead, most of the weapons remained here to decay until it was considered too risky to ship them anywhere. So now they only threaten what they were intended to protect.

A few of the arsenal's bombs, rockets, land mines, and shells were indeed sent to other places—to stockpiles in other states, to Johnston Island, to Okinawa to be on hand in the Far East, and to West Germany to help defend NATO. But they were not really wanted in those places either, any more than in Denver.

There were, of course, a few unfortunate accidents, notably the result of storage, handling, or disposal errors in Okinawa. A few dozen kids swimming near the depot suffered severe skin burns, and on another occasion a few soldiers had to be rushed to the hospital because of a leak. Okinawans rioted, and after several years of hemming and hawing and further threats and riots, the

United States packed up its many thousands of gallons of poisons in Okinawa and took them away to Johnston Island, where they remain today.

In West Germany, Chancellor Willy Brandt, for one, was caustically critical of this reintroduction of nerve gas to Germany, where it had first been discovered at the brink of World War II, and where the citizens of the Federal Republic would prefer not to be reminded. It made no sense to them to see America brandish a weapon that the Nazis had steadfastly refused to use even to save what was left of the collapsing Third Reich. But Washington simply dragged its feet until the next West German elections, and the nerve agents remained in the city of Hanau, at the eastern end of the great metropolitan area of Frankfurt, to this day—as they are in Denver.

Wherever the war poisons were taken, and the local population found out, the Americans were blamed as if they had brought phials of dreaded bubonic plague in the breast pockets of their aloha shirts. Therefore, most of it had to remain in Denver or at Dugway in Utah, far from any danger zone. It was no longer safe to move it in any case.

So, only a few years after rushing urgently into production of nerve agents and churning them out in vast quantities, America found itself in a "tar baby" predicament—unable to use it, unable to pass it on, and unable to get rid of it.

It is doubtful if the German general staff in World War II ever imagined that the day would arrive when their most virtuous conquerors, the Yanks, would adopt the one weapon that even the Nazis refused to use. Or that the weapon would become an issue to divide Americans and raise doubts about the judgment and fundamental morality of their leaders. For such it has been, and may be again, like an unmentionable social disease picked up on a foreign journey. But in the rubble of Germany's defeat, both the American and Russian conquerors were inclined to pick up anything shiny and take it home without realizing the consequences.

In 1968, twenty years after America secretly began to produce and stockpile these fearsome poisons, the public learned of their existence and decided that the Pentagon had gone too far. From the Vietnam War came horrifying stories about the effects of drenching the countryside with Agent Orange defoliant—not merely the devastation of the environment and the destruction of all its creatures but growing evidence that by-products of Agent Orange were causing deformations, stillbirths, and genetic damage. This, added to news of the 6,300 dead sheep at Skull Valley plus the increasingly severe earthquakes at Denver and a whole litany of other grim revelations, caused a remarkable public outcry. President Johnson had already stepped down because of the unpopularity of the Vietnam War, and President Nixon found himself in an office under public siege.

In a sequence of sweeping and dynamic decisions, the Nixon White House boldly announced that it was unilaterally banning all biological weapons from America's arsenal forever, and setting an absolute policy that America would never use poison gas offensively, but would work only on defensive measures and use chemical weapons only if an enemy used them first.

So far as most Americans were concerned, myself included, that was it for bugs and gas.

The Nixon ban took America out of the chemical and biological warfare business permanently. All the secret biological warfare research and development stations were going to be closed down or turned into centers of research for disease control. Most of the frightening arsenal of dread chemical poisons were going to be disposed of, particularly since so many of them were leaking or falling apart. The Pentagon vowed that it would dispose of its poisons safely on the bases where they were kept. Nobody wanted them trucked or trained around the country to get bashed up in freight yards or spilled in derailments.

Satisfied, the protesters went back to their daily lives. The Vietnam War ended, and there were psychic wounds to lick. There was Watergate. And a recession. Several years passed. The whole matter was forgotten.

Then, in the late 1970s, out of the remote hills of Laos came puzzling reports of hill people dying from poison gas. Of Vietnamese aircraft dousing villages with varicolored clouds of poisonous mist, and of a sickening yellow rain that left hundreds of people "drowning in their own blood."

It was at this point that the riddle of Laos began to fascinate me. After the better part of a lifetime in the Orient, I could make no sense of the stories. But I kept encountering thoughtful, well-informed people who were becoming alarmed. Among them were foreign journalists, China scholars, old Asia hands, expatriates, foreign service analysts, experienced military officers from the field, and a few diplomatic and military intelligence officers who were then in Washington or keeping up random correspondence from Bangkok or Singapore and Hong Kong.

They were becoming alarmed because they were beginning to be persuaded by the reports. Something was happening in Laos that had never happened quite that way in the world before. People who could not make themselves heard by the outside world were being systematically exterminated with a peculiar new kind of poison that did not leave any of the obvious traces left by mustard, phosgene, chlorine, and the nerve gases like sarin or VX.

There are two ways to resolve a mystery. You may ignore it. Live with it, assume that it was caused by circumstantial coincidence, or that—at worst—somebody (either your friends or your enemies) wanted you to be misled, to be intrigued by false clues. And you can assume that the consequences, however grim or shocking, can somehow be explained by other causes.

The other way to resolve a mystery is to assume that the reports may be true. To be prepared to believe some of the evidence, however circumstantial, providing that the coincidences are overwhelming and the circumstances are extraordinary. Set out, then, to investigate all the possibilities.

Because the recent accounts of poison gas attacks are so baffling, and have come from the most inaccessible corners of Laos or Afghanistan, there has been an overwhelming temptation to simply live with the enigma rather than somehow force the issue into the open. I chose instead to investigate and was led on an unexpected journey into a world that I only dimly realized existed.

It was a journey that led back centuries to the grim fascination of medieval poisonings and to the Dark Ages, when whole countrysides were erased of human life by sinister blooms that appeared in the food—blooms that would one day offer up a surprising answer to the riddle of warfare in our future.

The journey led to the muddy banks of the Mekong River and the opium country of the Golden Triangle, to the dusty coast of Somalia and the *gat* plantations of Yemen, to the spectacular snow peaks of the Hindu Kush in Afghanistan, and to the tidy corridors of the Swedish Foreign Ministry, NATO, and Scotland Yard. Many days were spent with the Hmong refugees on the border of Laos and the Mujahideen guerrillas on the border of Afghanistan, cross-checking their accounts of poison gas attacks and comparing the physical symptoms and medical signs from which forensic specialists and pathologists reconstruct probable causes of death. To my surprise, a pattern began to appear that soon led to some disturbing discoveries.

It led, for one thing, to the realization that nerve gas, for all its speed and dramatic effect, is only an antiquated and clumsy weapon compared to the new generation of fantastically deadly biological superpoisons that are being used now in the small wars that fill the deafening nuclear silence. It led to the realization that while the world was distracted by events in the 1960s in Vietnam, Israel, and Eastern Europe, unfortunate villages in other areas were already being sprayed, gassed, misted, squirted, doused, bombed, and dusted with these gruesome new poisons.

The journey led to depots hidden in the Laotian and Vietnamese jungles, stocked with Russian poisons and watched over by Soviet army officers. That led in turn to strange incidents on opposite sides of China in which Russian and Vietnamese troops sprayed these same awesome poisons on Communist Chinese military units, producing mass casualties that went unreported in the West. Ultimately the path led also to Cuba, to yet another stockpile of these same poisons, and to the eerie, primeval death of a Cuban secret agent who came too close to one poison and was transformed into a walking hemorrhage. For these new killers are old poisons dipped from the alchemist's cauldron, borrowed from the sewers of the black plague and the red death, compounded with eye of newt and toe of frog and dumped into the dawn of the space age.

When I was handed a copy of the autopsy on the Cuban agent, by an irreproachable European physician, and read the details of massive internal bleeding from the brainpan to the viscera, from all the body openings and beneath the skin all over the body, it was like reading the horrified account of a thirteenth-century German monk describing the ghastly end of a fellow cleric after eating black bread tainted by the powers of the supernatural. And yet it was an event taking place in Havana, Cuba, in 1980, just ninety miles from the walleyed tourist motels of Key West. By then I was aware that Cuban military officers were being given firsthand field experience with Russian chemical agents in Indochina, Afghanistan, and Ethiopia—possibly in Angola as well—and that Cuban armed forces I discovered were being trained in chemical warfare on the island by teams of Soviet instructors. But the death of the Cuban agent was the first positive confirmation I had of reports that Soviet war poisons were stockpiled in Cuba itself. The autopsy made it plain that these included the grisliest poison of them all—the same one that was causing Laotian villagers to vomit blood.

So long as these poisons remained a barbaric weapon wielded only by bellicose enemies and manufactured by the masters of the Gulag Archipelago, it was tempting to be righteous. There was a virtuous context for dismay and anger. The enlightened West does not stoop to these weapons.

But that, unfortunately, did not provide me with comfort for long. Inexorably, the realization dawned on me that America had once possessed the world's largest arsenal of poisons. All of the biological and chemical killers that were supposed to have been destroyed a decade ago, plus many new ones, might still be right where they were all along. Still in Denver, still at Dugway Proving Ground, still at Pine Bluff Arsenal in Arkansas and a score of other locations. For that matter, still in West Germany. I began to wonder if they were ever destroyed after all, or were they just tucked away a little deeper in secrecy? Did the Dr. Strangeloves of America's "bugs and gas" establishment simply pack up and move to where they could not be seen by their fellow citizens? Were all the factories that had supposedly been mothballed actually closed down? And what were we to make of the moves during 1981 to start up new factories to brew more and better poisons, for wars that are yet to happen but always hang over our heads?

So, like most journeys, this one led back to where it began. The famous Nixon ban turned out to be just another part of the intricate Watergate hoax. The Nixon ban was a fake. And the only difference between Washington and the Hindu Kush in the end is that in the wild, lunar mountains of Afghanistan you know your enemies.

This journey began, in Washington, in late October 1978, as the autumn wind whipped dead oak and maple leaves past the windows and stretched horsetail clouds across a cold pewter sky, when a man with a leg bone in his suitcase knocked apprehensively at my door.

2.
Medicine from the Sky

If I had first met the young American on the streets of Bangkok near his dingy rented room off Sathorn Road, I might have taken him for a Swiss tourist. There was nothing about him of the jungle. Nothing to indicate that he had just walked out of the rain forests of Laos with a man's leg bone—the femur—in his pack. No sign that he had swum at night across the muddy, broad Mekong River to elude the Lao Communist border guards, towing the pack with the leg bone behind him until he reached the safety of the steep mud bank on the Thai side. Instead, he was clean-cut, freshly scrubbed, his blond hair trimmed short in a style suitable for a vacationing accountant from Zurich.

It was autumn and the monsoon rains were long over. Bangkok cooked in microwave heat, and like the lean-legged Thais crowding the alleys converging on busy Silom Road, the young American was wearing neat shoes, crisp chino slacks, and an open shirt, the uniform of a city that should have been built in a more hospitable setting. He stepped nimbly around darting Datsun Bluebird taxis, crossed Silom Road without looking at the display in the windows of John Fowler's men's shop, passed a chromatic storefront featuring bolts of brilliant Thai cottons and smelling sharply of sizing, and entered the gloom of a fly-blown Chinese noodle shop that I had also frequented during my years in Thailand. Sitting by himself so that he could see the street, he stuck grimy chopsticks into a deep bowl of *kwetiao* pork noodle soup, poking away chopped green chillis and simmering leaves of fresh coriander to get at the gray bits of pork.

Jack Schramm was one of the Americans who had stayed on in Asia after the fall of Saigon in 1975. The older ones who stayed had conspicuous reasons: alcohol, drugs, despair, a woman, a passion for boys, a pension that could stretch a long way in the right part of the Orient, or a job with one of the multinational firms. For the younger ones who stayed, no reason was needed—and it was usually better not to ask, because they might try to explain themselves to you. After Saigon, concerned young Americans could be found all over Asia. But most drifted home in time, unable to find whatever it was that they were looking for.

Schramm had stayed because he was concerned about MIA bones, the remains of Americans missing in action that might still be found if somebody had the courage to go into the jungle, find the crash sites, and get the help of hill tribes like the Hmong in Laos, who were still fighting to keep from being overrun by the hated lowland Laotians. This is what gave Schramm the sense of mission that drove him back repeatedly to the Lao rain forests, where he had located the leg bone—and where he had encountered the four French mercenaries.

It was on his third or fourth or fifth illegal trip into Laos that Schramm's Hmong guides led him to the site of a U.S. Navy crash. In the wreckage he discovered the pilot's femur bone. By this time he and the Hmong were deep inside Laos. The Mekong River border was a few days away along the jungle trails, and they were alert to the possibility that they might be surprised at any moment by a Communist government patrol. But after locating the bone they relaxed. Schramm's escort of young Hmong resistance fighters was well armed with American M-16s and Chinese AK-47s. Most of them were barefoot, the rest wearing rubber thongs. All of them wore typical Hmong black pajamas.

Schramm saw no point in continuing deeper into the rain forest. He was eager to get back to Thailand with his find. The bone could be identified by experts in the United States, and the pilot's family informed that he was indeed killed in action rather than simply "missing." But the route back to Thailand had to be indirect, to skirt lowland Laotian villages and to bypass areas along the Mekong that were patrolled. So they headed inland toward the hills, unaware of being observed.

As they made their way along a trail through a stand of tall teak trees, where tiny white lilies grew in the sodden mulch on the jungle floor, they heard the unmistakable clicking of automatic weapons around them. Startled in midstep, Schramm looked quickly from side to side, searching for the ambushers, ready to plunge for cover. Suddenly, four large men wearing leopard-spot camouflage materialized from the foliage, each carrying an Israeli Uzi machine gun, each draped with ammunition pouches and grenades, each wearing a black beret. Their faces were smeared with char, but they were unmistakably "round eyes."

They disarmed the young Hmongs and the American, and then gestured for them to sit down. One of the ambushers took out a blue box of Gitanes French cigarettes and passed them around.

The ambushers were French mercenaries. They did not explain what they were doing inside Laos, but they were so at ease and full of jests that Schramm assumed they had passed this way more than once before. In fluent English, one of them quickly ascertained what Schramm was doing in Laos, and looked with only mild curiosity at the bone when Schramm held it out for their inspection.

Certainly, the commando said, there were a number of places where they knew remains of crashed U.S. pilots could be found. However, he warned, if Schramm was planning to continue traveling with his Hmong companions in the direction they were going— toward the mountains around Phu Bia, near the Plain of Jars—it would be extremely dangerous.

"Why?" asked Schramm.

"Because the Vietnamese are spraying the villages with gas," the mercenary said. He did not say what kind of gas, and it occurred to Schramm that there were many kinds, including tear gas, the defoliant called Agent Orange, and the incapacitant called Agent CS that American forces had employed in Vietnam.

"What kind of gas is it?" Schramm asked.

"Ypres," answered the Frenchman, as if the name should have obvious significance.

"You mean poison gas?" Schramm said. "What they used in World War I at Ypres?"

The commandos nodded. "That is what it looked like to us, from the way the Hmong died."

Schramm was carrying his battered suitcase with the leg bone inside when he appeared on my doorstep in Washington, D.C., several weeks later, in late autumn of 1978. A mutual friend who was employed by the government as a political-military analyst specializing in Southeast Asia had telephoned the day before to see if I could take a house guest from Thailand for a week or two. I was expecting someone with long hair and a feigned case of tropical fever, a plastic bag full of Vientiane premium-grade marijuana blossoms in his backpack, and a haggard touch of jaundice around the eyes from too many nights spent sleeping on the stone floors of Buddhist monasteries; I had not been looking forward to the guest. But the figure on my doorstep was still crisply dressed for the tropics, brisk and businesslike, clear-eyed and healthy. I marked him as the kind who sets aside a few minutes before sleeping every night to take out a book and note all the day's activities in a neat hand. After making him at home I left him to his own devices, and in the days to follow noticed him making phone calls for appointments, coming and going silently and intently. Outside it suddenly turned colder and began to snow.

Over meals and drinks the next few days, we talked, at first guardedly, comparing backgrounds in Asia, checking off people we knew in Thailand—journalists, government officials, assorted foreign diplomats, and the American or European intelligence gatherers whom everyone who has lived for long in the Orient soon comes to know. After a few of these conversations we had established a common ground, and neither of us was surprised by the other's fascination with the backwoods of the Far East. So Schramm began to talk about his trips into Laos.

In time I concluded that he was doing this on his own. Nobody was sponsoring his clandestine excursions, unless he was receiving contributions from MIA families. Maybe somewhere he had his own stash of family money that he drew on when needed. But he had more in common with a Seventh-day Adventist or Mormon missionary than he did with any secret agency.

He was in Washington to deliver his bone and to try to drum up some official support to look for other remains, lobbying any member of Congress he could get to, and I suppose on the side doing everything he could to stir up interest in the besieged Hmong.

It was then that he told me about his last expedition into the rain forest, and of his encounter with the four French mercenaries. He related their brief but provocative conversation about "Ypres," and I tried to pry more details from him about the poison gas. But Schramm was unable to add anything to the mercenary's cryptic remark, nor could he explain what the gas was—beyond "Ypres." To him it was important only that the gas was being used on his friends, the Hmong. This upset him very much because he felt that America had betrayed the hill tribes and put the Hmong into this predicament to start with.

During the Indochina war, the United States had enlisted the Hmong to fight the Communist Pathet Lao and the North Vietnamese. When the war had ended and the United States had pulled out, the Hmong had not given up. They had continued to fight. It was either that or allow themselves to be rounded up by the Communists and placed in prison camps where many of them would probably be killed in acts of revenge by the lowland Lao.

Schramm said that Lao ground forces and Vietnamese air force units had repeatedly assaulted the main Hmong stronghold in the mountains at Phu Bia, just south of the Plain of Jars in central Laos. While the Lao soldiers lobbed mortar rounds into the Hmong villages, Vietnamese planes splashed the defenders with napalm. After more than two years of unequal fighting, the trickle of Hmong refugees reaching the Mekong River and attempting to cross to safety in Thailand had grown to a flood. Many of the Hmong failed to complete the river crossing. As hill people, most of them did not know how to swim, so they had to pause to build clumsy rafts of dried bamboo torn from Lao fences. Even at night, when many of the families struggled across, pushing their children and meager possessions ahead of them on the rafts, they were seen and machine-gunned by border guards on the riverbank behind them. Those who safely reached the Thai side were interrogated by the reluctant Thai military or border patrol and then sent to refugee camps. Each of the camps had its collection of young guerrilla fighters. Periodically, small groups of these Hmong boys would make their way across the river with weapons and ammunition obtained in Thailand to rejoin the Hmong still holding out around Phu Bia. It was with one of these groups that Schramm had been crossing into Laos.

Schramm left Washington a few days later to resume his hunt for MIA bones. I wished him well.

If what Schramm said was true, the Vietnamese and Lao forces had given up using conventional weapons in their effort to force the Hmong into submission and in frustration had turned to smoking them out or exterminating them with toxic chemicals. It was a grotesque image, of a primitive hill tribe fighting for survival against clouds of poisonous vapors sprayed on them by enemy aircraft—the horrors of trench warfare and gas chambers brought to bear on villagers too remote for the outside world to notice.

There had been no mention of gas warfare in the press at the time, so these atrocities were going on without anyone having to answer for them. If the Hmong screamed when they died, nobody heard.

I began making guarded inquiries of acquaintances at the Pentagon and the Department of State, and was surprised to find that vague rumors of poison gas in Laos had begun to come in through several channels. They were starting with the Hmong refugees, who had been coming across in increasing numbers since the end of that summer's rains and the dropping of the flood tide on the river. The reports were picked up by Thais or international aid people working with the refugees and were passed on to the American embassy in Bangkok, or through other routes to the Pentagon and State Department. The reports were also picked up by knowledgeable staff aides on Capitol Hill and were added to the docket of the House Subcommittee on Asian and Pacific Affairs. No single person, then, had more than a few scant rumors to go on. These tended to be discounted because the use of ordinary tear gas is usually sufficient to stir reports of chemical warfare. Nobody was prepared to jeopardize his credibility in Washington by concluding anything on the basis of rumors about something so ridiculous.

But as more reports came in, the private cross talk and debate among analysts grew. From the outset there was a quarrel between State and the Pentagon over how to investigate the rumors, or whether they should be investigated at all. The argument raged even within State, where one contingent wanted urgently to find out everything possible and another contingent (in the majority) was afraid to upset the diplomatic tranquility by butting into an area that has been regarded, since Saigon, as off limits and strictly the concern of Bangkok and other governments of Southeast Asia.

In particular, the U.S. Embassy on Wireless Road in Bangkok did not want its Thai dominion upset by the intrusion of a bunch of Washington carpetbaggers looking for evidence of chemical warfare and charging around the undergrowth along the sensitive north and northeast borders of Thailand—the area adjacent to Communist Laos and Cambodia. Bangkok's control of that region was tenuous at best, and Communist cadres, supplied by Russian helicopters flown in by the Vietnamese, were in control of the deep woods. Nothing must be done to destabilize the delicate balance in that area.

After the blunders of the Indochina war, no diplomat wanted to forfeit his career by stirring up that pot again. Nor was it possible to simply bypass Bangkok and go straight to the Lao government. Since the American withdrawal from its so-called "secret war" run by the CIA in Laos, corollary to the fall of Saigon, diplomatic relations had existed with Laos only in the form of a U.S. chargé d'affaires and a small staff. The prevailing policy at the Department of State was that this toehold had to be maintained at all cost in order to sustain a "dialogue" with the Lao Communist regime. To any argument about the overriding importance of the use of poison gas the reply was simply "But you don't have any evidence." Without access, none could be obtained.

On the other hand, the Pentagon—not obliged to maintain even an illusion of relations with Laos—fretted over the larger meaning of the poison gas rumors. First, it was clear that there must be some foundation for the rumors because they were coming from people too unsophisticated to concoct such a baroque intrigue. Second, if the reports were true, the Vietnamese and the Lao were out to exterminate the whole hill tribe, which was a matter of military curiosity. Third, and most important, the military use of poison gas was supposed to be unthinkable.

If the Hmong were being gassed, it had to be with Vietnamese help, because the Lao on their own were not capable of mounting such an operation. If the Vietnamese were carrying it out, they were most likely using Soviet chemical warfare agents. This became no longer just a parochial question involving the niceties of diplomatic relations with Vientiane, Laos. It was a global question. The Vietnamese had not been signatories of the poison gas protocols signed after World War I because Vietnam was then a French colony, and the French had signed instead. Moscow had signed, but the protocols did not prohibit a nation from making chemical warfare agents available to a third party, in this case Hanoi. However you sliced it, the use of poison gas in Laos, if true, was an issue affecting global U.S. military policy.

By mid-1979, State relented and agreed to have two young diplomatic officers quietly investigate the rumors in the refugee camps of northern Thailand, and possibly obtain some physical evidence—if such evidence existed. Chosen for the mission were Ed McWilliams and Tim Carney. McWilliams was then a State Department desk officer in Washington with experience in Southeast Asia and fluent in Lao. A slim, dark-haired man in his thirties, he had an intense look about him and strong feelings for the plight of the hill tribes, the refugees, and all the human fallout in Southeast Asia. He knew Thailand well and liked the Thais, understanding their pivotal position in the region and the stresses this placed upon the government in Bangkok and the Thai monarchy.

Carney was equally sensitive to the region, and as the new U.S. consul in Udorn, in northeast Thailand, the hub of the refugee area, he was the diplomat primarily responsible for anything going wrong there. His bailiwick included the Cambodian refugee camps as well as people fleeing from Laos who sought refuge in America. And he was responsible for the actions of American journalists junketing through the refugee camps, for the celebrities who came to demonstrate their sympathy for the human wreckage, and to the wrath of the American ambassador if anything went amiss. Well over six feet tall, with the good looks and confident air of solid Anglo-Saxon New England, he had published studies of Southeast Asia at Cornell University. He was fluent in Cambodian—at ease in the Bangkok diplomatic circuit or the troubled northeast, and went about everything with an admirable air of certitude, relieved by good humor.

McWilliams and Carney quietly and inconspicuously toured the Hmong refugee camps, and talked with some hill people who said they had fled to Thailand after miraculously surviving gas attacks that had wiped out everyone else in their villages. The Americans saw several Hmong in a camp hospital who were covered with small, hard blisters that they said were caused by gas spread over their villages by aircraft. McWilliams took photographs of the blisters, but doctors later found them inconclusive without skin samples— because they did not look like blisters caused by mustard gas or any other familiar chemical agent. The doctors passed the word that they would appreciate some sort of samples of chemical residue from a village that had suffered a gas attack. In time that evidence was brought in. It consisted of odd bits of debris from a Hmong village, including leaves of foliage with curious burn holes and a small section of roofing from a hut, dusted with a yellow powder.

When it reached Washington, the plastic bag of debris was turned over to the Pentagon and was hand-carried by two army officers to the biomedical laboratories at Edgewood Arsenal in the Aberdeen Proving Grounds in Maryland.

After a preliminary examination, the chemists at Edgewood said that while the samples were too small to draw positive conclusions from, the holes could have been burned by a form of mustard gas—a blistering agent used in World War I at Ypres.

In the Pentagon, speculation then led to four conjectures. The descriptions provided by the Hmong refugees at this early stage indicated that death was caused in ways that could not be identified exclusively with the nerve agent called soman, which the Soviet Union was believed to have in large supply. It seemed likely therefore that a new compound of unfamiliar toxic chemicals had been developed and was being provided to Hanoi by the Soviets.

Granted, whoever was spraying the chemicals might have their own chemists capable of producing new compounds. But not on the large scale required.

There was always the possibility that the Vietnamese had discovered a cache of ancient World War I mustard gas left behind in Indochina by the French. Perhaps the Vietnamese had found such a depot and somehow combined the mustard gas with other chemical killers to produce the odd mixture of effects reported by the Hmong.

The fourth possibility was the most curious: that the lethal chemicals were extracted from a natural source, such as the deadly oil of the common tropical plant *Croton tiglium,* which grows all over Southeast Asia. Or it might have been extracted from a particularly poisonous coral formation common to the Pacific Ocean. Or from various poisonous snakes.

Of these four early conjectures, it was considered most likely that the Soviets were the providers, that the chemicals were a new compound of unknown ingredients, and that it was being delivered by Vietnamese jets and propeller aircraft with Lao ground support.

A fresh effort was begun by the Pentagon to get more substantial evidence, this time by sending a team of doctors to Thailand from Edgewood and other U.S. Army Medical Corps centers. Once again the U.S. Embassy in Bangkok objected, and the Department of State blocked the trip. The reason, as before, was the embassy's stated desire to avoid stepping on the toes of the Thai generals who held the real power within the government of Thailand. And once again the State Department was divided between those backing the position of the embassy and those who thought it was more important to find out conclusively about the poison gas. In the end, the matter was resolved by a blunt maneuver: the assistant secretary of state for Asian and Pacific affairs, Richard Holbrooke, simply sent a cable to the embassy telling it when the army medical team would arrive at Don Muang airport outside Bangkok. The issue was closed.

The medical team was led by Col. Charles W. Lewis, chief of the dermatology section at Brooke Army Medical Center at Fort Sam Houston in San Antonio, Texas. With Lewis were Dr. Frederick R. Sidell of the Army Biomedical Laboratory at Aberdeen Proving Ground, who had written numerous papers on nerve agents; Brig. Gen. William D. Tigertt, who had retired from the army to teach pathology at the University of Maryland; and Sp5 Burton L. Kelley, from Dr. Lewis's staff at Brooke Army Medical Center. They were to be escorted to Thailand by Lt. Col. Charles D. Lane, an army expert on Asia with many years of background in Indochina, Thailand, and Burma.

Since Jack Schramm's visit the previous year, I had been fitting together bits and pieces of rumors and reports and had started building background files. For the time being, it was little more than a hobby. Somebody else's baffling riddle to toy with. Perhaps in the back of my mind I had already decided to undertake the riddle myself and work on it until I reached a satisfactory explanation. But I certainly had no idea then that it would ultimately take me into the wilds of Afghanistan, or into secret police headquarters in Mogadishu, Somalia—that I would find myself on top of a mountain in the Hindu Kush within sight of Soviet helicopters, cross-examining Mujahideen rebels, or haggling with the Queen's coroner in London to get a look at the pathologist's report on a dead Bulgarian emigré. In the beginning, before the reports suddenly began converging with other circumstantial evidence, I was prepared to drop it all instantly. But once they converged—and all my intuitions told me that they would—I knew it would be impossible to stop short of a complete answer. That moment came a lot sooner than I expected.

On September 1, 1979, I learned that the army medical team was about to leave for Thailand. Their findings might well be conclusive. If the reports were found to be true, it would be a major story. I was scheduled to go to Thailand at about the same time on a magazine assignment to write about the hill people of the opium-growing area known as the Golden Triangle where the borders of Laos, Thailand, and Burma come together. The Hmong refugee camps were not far from there. When Dr. Lewis drew his conclusions about the gassing of the Hmong, I wanted to be present. His team left for Bangkok on September 28, 1979. I caught a plane two days later.

When I reached Bangkok I learned that the doctors had already left for Udorn in the northeastern plateau, where they would begin to have direct access to the refugee camps. It might take days to catch up by train or car, and I might not catch up at all if the doctors kept moving. Travel in northeast Thailand could be frustrating, depending on rickety Thai taxis and jungle jitney buses. But I was able to find a small plane for charter at Don Muang airport. We reached Udorn before noon, left the plane parked on an otherwise empty airport, and headed for town—only to discover that the army doctors had already left for the town of Loei one hundred miles to the west. Near Loei was the biggest Hmong refugee camp in Thailand, a town of 45,000 refugees named Ban Vinai, only five miles from the border at the Mekong River. I had just enough time to reach Loei before dark if we took off immediately.

At sunset, the Mekong appeared like a thread of silver filagree in the blackening hills far ahead. We were making our approach to the small airstrip at Loei. The town itself turned out to be little more than a few intersecting unpaved streets, bracketed by Chinese-style storefronts: a gaping shop on the ground level with living quarters on the floor above. Thai love songs poured from loudspeakers along the main street, and most of the traffic was of pedicabs. There were only two small hotels, modest structures with terrazzo floors and plastic shrubbery gathering years of dust from the street. After checking into one and finding no sign of the medical team, I climbed into a pedicab and headed for the other, moving silently on the whispering bicycle tires over the dirt road through the twilight of that strange town that bellowed its overamplified love at the surrounding emptiness.

Off the barren lobby of the second hotel, there was a dimly lit bistro with pink plastic curtains covering its plate glass door. The strong smell of shrimp paste, fish sauce, lemon grass, and burnt garlic held back the mosquitoes in the muggy heat. The glass door swung open toward me and out of the gloom inside the restaurant stepped Colonel Lane.

He was in a short-sleeved shirt, scowling at me though his glasses—a sinewy man in his late thirties with dark wiry hair that stuck out this way and that, and a British accent from growing up in England. He grinned. "Fancy meeting you here."

"Where are your doctors?"

He gestured at the restaurant. "Inside. We just got back from Ban Vinai. Come in. I'll introduce you."

I followed Lane into the gloom and found the four members of the medical team sitting around a pink plastic booth, all except Colonel Lane wearing civilian clothes, all looking exhausted and hungry. They had spent that day, and the day before, at Ban Vinai examining and interviewing scores of Hmong refugees among those who had recently arrived from areas that they said had been hit by gas attacks.

Dr. Lewis was a pensive-looking man of medium height and thinning hair who looked like he would be good-natured and easy to like if he was not preoccupied with an unusually grim assignment and weary from days of talking with death.

I asked him what he had learned so far.

"There is no question about it," he answered. "It is a nerve agent combined with other chemicals." He had talked to groups of survivors from widely separated regions in Laos, people with no contact whatever at Ban Vinai, including unrelated women and children. It had taken them so long to escape to Thailand that if they survived the trip the physical effects of the chemicals wore off before they got to Ban Vinai. The ones who had suffered stronger doses either died in the attacks or on the way out. So Lewis had to work on the basis of lengthy medical interviews, up to two hours with each refugee. But their stories were all essentially alike. The circumstances varied but the medical symptoms the Hmong described were basically the same. The medical conclusions, therefore, were necessarily the same.

"It is a nerve agent," Lewis said. "Probably combined with an internal hemorrhaging agent and a blistering agent."

"Is it something too sophisticated," I asked, "to be produced by anyone without an advanced chemical warfare program?" I meant the Laotians and the Vietnamese.

"Well, you could produce some of these effects with different agents," he said. "It might include chlorine or phosgene, one of the industrial chemicals—not the sort of thing that could be produced by anyone. And there may very well be some other poisons included. We can draw a medical profile based on the interviews so that we know how these people are dying, so we can tell what types of chemicals it would take to cause death in these ways. But we can't be certain exactly what the chemicals are."

I asked if he had been able to get any estimate of the number killed by gas.

"From the interviews alone, I would calculate upward of a thousand deaths that were witnessed by people we talked to. But as a whole, the Hmong say as many as ten thousand to fifteen thousand." Somebody, it appeared, was going to extraordinary lengths to wipe out the whole hill tribe. Turning to Colonel Lane, I asked if there was any definite evidence who was responsible.

"Nothing positive yet," Lane said from out of the gloom. "The Hmong all call the jets MIGS—but they tend to call all enemy jets MIGS." Then he added: "But there are some propeller aircraft that appear to be used in some of the attacks. L-19s."

I asked how they planned to proceed. They said they were hoping to get a better sample of chemical residue from across the Mekong, if the Hmong were able to bring it out. And they still hoped to find a Hmong who had been in a gas attack so recently that samples of skin tissue and blood could be taken along with other tests that could be conclusive in the laboratory. The doctors would continue to work in Ban Vinai for several days, then move north along the Lao border to smaller camps where there might be more recent arrivals.

For the moment I decided not to press them further, but to see for myself.

I arrived at Ban Vinai the following morning ahead of the cars rented for the doctors. I had driven for nearly two hours from Loei in a small Thai taxi, up through the jagged calcium karst formations with their sharp fingers splayed against a clean blue sky.

The karsts had been carved by some forgotten sea that once submerged this entire region all the way from central Burma in the west across Laos to China's Kwangtung Province near Canton and Hong Kong in the east. Among the eroded spires you could find seashells many hundreds of miles from the sea.

Most of the last hour in the taxi had been spent driving along the brown waters of the Mekong, sweeping through the jungle in a muddy surge carrying tree trunks along like twigs.

On the far side, the bank looked as innocent as the Mississippi, until you recalled where you were and how many people had died on the other side of the river during the Indochina war, and how many were dying now trying to escape the agonies of death by poison gas.

Once, during that war, I had set out in a teakwood pirogue from the royal capital of Laos at Luang Prabang to make my way to the royal caves at Pak Ou, where there was an array of Buddhist icons standing guard in the face of the cliff over the river. The area around Pak Ou was in the control of the Pathet Lao, but there was a rightist government outpost in the cave itself, protected by sandbags and affording a view of the river below that made it possible for only a few armed men to control boat traffic. I had intended to take photographs from inside the cave showing the implacable Buddhas overseeing the soldiers and the sandbags and the river.

Through the morning hours, the pirogue had moved steadily upriver under the power of its small outboard motor. I had sat in the bow enjoying the silence of the riverbanks and the stillness of the Chinese watercolor scenery. Then on my right a .50 caliber machine gun had begun firing at us from the treeline. It had stopped just as suddenly. No gun had been visible.

Now, breezing along in the taxi, I wondered how many eyes were watching from the far bank. At any moment, a raft might push off from the far shore, or I might see heads bobbing in the current.

The monsoons had ended in August, but the river was still swollen both from the rains and the summer melt of the Himalayan ice cap where the Mekong flows out of a glacial moraine just north of Lhasa, Tibet.

There is a legend about the Mekong. It is born just a few air miles from each of the other great rivers of Asia. But only the Mekong ends up forming the borders of nearly every country in Southeast Asia. It flows down from Tibet toward the east along with the Brahmaputra, the Irrawaddy, the Salween, the Yangtze, and the Yellow River. But those rivers all turn away to the north or the south or the west. Only the Mekong is left to run along the borders of China and Burma, Laos and Thailand, Cambodia and Vietnam. By the time it empties into the South China Sea it is full of many tears. So it is called The River of the Third Eye—the third eye being the eye of wisdom in the forehead of the Lord Buddha.

What stuck in my mind as I drove down the Mekong that afternoon in the Thai taxi was the marked division the river formed between the perils and cruelties of Indochina and the seductive tranquility of Thailand. When the Hmong had fled south from China a thousand years ago into the mountains of Laos, perhaps they had not fled far enough to find true sanctuary. Perhaps now they were paying the price.

Up a dusty side road, Ban Vinai suddenly appeared through a gap in the hills guarded by a Thai border police checkpoint. As we entered the gap, the refugee town spread out below in the bowl of a shallow valley, crowded with huts and houses, jammed with people busy with a thousand chores. Many were teamed to build rows of new cement block houses topped by corrugated metal roofs. Others gathered in open-air markets, squatting on the ground to sell their wares, clothing, fruit, bric-a-brac. Most women wore the traditional Hmong black wraparound skirts with black jackets and headdresses, decorated with silver rings and necklaces and red cloth waistbands. Women who were bathing at wells had adopted Thai sarongs with batik prints.

Here and there, young women with long hair were hauling buckets out of wells and dousing themselves, twisting and winding their tresses into buns and knotting them, slipping dry sarongs over wet sarongs and then, modesty preserved, letting the wet sarong drop to be washed next and hung up.

The older men wore black shirts and loose black trousers, the common garb of most Asian hill tribes. But many of the younger men wore olive drab military fatigue trousers with white or olive green army singlets.

Everywhere they seemed to be putting their shoulders together to raise poured concrete beams, using old rubber bicycle tires as harnesses. A great deal of building was going on.

I stopped first at one of Ban Vinai's small hospitals.

Inside, I found a little boy, no more than a year old, his legs and arms hardly as big around as my thumbs. His face was gaunt and ravaged, his eyes yellow and huge with despair. His movements were jerky and pointless, as if searching for something that his shriveled hands could not reach. On the wooden bed platform next to him his young father looked as if he had just aged from thirty-two to seventy-eight in the past few weeks. His face was stricken as he held the boy in his arms. He had lost one of his four children to pneumonia and exposure after pushing his family on a raft across the Mekong a few nights before. Now he passed the boy to his wife, who sat on the next platform exhausted and dazed. She was obviously once quite pretty. She might have been eighteen or twenty years old, perhaps even younger. She took the little boy from her husband and let him work at her breast. He stopped sucking to howl, and then returned to his work. His father brightened.

"The doctor says they are stronger if they can cry," he explained, speaking to me apprehensively through the young Hmong medic who was in charge of the clinic. The medic had worked at the American base in Long Xieng, Laos, during the war, and he spoke excellent English that was only slightly stilted from being spoken so carefully.

"What is wrong with the boy?" I asked.

The medic said: "They had to feed him opium to keep him quiet while they came across the river."

Through the medic I asked the father why they had fled to Thailand, and he began telling me about the day of the final raid.

"The MIGs came over the village with blue gas coming out of the right wing tanks and red gas from the left," the medic explained. "That is what he said."

"What happened after the red and blue gas?" I asked. There was an exchange in Hmong, then the medic translated:

"He says: We all felt sick in the village, and everyone began to fall down. Then the MIGs came back and dropped bags—he says like big rice bags—that exploded in the air and blew yellow powder all over the village. Then everyone began to die."

"How many died?"

"The village had fifty people in all. But some were not there, so thirty-four died immediately."

"How did he escape with his family?"

"He says: I was up on a hillside across a stream from the village, tending my poppies. My children came with my wife to give me some food, and while we were all on the hill across from the village the MIGs came. We saw the colored gas, and the people in the village began to lie down and go to sleep. Then the MIGs came back and dropped the bags. When the bags burst, the powder inside turned into yellow gas like a cloud. When it came down it was like yellow rain.

"We were frightened, but we had many relatives in the village. We wanted to help them. So we went back. Most of the people were already dead. There was blood coming from their noses and ears and blisters appeared on their skin. Their skin was turning yellow. All the chickens, dogs, and pigs were also dead. The people who were not dead were jerking like fish when you take them out of the water. Their skins were already yellow. Soon some of them turned black and they got blisters like the others. Blood came from their noses and they died.

"There were others like me working up the hill. When the bag burst and spread the yellow cloud it was at treetop level. But there were some of us who were up the hill above the trees, so we did not get covered by the cloud or breathe it. But later when we came down the hill to the village, the ones who drank water from the well also became sick. They turned black and got blisters and died jerking and bleeding. I took my wife and children away to another village and we drank none of the water before we left. But we all felt short of breath and sick in our stomachs.

"We walked through the forest for six weeks. The last two weeks we had nothing to eat except what we could find in the forest, because we were no longer in the mountains. We were in the plains where the Lao live, and we were afraid to ask anyone for food. That is why my son is so thin. We are afraid that he is going to die also."

I asked him what he meant by "also."

"When we got to the Mekong we tied ourselves to some pieces of bamboo fence and floated across at night. My youngest daughter was very weak and had been sick from the gas. When we reached this side, she became very sick and died in the camp where the Thais kept us before sending us here."

The medic explained that the girl had died of pneumonia, but she had been suffering from some kind of lung disease ever since the gas attack, and she had been weakened further by starvation and exposure.

"This boy may survive," the medic added, "but they fed him so much opium to keep him from crying when they crossed the river that he was overdosed."

The story that the refugee father had related was not unusual. The medic said he had heard other Hmong tell similar stories.

Sometimes the gas was blue or red, sometimes green or yellow or pink. The medic said he thought the blue-colored gas was used in part to knock the people unconscious so that they could not take shelter, and he thought that the other colors were added to mark the target so that the pilots could make their turn and easily find the same village again. Then they dropped the bags that had the killing agents—a red mist or a yellow rain—and these were said at different times to explode anywhere from one thousand or two thousand feet above the village to as low as treetop height, so the attackers must be able to adjust the detonator according to altitude, wind conditions, and the area they wanted to cover.

"You must understand," the medic explained, "that the Hmong have different ways of seeing things and measuring things than Westerners. In our language we do not use terms such as yards or meters, so when I translate I have to make an approximation. Also, as Dr. Lewis and the other American doctors have learned when we helped them with their interviews, the situation is not always the same. That is why we think that the Russians are doing this as an experiment to test their chemical warfare in the field with different chemicals under different conditions. They are just using the Vietnamese and Lao to carry it out, although some of the Hmong say they have seen round eyes in the L-19s. They fly more slowly than the MIGs, so sometimes you could see their faces looking down from the plane."

I asked where the attacks were taking place.

"His village was near the Phu Bia Mountain, but on the Vang Vieng side. Closer to Vang Vieng. That is why it took him only six weeks to reach the river. The others take eight weeks or longer. By then they are either dead from the chemicals or the chemicals are worn off. Most of them do not understand what it is that is making them sick. The Hmong people call it medicine from the sky."

I wandered later through the huge resettlement camp, talking with people in broken Thai or French or English. Old men approached me with expansive smiles and insisted on shaking hands like old friends, as if we had served together in the war. All the hill people are like that. Dr. Lewis and Dr. Fred Sidell of Edgewood arrived from Loei to resume their interviews, using a specially prepared questionnaire.

What happened to the questionnaires later in Washington was a fascinating exercise in bureaucracy at work, and helps to explain why it is so difficult for government leaders to get a grip on reality in the field. It also helps to explain why simple, straightforward details offered up by earnest hill people get garbled by the time they reach Washington, and then do not make much of an impression. When the details are then picked up by the press and reported in newspapers and television, it is like the Six Blind Men of Hindustan groping at various parts of an elephant and describing what they think it is—the one holding the tail says it's a snake, the one feeling the legs says it's a tree, and so forth.

First, Dr. Lewis got a strong, tactile description of an attack and the victims from somebody who was there. Then he was obliged to record only the "pertinent" data in a very simplified form, eliminating all significant undertones and colorations. Then the forms were all bundled together and submitted to the Army Surgeon General's Office, with a summary by Dr. Lewis on top. The summary was kept terse and flavorless in the manner favored by the army. It embodied the conclusions reached by Lewis after all the interviews, and after lengthy discussions with Fred Sidell and other team members. But it was depersonalized. The Surgeon General's office passed copies on to the Pentagon where it was scanned by the Office of the Joint Chiefs of Staff and then passed on to other branches of the government. At some point along the way, two of Dr. Lewis's three conclusions were absorbed by the bureaucrats while the third—and most provocative—was misunderstood and ignored. At the same time, the bureaucrats saw the figures Dr. Lewis gave for the number of deaths from gassing actually witnessed by people he interviewed in Laos. The bureaucrats then made the mistake of using this number as the total of all gas deaths in Laos, not merely the deaths witnessed by the 43 people interviewed. That figure—of 800–1,000 dead—remained fixed in American government documents for the next three years and was cited repeatedly in State Department, White House, Pentagon, and congressional statements, and in the press as a result. The mistake became institutionalized. The actual number of gas deaths in Laos was more on the order of 15,000 to 20,000 *at that time* (autumn 1979). When some European critics then suggested that Washington was exaggerating the gas reports, they would have laughed if they had known how right they were—the number was exaggerated downward unwittingly.

Eventually, Dr. Lewis would end up testifying before the House Subcommittee on Asian and Pacific Affairs. His report would be declassified after the names of the Hmong refugees were deleted to protect them from reprisals. Because of the complexity of the report, and its technical language, only a few people would bother to wade through it, and then sit bolt upright as they began to comprehend such dispassionate interviews as this extract:

1. Date: 28 September 1978
2. Location: Pha Na Khun at foot of Phu Bia.
3. Name: DELETED, 50 year old man, village clerk, French Foreign Legion in 1950s. Wrote out a list of family names, number of people killed in each.
4 & 5. Mode of attack and Material/Agent used: Two L-19 airplanes—first one sprayed yellow and green powder that was not wet like rain—but fell to ground. Second plane few minutes later—fired rocket that exploded about 20 meters overhead releasing a red smoke/gas.
6. Number of people in village/unit: 300 (about 50 were out of village at time of attack)
7. Number of people affected: Only 19 or 20 survived.
8. Number of people killed: Approximately 230.
9. Animals: All animals died.
10. Miscellaneous: The yellow and green powders made everyone feel dizzy, confused actions, blurred vision, difficult to move, people fell down, jaws were stiff (clamped shut), could not speak and had almost immediate vomiting and diarrhea before the red smoke came down.

Red smoke caused all to start coughing, have massive nose bleeds within five minutes; blood came from nose and mouth and people fell down and were dead in less than 15 minutes.

At onset of attack, he ran with 12 year old son about 50 meters out of village to small cave where he could see people dying. He and son were made very ill by smoke.

MEDICAL FINDINGS: His symptoms—dizzy, headache at temples. Eyes—no pain, no tears, blurred vision—could not see beyond 10 meters; son's eyes were very red and the black part of eyes (iris) was smaller and lighter in color. Throat—very sore, could not talk, voice weak and hoarse, larynx felt tight. Coughed repeatedly and coughed up blood. Burning pain in chest with coughing. Marked shortness of breath—could say only one or two words. Substernal pain with breathing, very difficult to breathe because he was so weak. No vomiting or diarrhea. Skin—yellow material got on legs—caused much itching —scratched skin off—10 days later had crusted lesions. Sleep—unable to go to sleep for five days. Muscles—so weak he could not move or even pick up a pack of cigarettes. Lasted two days.

Several hours after attack a military unit of ethnic Pathet Lao soldiers with AK rifles and B-40 rockets entered the village. Carried all those alive (19 or 20) into center of village—gave them an injection into upper arm. Next morning they were carried one or two kilometers to Muang Oom Village. Kept in a hospital five days and given injections on second and fifth days. Was very weak but could walk short distance. Sent to a detention center.

Soldiers wore a "cloth mask" (like dressing pads) over nose and mouth. Describes five of his group that acted "crazy" and two died on 8th day and three more died 10th day after attack (all in their twenties). States the skin peeled off in sheets, very large sacs of skin with fluid in them and very sick. Their bodies (skin) turned black within three hours of death. Sounds like Toxic Epidermal Necrolysis.

Dr. Lewis stated in the report that "the team was prepared to obtain blood and skin samples (for cholinesterase activity and study of pathological changes, respectively) from those exposed to chemical agents. For such samples to yield meaningful results they must be taken within 6–8 weeks of exposure. Since the last reported exposure was in May 1979 no samples were collected."

The team interviewed forty men, two women, and a twelve-year-old girl, taking one or two hours for each interview.

"The chemical attacks," wrote Dr. Lewis, "reportedly occurred between June 1976 and May 1979. The absence of reports of attacks after May 1979 may be because very few refugees crossed the Mekong River after that time because of heavy rains and flooding from June to September 1979. Most of the early reports were of the use of rockets releasing the agent, but beginning in the fall of 1978 the majority of the attacks were carried out by aircraft spraying a yellowish substance which 'fell like rain.'

"The team was given a plastic vial containing pieces of bark stained by a yellow substance which several Hmong refugees claimed was residue from an aircraft spray attack in April 1979. Preliminary chemical analysis of the sample indicates that no standard chemical agent is present, i.e., an agent listed in TM-8-285 (U.S. Army, May 1974)." (This is a technical manual that lists the various chemical warfare agents used during World War I, the first-generation agents, and the newer chemical warfare agents developed before, during, and after World War II, or the second-generation agents, which includes the nerve gases.)

The tests demonstrated that none of these first- or second-generation agents were on the leaves or the bark. This did not mean absolutely that agents of those two categories were not used, although most of them would leave residues of arsenic or other chemicals that could be detected. The only substance on the bark was in itself very curious: It was a chemical "surfactant" called laurel sufonate commonly used in liquid soaps or detergents to help them penetrate easily. (Not the sort of thing common to remote hills in Laos.) Whatever killer poison had been there with the surfactant had long since washed away.

Dr. Lewis concluded that "at least two, and possibly three, different chemical agents" may have been used, including a nerve agent, an irritant or riot-control agent, plus one or more other chemicals that produced symptoms "that it is difficult to attribute to a single known agent."

The signs and symptoms suggesting a nerve agent included sweating, tearing, excessive salivation, difficulty in breathing, shortness of breath, nausea and vomiting, dizziness, weakness, convulsions, and death occurring shortly after exposure.

The signs Lewis thought suggested a riot-control or irritant agent included irritation or burning of the eyes with tearing and pain; irritation and burning of the nose and throat; coughing and burning and tightness in the chest; headache; nausea and vomiting.

But the symptoms that could not be attributed to a nerve agent or riot-control agent, or any other known single chemical agent, were a mixture of the above, plus profuse bleeding from mucous membranes of the nose, lungs, and gastrointestinal tract with rapid death.

Dr. Lewis was working very much like a forensic pathologist at the scene of a murder. First he determined how the victims died and exactly what their symptoms and medical signs were. Then he traced backward to the scene at the time of the murder to establish what was curious or significant and revealing about the incident as it happened. From these two groups of information he then made a projection of the probable cause of death—as a coroner would after doing an autopsy on a corpse dragged out of the bay. For example, if the victim's lungs were full of water, death probably was from drowning. If the lungs were not full of water, the victim may have been killed before being dumped in the bay, so foul play can be suspected.

In Laos, Dr. Lewis established that the victims had three basic groups of symptoms and signs. They had terrible skin burns and burns to eyes, nose, and throat. They spewed blood from all their body openings. And they died in spasms and convulsions. These were the three main indicators, although scores of other lesser signs added to the conclusions.

There were only a few *known* chemical agents that could cause these symptoms. The burning would have to be produced by a vesicant or blistering agent. The convulsions by a nerve agent. At least, those were the only known types of agents that could produce exactly those effects.

Neither a blister agent nor a nerve agent, however, could produce the third effect of extraordinary bleeding. Such hemorrhages, Dr. Lewis assured me, were a "medical anomaly"—meaning that they are abnormal in the extreme.

If the bleeding was not produced by a nerve agent or blister agent, what was it produced by? A new killing agent? In that case could the new killing agent also be producing the burning and the convulsions? Possibly. But aside from the initial blue or other bright-colored gases apparently sprayed to knock out the villagers and pin-point the target, the killing agents seemed to fall in two types—a red gas and a yellow powder. Sometimes they were delivered together, sometimes separately. The yellow powder, which came to be called "yellow rain," seemed most often to cause the convulsions. The red mist seemed to cause massive hemorrhage. Or were they just different variations of the same chemicals?

On the basis of these findings, Dr. Lewis recommended that the Army Medical Corps develop a system using a computerized questionnaire that would help to better identify the chemical agents involved. Three years passed before such a basic questionnaire was finally devised by the Arms Control and Disarmament Agency. Lewis urged that a channel be established to collect and rapidly transport blood, tissue, and other specimens from any suspect area to the U.S. Army Biomedical Laboratory at Edgewood for analysis. He proposed also that every effort be made to obtain samples of indigenous plants that might be a source of some of the toxic compounds that could cause the Hmong deaths. He mentioned in particular *Croton tiglium,* abrin (the crab-eye or jequirity pea), *cryptopleurin,* ricin (castor bean), and pinene. He also suggested that simple, commercially available toxic agent collection kits should be distributed for use in any area suspected of coming under chemical attack, and that a medical team should be kept on stand-by ready to travel to the scene to investigate any future gas reports. Not one of these proposals was acted upon for over a year.

"From a military defense position," Dr. Lewis concluded in his report, "it would seem to be an extremely urgent mission to initiate every effort possible to identify the chemical agents that have been used and to develop appropriate countermeasures, antidotes, etc."

Certain things were clear. Neither the Lao nor the Vietnamese, with their industry (such as it was) still attempting to recover from the protracted war, were capable of developing the complex poison compound being used on the Hmong.

Some of the lethal agents in the compound might be industrial chemicals such as chlorine or phosgene that could be purchased commercially, but a mustard gas—or similar blister agent—was probably incorporated in some of the attacks in Laos, and mustard is not simple to manufacture.

Although Dr. Lewis's report was ultimately reduced to arid, bureaucratic terms, its substance was clear. I had been able to listen to the Hmong accounts first hand, which filled in the tragedy and drama left out of the documents. With a solid medical framework provided by Dr. Lewis, I went on by myself through Ban Vinai, filling in the bits and pieces from eyewitnesses. While the medical team looked for basic forensic signs and symptoms, I looked for telltale signs of a less tangible sort. Both at Ban Vinai and back in Bangkok, they began to add up.

While I was in Thailand, both Thai military intelligence and American radio monitors picked up radio intercepts from Russian and Vietnamese military transmissions inside Indochina mentioning four separate chemical warfare depots. One of the Thai radio intercepts, passed on to the American embassy in Bangkok, identified the Soviet Union as the source of the chemicals in the depots. This merely confirmed what was by then obvious to anyone giving the matter serious thought.

There was no longer any question that the Hmong were being wiped out with a chemical compound containing not merely a form of nerve gas or something producing similar spasms, but some very exotic other chemicals that could not be identified by American experts. And these compounds were not being mixed up in the jungle and stirred with twigs in rusting oil drums. They were the products of high technology and of advanced laboratories with years of experience in chemical warfare development.

According to very well informed U.S. Government sources, satellite photographs of the places identified as chemical warfare depots in the radio intercepts showed them to be high-security areas surrounded by barbed wire and chain link fences. In two of the intercepts, Russian officers were heard giving instructions for the movement of a shipment of chemical warheads from one depot in Laos up a highway toward the Phu Bia Mountain attack sites. In another, a high-ranking Soviet general was touring the chemical depots. These brief transmissions, known in espionage as "secrets spoke," were recorded and translated.

Publicly, the State Department was still being very cautious, acting as if nothing had developed from unfounded rumors. But when pressed, State Department officials would concede that Assistant Secretary Richard Holbrooke in 1979 had made "representations" to the governments of Laos, Vietnam, and the Soviet Union about the use of toxic chemical on the Hmong. All three governments denied knowing what Holbrooke was talking about.

On my way back from Thailand that autumn, I stopped in Paris to see if I could take care of one loose end that bothered me—the presence of the four French mercenaries inside Laos.

In Paris French government officials knew nothing about the mercenaries or poison gas, they said. But one French journalist found an explanation for the mercenaries. Since the Communist victory in Indochina, he said, the Corsican heroin brokers of Marseille had been cut off from their main line of supply from the opium-growing regions of northwestern Laos. It would not be at all surprising, he observed, if the brokers periodically hired a small group of mercenary jungle experts to go into Laos and bring out a few pounds of refined No. 4 heroin. Because of the meager rainfall the past year, the price of opium base in Thailand had risen sharply from 3,000 baht (U.S. $150) a "joy" (3.5 pounds, or 1.6 kilos) to nearly 20,000 baht ($1,000) a joy. A few pounds of No. 4 heroin would be worth millions in Europe or America.

As I walked back toward my hotel on the Left Bank through the cold drizzle of late October, shivering in the unaccustomed cold after Thailand, I noticed a color poster on a news kiosk. It was a huge enlargement of the current cover of Le Point, showing an emaciated Cambodian infant with the bold black headline, "Cambodge: Holocauste." Someday soon there might be a similar poster with the headline "Laos: Holocauste"—perhaps with the face of the little Hmong boy who had swallowed too much opium. I looked away from the gaudy kiosk to the cold, muddy River Seine as the drizzle swept by me on the wind from the east, and I thought not of the Seine but of the warm and muddy Mekong. And I shivered. Not from the cold. Maybe it was because the drizzle felt like yellow rain.

I wondered if it was falling also on the chill Belgian countryside at Ypres, where it all began.

3.

Pilgrimage to Ypres

The trees lean eastward at Ypres, bent by the same prevailing winds that have driven sailing ships up the nearby English Channel since time forgotten. The Channel at Dunkirk is only thirty miles from Ypres through the low, rolling green hills. Here in the soft countryside of Belgium is where chemical warfare really began on a massive scale—in the Great War of 1914–18. If the mystery of Laos had an answer, the path to that answer would begin here among the hedgerows and wild roses of Ypres. So, after digesting all I could of the medical analysis of the victims in Laos, and sifting through the intelligence agency scuttlebutt in Washington, I gathered all the historical records I could find in the Library of Congress and set out for a pilgrimage to Ypres. I still knew very little about phosgene, chlorine, adamsite, and other first-generation chemical agents that played such a large part in World War I. And all I knew of mustard was that it burns like hell and makes great blisters that peel off in sheets, particularly in the armpits and crotch. I had heard stories of secret agents spraying each other with tiny jets of mustard from pencil-size dispensers, as a sort of nonfatal punishment. But what happened if you were a doughboy in the trenches and green clouds of chlorine and mustard descended upon you? What was it like? How did you die, if you died?

It was typical of popular literature to cast the poison gas of World War I in terms so horrible that they evoked images of charnel houses, grisly evil, and unspeakable fear. They seemed wildly exaggerated. How much of it was propaganda? The numbers killed by gas in that war were different in nearly every book and magazine article. How many really were killed, and what befell those who did not die?

There are many misconceptions about chemical warfare that are traceable back to World War I. They were the result of propaganda by both sides, and the lies and exaggerations were perpetuated after the war when the powers sat down to talk. The people responsible are long since gone, but their distortions continue to interfere with everything we see and hear about poison gas. Among the archives, however, there are eyewitness accounts from soldiers and officers. There are genuine medical statistics underneath all the false ones. Some of the real stories are grisly and frightening, but the overall impression that emerges is not one of death but one of unbridled fear—fear beyond all bounds of reality. Of frightened men stampeding across blasted no-man's-land, flinging their weapons aside in their terror to escape from pursuing clouds of choking, burning vapors. As this legitimate picture of gas warfare began to take shape for me from out of the mountain of propaganda, it became amazing for entirely unsuspected reasons. And the inspiration for all that fear began to have a focus in the person of a single, rather pathetic German scientist who performed extraordinary feats of invention to save his fatherland, and in the process gave us chemical warfare as we knew it half a century later. In appreciation of his patriotism he was given the greatest honors by one German government and then was victimized by the next for being a Jew.

The history of chemical warfare turns on this curious scientist, and on another superpatriot very much like him—an American. These two men, now largely forgotten, were fired by misguided zeal. They learned how to bend popular resistance to the poisons of war, and to mold generals and citizens alike behind the cause of gas warfare. Thanks in large part to these two men—Fritz Haber and Amos Fries—the German people in World War I and the American people, fifty years later in the Vietnam War, accepted the military use of deadly poisons as if they were a normal part of human warfare. Haber and Fries left a legacy that haunts us today, and set forth ways of manipulating popular fears that others now seek to exploit. More than anyone else, it was Fries and Haber who duped us into accepting the "unthinkable."

Both men seemed to be driven by noble instincts, though neither of them apparently intended to become a demagogue. In fact, without Fritz Haber, Amos Fries might have led just an ordinary career as an army engineer. But once Haber acted, Fries had to over-react. So it is with Fritz Haber that we must begin—back in the trenches at Ypres.

The road south from Amsterdam took me two hundred miles across the Low Countries, through some of the most embattled landscape on the face of the earth. The route led across Holland to Belgium, along the edge of the Ardennes Forest, through the shallow valleys of Waterloo, and past the pubescent hills of Mons, presently the headquarters of SHAFE—Supreme Headquarters Allied Forces Europe, the senior military command of NATO. Along the way the countryside was peaceful, green and moist. Small towns peeked over the curve of hills, and tidy villages were tucked like lace handkerchiefs into deep cleavages. All along there were cows, staring back at me unmoved. The cows, I mused, are always the first to die in a war. And the bent trees go soon afterward, torn up by the roots and flung through the air like dog's bones by the impact of artillery and bombs. Many of the trees left standing at Ypres still retain the memory of the chemical warfare in World War I. They retain it very clearly, judging from the experience of farmers here. One farmer at Ypres cut down a tree, a task that took him all of the morning, and when he sat down on the stump to wipe his brow, the tree shared its memory with him. His rump began to burn that afternoon, and by evening there were huge welts and blisters all over his backside. The residue of World War I mustard gas had been preserved in the wood of the tree.

Here at Ypres, in the drizzle of a day not unlike a cold day in early spring of 1915, it is possible to see why the generals always seem to choose places like this for carnage on the grand scale. The terrain is so innocent in its undulations that the landscape resembles a vast military plotting table from staff college. Troops can be moved around on it like tin soldiers. Command posts can be situated on the brows of ridgelines, the officers wielding spyglasses. A man on horseback can see a long way at Ypres.

For the men in trenches on that awful spring day in 1915, it was another story. They did not know what was coming. And when it hit them, they did not know what it was. They tried to run, throwing down their weapons, but it did no good.

They should have known that something grim was being planned for them because of all the activity over in the German lines. But the men on both sides were numbed by the long winter, and the grisly slaughter, the lice, the fungus, and the unending hunger. Even the German footsoldiers little understood all the strange comings and goings through the midwinter and early spring. First, there were the wagons. Hundreds of caissons rolled up to deliver odd-looking cylinders from the I.G. Farben factories. They were unloaded by the infantry and were placed in the care of the Pioneers— the specially trained chemical troops—with their strange equipment. It was all carried out under the close personal scrutiny of the gloomy scientist Dr. Fritz Haber, the head of Berlin's Kaiser Wilhelm Institute of physical chemistry and electrochemistry. Dr. Haber was everywhere in his civilian suit and vest, with a black bow tie at the winged collar, brooding over his cylinders as if they were incubating eggs about to hatch. His dark, sunken eyes peered out sorrowfully from above his fat mustache. Frequently he removed his homburg to wipe his balding dome, nervously inspecting the labor in progress to prepare proper nests for his precious eggs.

Of course, it was the infantry that did the work. First the digging, always carried out at night so that it would be unobserved by spies in enemy observation balloons and scout planes. The soldiers carved deep, narrow slits into the bottoms of the trenches. Thousands of slits were dug, because there were nearly six thousand metal cylinders. Each cylinder weighed nearly ninety pounds, and it took a detail of four soldiers to wrestle each one along the zigzag trenches, each trench bending every few yards so that incoming artillery rounds could not extend their concussion and shrapnel beyond the next bend.

There were so many cylinders that before long the soldiers were exhausted and prepared to risk their lives to take shortcuts by going over the top—dashing across exposed ground to their destination with each cylinder, preferring enemy fire to traversing the stinking trenches.

At each pit, the Pioneers watched closely as the soldiers lowered each cylinder gently into its slit nest, so that the domed valve cover at one end of the cylinder was just level with the bottom of the trench. Then the cylinder was cushioned with salsdecke—a long, sausage-shaped bag stuffed with peat moss that had been soaked in a potash solution to absorb any leaking gas. A board was placed over the slit, and this in turn was covered with three layers of sand-bags to shield the cylinder from all but a direct hit by enemy artillery. Until the time came to release the gas, the infantry could stand on the sandbags as a fire step. Soon many of the soldiers even forgot there was a cylinder underneath their feet.

Night after night, the strange noises could be heard by anyone with ears: the clinking, grunting, scraping, banging, and cursing. The cursing of the German infantrymen should have alerted the entire Western front.

It did not. German radio broadcasts and official communiqués accused the French, the British, and the Russians of using poison gas, but it was only propaganda to prepare the way. Nobody believed it.

The rumors about gas were so discredited that when French intelligence interrogated a German prisoner and learned that a gas attack was about to be launched, the French decided that it was an effort to plant false information. The German prisoner described the activity in his trenches in detail—a revelation that ultimately became known to his own countrymen, who labeled him "The Traitor of Ypres." But nobody reacted to his information. On April 9, 1915, a British newspaper ran a foolish story snickering about the preposterous rumors of an impending German gas attack. On that very day, the orders were issued to set off the cylinders and release their poisonous contents.

But the winds were wrong. Where the line of trenches bulged around the town of Ypres, there was a stretch where the trenches ran from northwest to southeast. And the prevailing wind from the west was strong that day. If the gas had been released, instead of rolling out of the German trenches toward the enemy lines, it would have stayed inside the German trenches and crept around the zigzags to exterminate their own men.

What the Germans needed was a wind from the north. Dr. Haber was certainly a brilliant chemist, but he was not a very shrewd meteorologist, or he would have known that Ypres was not the best place to find a wind from the north.

Day followed day as the Germans waited. The killing went on with ordinary weapons—bullets, artillery shells, and grenades—and replacements arrived in the German lines who had no idea what lay beneath their feet, under the sandbags. In the rear, Dr. Fritz

Haber waited tensely with his Pioneers. At last, on April 22, the wind came from the north.

All afternoon the Pioneers jostled into the trenches to make final preparations. Each Pioneer assumed his position beside a battery of twenty buried cylinders. Each battery was uncovered. The sandbags were removed and the boards were taken up. The protective domes were taken off the protruding cylinder valves. Lead pipes were attached to the valves and the opposite end of each pipe was directed up over the lip of the trench. A nozzle on the top end of each pipe pointed toward no-man's-land. To hold the nozzles and pipes securely in place, a sandbag was placed on each nozzle where it stuck up above the trench. This also served to hide the nozzles from anyone in the enemy lines who became curious.

Nobody was especially curious in the French lines opposite because on the previous day the crack French XX Corps had been withdrawn from that section of the line and replaced by seventeen companies of untested African Colonials and two battalions of the Forty-fifth (Algerian) Division. To the right and left of the black Africans were Belgians and newly arrived Canadians.

At 4:00 P.M. on April 22, 1915, as the gathering chill of dusk stiffened the blasted mud in the trenches and across the pockmarked no-man's-land, a small German plane flew along the front dropping flares, to the utter mystification of the French Colonials. At the sight of the flares, the German infantry fell back from their trenches, leaving the Pioneers to face the risk of something going wrong with the cylinders and their plumbing. It was very quiet.

With eerie slowness, a thick cloud formed and rolled out from the German line. It was a sickly green.

"Surprise and curiosity riveted us to the ground," said a Belgian grenadier. "None of us knew what was going on. The smoke cloud grew thicker, which made us believe that the German trenches were on fire!"

A Captain Pollard, watching from British trenches not far away, saw the "strange green cloud of death." A light northeasterly breeze wafted it toward him. In a moment death had him by the throat.

"It was a new and devilish engine of warfare," he wrote. "One for which white troops were wholly unprepared, and which held for these brave Africans a sheer terror of the supernatural—one cannot blame them that they broke and fled.

"In the gathering dark of that awful night, they fought with their terror, running blindly in the gas cloud, and dropping with breasts heaving in agony and the slow poison of suffocation mantling their dark faces. Hundreds of them fell and died; others lay helpless, froth upon their agonized lips and their racked bodies powerfully sick with tearing nausea at short intervals. They, too, would die later—a slow and lingering death of agony unspeakable.

"The whole air was tainted with the acrid smell of chlorine that caught at the back of men's throats and filled their mouths with its metallic taste."

A French army doctor in the path of the cloud hardly had time to see it coming before he felt its effects. "I had the impression that I was looking through green glasses. It burned my throat, caused pains in my chest, and made breathing all but impossible. I spat blood and suffered from dizziness. We all thought we were lost."

The Allied line melted away before the awesome green cloud. It oozed across no-man's-land and flowed into the Allied trenches. In the rear, an exhausted London battalion—Queen Victoria's Rifles—had just disengaged from the fighting for Hill 60 near Ypres when, as one of them recalled, "over the fields streamed mobs of infantry, the dusky warriors of French Africa; away went their rifles, equipment, even their tunics, that they might run faster. One man came stumbling through our lines. An officer of ours held him up with levelled revolver. 'What's the matter, you bloody lot of cowards?' says he. The Zouave was frothing at the mouth, his eyes started from their sockets, and he fell writhing at the officer's feet."

"The cloud around us was clearing," reported the Belgian grenadier from his lines to the left of the area under gas attack. "Ahead of us and to our right, whole enemy ranks were moving up with fixed bayonets behind the cloud."

The German infantry had been equipped with crude saturated cotton gauze respirators but were nonetheless highly reluctant to move into the gas area. "I could distinctly see the German officers hitting their men with the blades of their sabers, in order to make them advance faster," said the Belgian. "Hell now broke loose from our lines as we opened fire on the enemy. My rifle burned my fingers, but those damned Boches kept advancing, and moved beyond the French trenches."

The chlorine gas cloud had stifled all opposition along nine kilometers of the front; despite desperate flanking fire from the

Belgians and Canadians, the Germans pushed easily through. But they had advanced only two hundred yards when they stopped and began digging in, because night was falling and that was their standard operating procedure.

When their officers frantically called for reinforcements to exploit the breakthrough, they were told by German field headquarters that there were no reserves available. The German high command had not expected the gas to work, so no reserves had been prepared to support a breakthrough. The way to the Channel ports was open. The Allied lines could be cut. All major supply lines to Europe could be severed. England would be within artillery range, and a German triumph would at last be assured. But the Germans could not move.

By midnight the Allied command had figured out what had happened. The Canadians were wheeled into position to block any further German advance. By morning on the twenty-third, the French had reorganized, and the Allies counterattacked.

With no protective trenches and no reinforcements, the Germans fell back in bitter fighting to the original line they had left the previous day. The Second Battle of Ypres had ended without changing the position of the western front.

The novelty and the unexpectedness of the poison gas onslaught had produced very real terror at the front. The utter lack of a defense against poison gas stirred serious fears in the Allied command. There was clearly a need to galvanize the public to this new threat, so the propagandists quickly amplified the horror. Even now, after many decades, it is nearly impossible to cut through the distortions and arrive at any simple judgment of the military effectiveness of the gas attack. For years after World War I, popular estimates of the casualties at the Second Ypres mentioned 15,000 gas casualties including 5,000 dead—a wild exaggeration. According to the official British medical history of the war, 7,000 gas casualties passed through the field ambulances and casualty clearing areas in the Ypres sector on the night of 22 April. Of these only 350 died. The British figures may not be all-inclusive, but they are accurate so far as they go, and they reflect the proportions of those who died out of the much larger number who were sickened or disabled.

The misery of the survivors stirred the sympathy of even battle-hardened veterans who had grown accustomed to the sight of bodies mangled by shot and shell.

"There was no difficulty in finding them," wrote an officer of the wounded Territorials, when he came upon them in a field hospital on April 23. "The noise of the poor devils trying to get their breath was sufficient direction. Twenty of the worst cases were on mattresses, all more or less in a sitting posture, propped against the walls. Faces, arms, hands were a shiny gray-black. With mouths open and lead-glazed eyes, they were all swaying backwards and forwards trying to get their breath, struggling, struggling for life. There was nothing that could be done except to give them salt and water emetic. The gas fills up the lungs and bronchial tubes with froth, which finally suffocates the victim. It is like slow drowning, taking sometimes two days."

The frightful impact of chemicals on the unsuspecting soldiers of Ypres was actually part of a great sea change in warfare then taking place. This sea change had vast undercurrents that were only dimly perceived at the time. Industrialization in Europe and America was making the world a far more threatening and complicated place. There was no longer any simple cause and effect.

When something occurred in Europe before 1915, it could be ignored by people elsewhere. When World War I began, it was thought to be a matter for settlement by the usual professional soldiers. When it ended, however, war between countries had become total war, with every human being a combatant and every family residence and every farm in jeopardy. In such a new total war, tactical brilliance, which had been sufficient to ensure victory in earlier wars, was sufficient no longer. Victory in the modern unlimited war would depend instead on a country's ability to invent, manufacture, and deploy the industrial machinery of war. Victory would belong to the generals of production and their armies of technicians.

Ignorance of this concept almost lost World War I for Germany at the outset. Her aristocratic general staff was still approaching the battlefield with a medieval mentality. They regarded the crude realities of industrial production with arrogant contempt. It was their neglect of these realities that led directly to the green cloud at Ypres.

The German generals had faith in the military inevitability of the von Schlieffen Plan, which called for a massive attack and a quick victory. The von Schlieffen Plan simply did not allow for the vigorous opposition of the Belgians and the French. It did not allow for bogging down on the battlefield, for the onset of trench warfare, and for the numbing, discouraging slaughter to follow. Also, it did not allow adequately for the British navy blockade that quickly cut off vital supplies of raw materials such as rubber and petroleum. Not only had quick victory eluded Germany, but she was now faced by the peril that she would not be able to maintain the war because she lacked essential raw materials. Rubber and petroleum, the generals discovered to their dismay, were not the only raw materials a war required. There was also the matter of gunpowder.

The inescapable fact was that Germany, like the rest of the world, depended for its manufacture of gunpowder and high explosives on a single source—the saltpeter deposits of Chile, on South America's west coast. These saltpeter deposits in the Chilean deserts, far away from the industrial centers of the world, were the best and largest source of nitrates—which were essential for explosives and for agricultural fertilizers. When the British blockade cut off Germany's access to nitrates from Chile, the Germans found themselves with less than six months' supply of explosives, and no way to get the raw materials for more.

The prominent German industrialist Walther Rathenau had foreseen this crisis. But when it occurred, he was not able to find a single general staff officer who even knew what gunpowder was made from—much less the significance of the Chilean connection.

Germany's increasingly desperate situation prompted a frantic attempt to breach the British naval blockade and to reopen the nitrate supply line from Chile. The German navy assaulted the British base in the remote Falkland Islands, in the south Atlantic, which commanded the shipping lanes around Cape Horn to and from Chile. The British were thoroughly mystified by the motive for the attack. Years later, when Sir Winston Churchill wrote his history of the war, he confessed that he never understood what the Germans were doing down there.

The attack failed, and the supply of Chilean nitrates remained blocked. The German offensive in Europe might have come to an ignominious end, and World War I might very well have stopped,

if it had not been for Germany's inventiveness in two totally unrelated fields: the manufacture of dyes for bright-colored clothes
and the solution of the age-old human problem of famine. For in
these two unlikely areas lay the answer to synthetic gunpowder—
and, ultimately, to chemical warfare.

Just as the world depended largely on Chile for nitrates, it
depended on China for blue cloth—until the last half of the nineteenth century. For only China had the source of natural indigo dye
—the indigo plant—to meet the demand of an increasingly stylish
world. The production of dyes for clothing had become a major
German enterprise, and commercial agents for the German dyestuffs industry had worked hard for decades to corner the market
on natural sources of dyes all over the world. The majority of
China's production of natural indigo dye was controlled by a German company called BASF (Badische Anilin und Soda-Fabrik, of
Ludwigshafen). A great deal of money was paid to Chinese indigo
merchants each year by BASF. So it was a matter of serious priority
at BASF to find a way to produce indigo artificially. Its staff scientists had long been engaged in research toward that end when, at
the end of the nineteenth century, they succeeded at last. A way
was found to create synthetic indigo by the reduction of nitroben-
zene. (One of the by-products of the process was the generation of
forty tons of liquid chlorine each day.)

With this achievement, Germany's grip on the world supply of
dyes was complete. In order to take full advantage of their monopoly, and to eliminate pointless competition among themselves, the
German dye manufacturers (or *farben,* meaning color producers)
joined together into a cartel. The cartel was called an *interessen
gemeinshaft,* or community of interests, and became known as the
color producers' cartel, or I.G. Farben.

I.G. Farben's objectives went far beyond the mere pooling of
profits from the German dye industry. It wanted to eliminate all
competition throughout the world and to gain a total monopoly.
Ruthlessly the cartel members drove competitors from the field.
Their mutual strength permitted them to slash their prices as low
as necessary to undercut a competitor for as long as necessary to
drive him out of business. Wherever they found a need for materials, the I.G. bought out the supplier or underwrote major scientific research to develop a synthetic alternative.

The mastery of the chemistry of textile dyes gave the cartel immense strength. It also offered a scientific base that was available to each of the companies in the I.G. They were free to pursue their own specialties outside the cartel. From the prolific laboratories of the I.G. came an outpouring of chemical and pharmaceutical advances that substantially affected life on the planet: aspirin, sulfa drugs, Atabrine (for malaria), heroin (as a treatment for morphine addiction), and later methadone (for treatment of heroin addiction), all from Bayer; a cure for syphilis from Hoechst; photochemicals and film from Agfa; and from a balding instructor at a technical school, working under a grant from BASF, a process for artificially fixing the nitrogen from air as a source of nitrates for fertilizer, thereby substantially reducing the threat of famine in the world.

The man who achieved this major victory over human hunger, and who would one day receive the Nobel Prize for his feat, was Fritz Haber.

He was born on December 9, 1868, in Breslau, where his father was a chemical merchant. But as a young man he found himself ill equipped to be a merchant like his father in the family business. He was also not a particularly good student, but he stuck to his studies at the Technische Hochschule in Berlin and took his doctorate in organic chemistry. The so-far undeveloped field of physical chemistry interested him a great deal more than organic chemistry. So, as soon as he was able to secure a teaching job at the Karlsruhe Technische Hochschule in 1894, Fritz Haber turned his energies to the study of electrochemistry and thermodynamics, and began to bloom. In 1906 he became a full professor at the school, and in 1909 he developed a glass electrode of a type now commonly used to measure the acidity of a solution by detecting its electric potential across a thin piece of glass, a simple way to determine the acidity or pH factor.

Haber was especially interested in how different gases react under heat or flame. Because his research had potential industrial application, he was able to obtain a grant from BASF. His project was to find a way to convert elemental nitrogen into compound form, and to be able to carry it out cheaply and on a large scale.

Although the best source of nitrates then lay in the Chilean deposits, the atmosphere of the earth was four-fifths nitrogen, and plain air could provide an inexhaustible supply if only somebody could learn how to convert it at low cost. Two prohibitively expensive ways had been found already—the electric arc process and the cyanamide process—but they required large supplies of cheap electrical power. Haber found a way to combine nitrogen and hydrogen under pressure, using iron as a catalyst, to form ammonia. The ammonia could then be converted into fertilizer—or explosives. It was ingenious, and the consequences were literally earthshaking.

In 1908 Haber informed BASF of his success, which had such impact that practically overnight he became one of Germany's foremost scientists. In no more than three years, in 1911, he was rewarded with the directorship of the prestigious Kaiser Wilhelm Institute in Berlin. It remained for BASF to find a way to develop the Haber process into a practical industrial method. This was carried out for the company by the engineer and chemist Carl Bosch, from Leipzig. By 1913, the Haber-Bosch process was a commercial reality. Initially it was used to produce commercial fertilizers, but it was only a matter of time—and innovation—before more sinister uses were found.

Haber was not merely a patriot. He was a chauvinist of such zeal that he dedicated himself, as director of the Kaiser Wilhelm Institute, to a fanatical support of the fatherland on the eve of World War I. The institute was deeply involved in work on military problems, and Haber led the way. He was full of ideas on how poisonous chemical vapors could be employed as weapons on the battlefield. As a senior chemist of BASF and the I.G. Farben, Haber was intimately informed of the enormous industrial and scientific resources available. He gladly accepted the post as head of Germany's chemical warfare service. But he found the general staff unreceptive to his ideas. To the old war-horses of the German Imperial Army, the notion of using poison in combat was demonic.

All that changed after the British naval blockade. With Chilean nitrates cut off, and only six months' worth of explosives left with which to carry on the war, a crash program was launched to adapt I.G. Farben's manufacturing plants from fertilizer production to gunpowder production. The crash program involved the best chemical and industrial brains in Germany, and came under the direction of Bureau Haber, putting Fritz Haber for the first time in a powerful position where he had the undivided attention of the general staff. As the gunpowder project neared success, holding out the promise of limitless supplies of explosives for the war machine, Haber went before the general staff with some additional ideas on how to break the deadlock at the front. This time they listened.

The enormous quantities of poisonous chemicals generated by the dye industry, he argued, could be a devastating new weapon. The idea was distasteful to the generals, but in their frustration they were willing to permit an initial test. However, they would not endorse the project to the extent that they would draw troops away from other combat areas to provide Haber with reinforcements—it seemed highly unlikely to the general staff that Haber would succeed, despite his fanaticism. They would wait and see.

In 1915, as in the 1980s, poison gas was something people talked about but nobody really believed anyone would dare use. While we consider it to be outlawed by the Geneva Protocol of 1925, the public of 1915 thought it was outlawed by the Hague Convention of 1899.

All the belligerents in 1915—except the United States—had signed the Hague Convention, Article 23 of which forbade "the use of projectiles the sole purpose of which is the diffusion of asphyxiating or deleterious gases." The United States did not sign because it did not believe that such a restraint would have any effect in wartime.

The British had authorized the use of noxious sulfur fumes in the 1894 Siege of Sebastopol during the Crimean War. And during the Boer War from 1899 to 1902 the British had hit Boer guerrilla redoubts with experimental artillery shells containing picric acid, a toxic agent that causes vomiting.

In France, the police had developed tear gas rifle grenades and hand grenades for use in riot control.

But these were all rather primitive experiments. The green cloud at Ypres on April 22, 1915, found the Allies utterly unprepared for gas defense or retaliation in kind. Once the chlorine attack had taken place, and its results were exaggerated by Allied propaganda, the outraged public quite naturally demanded horrible reprisals.

The first priority was gas defense. Perhaps the Germans had not been prepared with reinforcements to take advantage of the unexpected success of the chlorine cloud the first time, but a repetition could prove disastrous. By April 23, the day after Fritz Haber's triumph, the British Medical Service had sped buckets of sodium bicarbonate solution to the trenches with instructions for the troops to soak handkerchiefs in it and tie them over the nose and mouth the moment there was a gas alarm. Within a week, thousands of British women were at work in their homes making copies of a captured German mask—very unreliable copies.

The initial problem was to filter the airborne contaminants from the air being breathed by a soldier. That was easily solved. The secondary problem was to leave a man thus protected free to take part in combat. The first official British mask, the "Black Veil Respirator" issued in mid-May, was hot, smelly, and uncomfortable. It, and subsequent variations, consisted of a long flannel hood with acetate eyeholes, and a pocket below the face that contained a wad of cotton impregnated with absorbents.

Britain's efforts were rewarded on May 1 when another of Fritz Haber's green clouds rolled down across no-man's-land, followed by German infantry. They were stopped cold by soldiers prepared for the gas and able to function despite it.

By autumn, the British had achieved a design breakthrough that solved all the technical problems sufficiently to produce a gas mask that remained in service for thirty years. This was a rat-faced mask connected by a hose to a canister of absorbents carried in a satchel on the soldier's back.

Defense was one thing. Retaliation was another matter. It would mean unleashing a chemical monster whose potential for destruction was only dimly comprehended. For nearly a month the British agonized over the decision, debating their responsibility as a signatory of the Hague Convention, the morality of gas warfare, the chivalry of poison, and the effect on troop morale if Britain failed to retaliate. Some quarters proposed that Britain should offer not to use gas if the Germans promised to stop using it. Only a month was needed to exhaust the various arguments. By May 18, 1915, barely a month after Haber's first strike at Ypres, the British decision was firm: If Germany wanted chemical warfare, so be it.

A thousand committees, societies, departments, and subunits became involved in surveying a thousand chemical compounds. The British army scoured its ranks for chemists and created "breach organizations" to prepare gas defenses, and other field gas units to train troops, advise commanders, and carry out gas attacks. People working on gas defense had no idea what was being done by people working on gas offense. It was all very democratic.

In contrast, the German chemical organization was simple and vast. Fritz Haber was in charge. He worked out strategy with the German general staff. He also commanded the vast resources of I.G. Farben, and trained his own chemical corps Pioneers in field use. At his urging, chlorine clouds were put to use on the eastern front as well as at Ypres, and gas-filled artillery shells were tested in the Argonne.

In England, as in France, the question of which gas to use resolved itself to four compounds: chlorine, phosgene, chloropicrin, and mustard. But there were production problems to surmount. Unlike I.G. Farben, which had been processing toxic chemicals in large quantities for many years, the Allies lacked factories, equipment, and experienced workers. But within five months, the Allies were ready to strike back.

The reprisal came at Loos, on September 15, 1915. There, the Allies rolled out a green chlorine cloud exactly like the one Fritz Haber had first produced at Ypres in April. Incredibly, it caught the Germans unprepared. The British seized and held twelve kilometers of the German line.

Once the element of surprise was gone, the gas war entered a new phase. When enemy troops learned what it was and to expect it, and possessed enough gas masks and training to take it in stride, the green clouds ceased to be effective. While scientists in the labs worked on new gases and new methods of delivery, the field commanders sought ways to gain the chemical advantage. There were two types of attack that proved effective—a surprise shoot to catch the defenders off guard, and a high dosage shoot to overcome the defenders even if they donned their masks. The British specialized in the latter when they learned of the limitations of the German mask. And they gained the advantage in surprise as well with the introduction of the Stokes Mortar and the Livens projector—variations of which exist in Soviet chemical service today.

The Germans had experimented with delivering chemicals by ordinary artillery shells, but a liquid chemical load changed the ballistics and altered the trajectory of the rounds when they were fired. It was difficult to be accurate. And the heat and force generated by high-explosive charges in artillery often caused the chemical to puddle uselessly in the bottom of the shell crater or to dissipate entirely.

The British, instead of adapting existing weaponry, designed the

Stokes mortar—a four-inch tube that could fire twenty rounds a minute and deliver three or four kilos of chemical effectively and accurately up to one thousand meters. It was first used in the battle at Loos to supplement the green cloud released from chlorine gas cylinders. But it was not long before ways were found to improve upon it.

A British engineer named Livens, embittered by the loss of a relative aboard the *Lusitania* when it was sunk by German U-boats, was determined to exact revenge. He did it by designing a simple, effective way to deliver a massive poison gas dose suddenly and accurately up to two kilometers. The Livens projector was a battery of large mortar tubes that discharged simultaneously on an electrical impulse. The tubes were improvised from oil drums or lengths of pipe, into which bags of explosives were stuffed. The gas cylinders with their bursting charges were placed on top of the explosive, and the simultaneous discharge of the mortars placed a gas cloud directly over the heads of the enemy, without regard to wind or weather.

These devices yielded momentary battlefield advantages in the gas war, but they were not decisive for a knockout blow. Germany thought it had found the answer in phosgene, another of Fritz Haber's potions from the I.G. Farben dyestuffs pharmacopeia. With phosgene, the Germans hoped to break the stalemate of the war in December 1915, again near Ypres.

Like chlorine, phosgene was an asphyxiating gas that caused lesions and congestion in the lungs, leading to death by asphyxiation. But unlike chlorine, which acted immediately, the effects of phosgene were delayed up to twenty-four hours. A story became legendary along the front of a German soldier taken prisoner after a British phosgene attack: During interrogation at various command levels, the soldier told again and again how feeble the British gas had been in its effect, and how he had come through it unscathed; the next day he dropped dead.

Determined not to make the same mistake they had made at the Second Ypres, the Germans prepared a massive infantry attack to follow their phosgene gas assault. This time, they expected to break through Allied defenses and go all the way to the Channel. But the British had also been experimenting with phosgene, had developed a gas mask that was effective against it, and had thoroughly indoctrinated their troops. The German phosgene attack, when it came, was stopped cold. The Allies responded with phosgene attacks of their own, and the stalemate continued.

It lasted until July 12, 1917, when the Germans came up with a devastating surprise, again at Ypres.

This time they did not use an asphyxiating gas. Drawing on the endless inventiveness of Fritz Haber and his team at the Bureau Haber, and on I.G. Farben's chemical closet, the Germans came forth with mustard. It was a blockbuster.

The Allied troops were by now experienced in gas and disciplined in their reaction to gas attacks. "We met a terrible strafe of high-explosive and gas shells in Nieuport," wrote a British officer whose party was digging in Livens projectors at the time. "When things quietened a little I went up with three wagons, all that were left, and the carrying parties. I must say that the gas was clearly visible and had exactly the same smell as horseradish. It had no immediate effect on the eyes or throat. I suspected a delayed action and my party all put their masks on." They had no real idea what was about to occur, and despite their calm acceptance of the gas realities on the Front, they were not prepared.

"On arriving at the emplacement," he continued, "we met a very thick cloud of the same stuff drifting from the front-line system. As it seemed to have no effect on the eyes I gave orders for all to put on their mouthpieces and noseclips so as to breathe none of the stuff, and we carried on. Next morning myself and all the eighty men we had up there were absolutely blind. One or two of our party never recovered their sight and died."

At that, his experience was comparatively mild. Elsewhere, soldiers emerged from their dugouts not knowing that a chemical agent had been delivered. An hour or two later strange symptoms began to appear—eyes swelled shut and great blisters appeared under their arms and between their legs. There was almost universal hoarseness and coughing.

Mustard gas was a vesicant—a blister agent. It could affect exposed skin to such an extent that it disabled even a man in a gas mask. Its effects were even worse, of course, on an unmasked man. Internal blisters caused by inhaling or swallowing mustard gas particles were often fatal. Blinding was common. Because the effects were delayed, it caught by surprise many men who were completely prepared for phosgene or chlorine.

Mustard also persisted on the ground, foliage, equipment, and buildings, where it could cause casualties long after a gas attack—hence the story told in Ypres sixty-five years later of the farmer wounded in the rump by the tree he cut down.

The Allies soon learned that when the Germans planned to attack in force, they would lay down mustard gas only on the flanks of their intended route, hampering Allied movement in those areas but leaving the German path free of contamination.

Mustard gas was by far the most effective chemical agent used in World War I. It produced eight times the casualties of all other German chemicals used. During the first three weeks that mustard was in play, it accounted for 14,276 British casualties, compared with fewer than 1,000 during the previous three-week period.

Strategists realized that it was militarily more effective to create a casualty than a corpse. A disabled man was not only removed from action, he occupied several other people in transporting and caring for him. No effective defense was ever developed against mustard, although such things as oilcloth clothing, barrier creams, and decontaminant powders were tried.

Although they had gained the initiative with poison gas, the Germans found themselves increasingly on the defensive toward the end of 1917. That spring they had given up an area northeast of Paris measuring seventy by eighteen miles in order to withdraw to a shorter and stronger line, which was known as the Hindenburg Line. In early summer the British and Australians overran part of the Hindenburg Line, and in late summer drove the Line back five miles from the area of Ypres. Meanwhile, the French were making gains at Verdun and the Aisne. And the Americans were coming.

The United States declaration of war on Germany that April 6 was followed by the arrival in June of Gen. John J. Pershing and the first organizational units of the American Expeditionary Forces in Paris. It was late in the year, however, before significant numbers of American troops were on the battlefield.

Although the United States Army had enjoyed the opportunity of studying the ongoing war for two years, it came into action utterly unprepared for chemical warfare—a situation not unlike the 1980s. The War College studies on which the War Department had based its preparations, and on which Congress had prepared its readiness legislation, included a "Statement of a Proper Military Policy for the United States." It was completed after several chlorine assaults had been carried out by the Germans, and also after the British phosgene attack at Loos. But it did not so much as mention the use of chemicals in combat. In the same tradition, the Pentagon refused to act on a single one of Dr. Lewis's recommendations from Laos.

As one historian marveled: "We had no masks or other protective devices, we did not know how they were made. Our soldiers had had no gas training and there was no one in this country with sufficient knowledge of training to pass it on to them." Such a statement could just as well be applied to the same army more than six decades later.

In the midst of this American indifference, there was one notable exception—nonmilitary in origin. In February 1917, the secretary of the interior and the director of the U.S. Bureau of Mines started a research program in gas defense based on the bureau's experience with gases in mines.

General Pershing realized soon after he reached Europe in 1917 just how serious the gas threat was. Had there been any doubt in his mind, it was dispelled by the appearance of Germany's new mustard gas that July. In August, Pershing turned to Lt. Col. Amos A. Fries, one of his staff officers, and placed him in charge of the U.S. chemical warfare effort. With remarkable efficiency and speed, the Americans assimilated everything that the British and French could tell them about chemicals in combat, and realized (with pure mercantile instinct) that the heart of the strategic problem lay in production. It was a problem that the United States, undamaged by the war and bursting with industrial innovation and manpower, was admirably equipped to tackle. By November 1, construction of Edgewood Arsenal began in Maryland. Soon it would have production plants to manufacture every chemical agent then in significant use, including a chlorine plant described as "probably the largest in the world" by a British authority. Edgewood also would have a filling plant for gas munitions capable of filling 200,000 shells and bombs per day. The month that construction began, the American Expeditionary Force had already requested that 10 percent of all its artillery shells be filled with gas. Pershing and Fries were moving rapidly to plug an astonishing gap of ignorance.

Despite these corrective measures at the top, American troops still went into chemical combat totally unprepared. Their baptism took place on the night of February 25, 1918, more than six months after the introduction of mustard by the Germans. The setting was the Bois de Remieres near Seicheprey. Over in the enemy lines, hammering and increased activity gave adequate warning that a gas attack might be imminent. The American troops were lectured by their officers on what might happen and how to meet it. The American soldiers did not take it seriously.

It came at 1:20 A.M.—a German projector attack using asphyxiating phosgene and chloropicrin, the vomiting agent. Total lack of gas discipline in the American ranks led to 95 percent casualties. And the attack was only a minor one of the sort that had become commonplace and inconsequential to British and French units. There had been a standing order that gas masks would not be removed until a responsible officer issued those instructions. This standing order was completely disregarded, and subsequent investigation showed that 75 percent of the casualties were a direct result of the disobedience.

It emerged that during their three months of combat training, the troops had been given only two days of chemical instruction, and that was soon reduced to six hours. Fries, the new chief of the U.S. chemical forces, found that despite all other efforts, he still had to "sell" gas to the combat troops.

"We had to adopt much the same means of making gas known that a manufacturer of a new article adopts to make a thing known to the public," he remarked.

A senior U.S. Chemical Warfare Service officer inspected a front-line infantry regiment in March, one month after the Bois de Remieres attack, and reported that "many soldiers and officers were found without proper gas protection, that is, the respirators either not in the 'alert' position or no respirators at all. None of the dugouts were properly protected against gas. No first aid appliances for the treatment of gassed men were observed." One week later the regiment came under attack for one hour and suffered 424 casualties, including almost 100 percent casualties in one particular company. In 1980, front-line U.S. Army troops serving in NATO could not get their gas masks on properly even in front of television news cameras.

The same negligent attitude applied to the offensive use of gas. When a chemical officer recommended a gas attack during the battle of the Argonne, the U.S. commander refused unless guaranteed in writing that the gas would not cause a single American casualty. Colonel Fries characterized this attitude as "perfectly absurd."

The final crisis of World War I was at hand. Along with it came a dramatic and unprecedented increase in chemical attacks. After a year of being pressed backward all along the western front, the Germans and their Central Powers allies were growing increasingly desperate. Austria, Bulgaria, and Turkey were nearing the breaking point. Their only good fortune came when the Russian Revolution took that country out of the war. More than 400,000 German combat troops were freed from the eastern front to transfer to the western front where their arrival helped produce a numerically superior German army for the first time since the earliest days of the war. To take advantage of that imbalance, the Germans launched their most savage offensive of the war thus far.

In the process they loosed their entire chemical arsenal, backed by the full productive facilities of I.G. Farben. There had never been anything like it in warfare. For twelve days in March 1918, the Germans saturated with mustard gas all the areas that they did not intend to cross during the coming attack. On one day alone of the bombardment, March 9, they used 200,000 rounds of mustard gas. The areas that they did intend to cross they drenched with asphyxiating and vomiting chemicals.

The British chemical liaison officer, Maj. Victor Lefebure, estimated that a million gas shells were used in the preliminary barrage. The very nature of the war had changed.

"The 1918 hostilities," he wrote, "were no longer a war of explosives. German guns were firing more than 50 percent of gas and war chemicals."

Colonel Fries requested that 50 percent of American artillery shells be filled with chemicals (he was already asking for production of up to 4,525 tons of chemicals per week), but U.S. production simply could not meet his demands.

In each of the belligerent countries, chemical warfare was then being assigned ever higher priorities.

"At the Ministry of Munitions," wrote Winston Churchill, "we were the bees of Hell, and we stored our hives with the pure essense of slaughter. It astonishes me to read after these years the diabolical schemes for killing men on a vast scale by machinery or chemistry to which we devoted ourselves."

In two months the British suffered 33,000 casualties from mustard gas. With the gift of understatement traditionally attributed to British officers, one general described the horror as "a source of serious embarrassment to us."

Still, the German attacks with mere asphyxiating gases proved ineffective because of growing gas discipline among the Allied armies, including the Americans, and the superior masks available to them. The Germans never did achieve an effective artillery shell to deliver the vomiting and penetrating gases on which they relied to get around the Allied masks and to force the men to remove them.

The French countered with their own mustard gas—called "Yperite"—spreading panic among the Germans who had used it but never before had it used on them. By July the German offensive was running out of momentum, and slowly the Allies began to roll the German lines back toward Germany. In desperation, the Germans saturated the path of the Allies with mustard. By September the British were ready with their own mustard, and in America Edgewood Arsenal was about to commence chemical agent production at last. New chemicals including incendiaries and defoliants were being developed, along with new systems of delivery—aircraft, balloons, and flamethrowers among them. Then, with breathtaking suddenness, the German war machine bent, cracked, and broke. It was November 11, 1918, and the blasted battlefields fell silent. Around Ypres, fresh westerly breezes began to dissipate the acrid fog of chemicals that had turned the air a sickly green and yellow, soaked into the sod, saturated the wood of the few remaining trees, and poisoned the soil. Soon healing grasses began to mend the soft, rolling hills. The men on horseback were gone.

The chemists also went home. The war chemical factories of the Allies, which had no industrial application, fell into disuse, disrepair, and oblivion, including—for the time being—new Edgewood Arsenal. In defeated Germany, the I.G. Farben regathered its worldwide monopoly on the dye industry, blocked Allied efforts to dismantle its capacity for production of toxic chemicals, locked up its secret formulas, and waited for another day.

Just before Germany was defeated, as its armies were in full rout, spreading mustard gas in the wake of their retreat, Dr. Fritz Haber made a brief trip across the Baltic Sea from Berlin to Stockholm, Sweden. The Nobel Prize committee had chosen him to be the recipient of the 1918 Nobel Prize for chemistry. Not for masterminding the introduction of poison gases to warfare, or for developing the process that put an endless supply of gunpowder in the hands of the general staff, but for his exceptional contribution to an ultimate end to human hunger with synthetic nitrate fertilizers.

Fritz Haber was deeply moved by the Nobel Prize. He was also deeply moved by Germany's defeat weeks later. He set about immediately to help pay off his nation's huge war indemnity. To do it, he had in mind extracting gold from seawater.

The legacy of World War I was, of course, one of broken promises. By the introduction of poison gas, all the traditional codes of military etiquette and chivalry were betrayed. The Hague Convention proved to be only a piece of paper to be violated whenever it served a national interest. This cast serious doubt on whether any such ban or international protocol outlawing poisons would ever be effective.

The war demonstrated also the mischief that burgeoning science and industry could get into when their self-interest coincided with military policy—a sobering thought in our own time of advanced microbiology and genetic engineering. The war loosed upon the world a number of frightening chemicals that choked, burned, gagged, sickened, and produced a slow and hysterical death—nothing clean and neat. It was on the order of death by executioner's knout or burning at the stake. These were not poisons in the popular fictional sense, these first-generation agents. Unlike cyanide, strychnine, or curare, they did not get straight to the point. They were chosen by Fritz Haber as much to maim and sicken as to kill. The real killers would come along next, in the second-generation agents. And then they, too, would be surpassed by further strokes of scientific genius in yet a third generation of biological poisons in the 1970s and 1980s.

World War I proved that chemical warfare was most effective when it came as a total surprise. But the matter of surprise was one that could be arranged either by the attacker or the defender. Troops properly prepared for chemical defense were invulnerable. But, as the Americans demonstrated, a little knowledge was a dangerous thing; a cocksure attitude and slapdash preparation or training was tantamount to handing the element of surprise right back to the enemy.

Chemical weapons were vague and hard to control, dependent on winds and other environmental circumstances that were always changing. So to many soldiers, poison gas was more nuisance than it was worth. But for other officers, once the civilian constraints were bypassed, poisons were just another weapon. This left the military divided about poison's real value. In that division, and in the confusion of the public about the morality of it all, there was room for another demagogue to make his appearance. The stage was set for a postwar reaction to Fritz Haber. All the disputes, doubts, fears, and "issues" were there waiting for another zealot like Haber—some Elmer Gantry out of a derisive novel by Sinclair Lewis who would rail at the devil while building a great revival tent of his own. Such a man was already waiting in the wings.

4.

The Gas Protocols

The sand dunes of Normandy are modest affairs, barely affording shelter for fiddler crabs from the howling wind off the slate sea. The Atlantic horizon is a vast flat pan, swept clean of all but a few threads of cirrus, and the stormy petrels and terns maintain only erratic flight over the hurried wavelets. Long gone are the tall cane shelters of the bathers at Deauville to the east. The French have gone home and left the Atlantic beaches to winter and to history. Judging from the numbers of brief warriors who have come long distances to die here, including the army of Henry V on its way to Agincourt, this stretch of Atlantic seascape is a good place to die. This particular stretch of beach had seen even more tragedy than its flanks. I had found it only after a good deal of backing and forthing after driving down from Ypres, taking the road to Caen and then poking along the oceanfront villages of Port-en-Bessin, Saint Laurent, and Vierville. The villages sat at the edge of a farming plateau overlooking the sea, the plateau coming to the water's edge in many places and dropping sheer into the sea 150 feet below. At the western end of the beach was a sharp promontory called Pointe du Hoc. Back near Saint Laurent the cliff gave way to a mound of scrabble and the low dunes, bedraggled with grasses. There, I picked my way down to the water's edge and stared out to sea, visualizing the solid wall of destroyers, battleships, and cruisers that appeared at dawn on June 6, 1944—D day at Normandy. This was Omaha Beach, where two American divisions, the First and the Twenty-ninth of the U.S. V Corps, battered their way ashore as a vanguard for 34,000 soldiers.

In the course of their landing, beginning at exactly 6:30 A.M. and lasting till 11:00 A.M. when the battle turned in their favor, the Americans were pinned down, hammered to pieces by German fire from bunkers and pillboxes on the cliffs. The first, second, third, fourth, and fifth waves to hit the beach that morning lay where they fell or clung to cover among the obstacles placed by the Germans. As the battle raged around them, one soldier in panic shouted "gas," and the entire First Infantry Division on the beach was thrown into disorder. What little command discipline remained as the men huddled or tried to crawl back into the shelter of the sea was lost. For three hours it could not be restored. At no point was gas actually used. But in one of the most extraordinary events in military history, the very idea of gas froze a crack, battle-hardened division in the midst of a crucial invasion. As if in confirmation of their fears, the soldiers could see, down the beach to the east, several units of the First Battalion, 116th Infantry, putting on gas masks and making their way through clouds of dense smoke pouring over the mound of dunes and scrabble. They did not know this was burning grass ignited by the naval bombardment.

Everybody expected gas. They had been issued gas masks and drilled to be ready for clouds of mustard and perhaps worse. Just how much worse, nobody knew. At that time the Allies were still unaware that Germany had developed nerve gases that could kill in minutes by paralyzing the nervous system. Allied intelligence had learned at the last minute that the crack German 352d Infantry Division from the eastern front had moved up to Omaha Beach, bringing stocks of war chemicals to supplement the depots already in the area. But what the Allies did not know was that these stocks included not only mustard, chlorine, and phosgene, the first-generation agents of World War I, but far more lethal canisters of tabun that could have wiped the entire beach clear of life like a giant hand.

Why the Germans did not use their nerve gas to save the day and block the Normandy invasion is a puzzling story of disputes between Hitler and his general staff, turning on Hitler's personal aversion. Although Germany had thousands of gallons of the nerve gases tabun and sarin, Hitler refused to use them to avert defeat at Stalingrad, at Normandy, and as Germany fell, despite the urging of his closest advisers.

Here in Normandy, its use most certainly would have had a

devastating impact on the Allied invasion, probably turning it into an unparalleled disaster with untold consequences on the eventual course of the war. As it was, without even Allied awareness of the existence of the nerve gases, just the suspicion of mustard gas and chlorine at Omaha Beach was enough to bring the landings to a halt for three hours, which caused Gen. Omar Bradley, commanding the American units in the invasion from the U.S.S. *Augusta* offshore, to decide that the situation at 9:00 A.M. was hopeless and send an urgent message to Allied headquarters asking permission to abandon Omaha Beach and attack elsewhere. By the time the message reached Allied headquarters, First Division officers had at last rallied their men, restored the beginnings of command discipline, and begun to move forward at 11:00 A.M. to attack the German positions.

Omaha Beach seemed to embody for me the whole contradiction of poison gas in World War II, so very different from what had happened thirty years earlier at Ypres.

In World War II, everybody was prepared for gas. Chemical corps units were dispatched everywhere, and chemicals were shipped back and forth to keep them ready near the shifting fronts. The fact that nobody used chemicals leads military historians to conclude that chemical preparedness serves as the only effective way to deter an enemy from using them. But it is doubtful that the soldiers who panicked on Omaha Beach would agree. For them, just the idea was enough.

The ironies are intriguing: No country in World War II was better prepared to wield chemical weapons than the United States. And yet it was totally unprepared for the second-generation agents that Germany had. No army was better prepared than the U.S. Army with defensive equipment that could protect its troops in the event of attack with familiar first-generation chemicals, yet the idea alone immobilized them. No country was in a better position than Germany to stun its enemies with radically superior chemical weapons and save the day for itself—but Germany did not use them. These and other contradictions raise serious questions about whether we are correct in our basic assumptions about chemical warfare, or whether we have been misled by decades of wishful thinking and self-propaganda.

The basic assumptions America has made are largely the product of one man, Amos Fries, and his strong prejudices. He was a good man and true, like Fritz Haber a god-fearing, upright patriot, a brilliant engineer widely admired for his improvements to Los Angeles harbor, and a leader in the effort to keep America armed and vigilant between the world wars.

However, in his zeal and utter conviction, Amos Fries set his country upon a course that has cost many millions of dollars with questionable results, left it with great stockpiles of poisons it cannot conceivably use, and now threatens to plunge the nation into another spending binge to buy billions in binary chemical weapons. Years after his death, Fries continues to wield tremendous influence in Washington where his successors periodically reenact his role in playing upon public fear of chemical warfare. Yet Amos Fries himself is virtually unknown.

In December 1918, the Great War over, two U.S. Army officers headed urgently for Washington, burning with the zeal of prophets and eager to offer themselves for the sacrifice of leadership. Each had seen a personal vision of future warfare and wanted his country to lead the way.

One was Gen. Billy Mitchell, who lost his personal battle and yet became famous. The other was Col. Amos Fries, who won his personal and equally significant battle but whose name has vanished from memory as quickly as a cloud of phosgene. There are important lessons to be drawn from what their melodramas reveal of fickle and expedient power as it is malpracticed along the Potomac.

Billy Mitchell had seen the airplane develop from its first stuttering flights as an observation platform, to its application in World War I as a weapon of massive destruction. He grasped the realities of what he had seen, and knew what this could mean in future wars and that somebody had to marshal resources toward that end. His mission in Washington was to gain command of the Army Air Service and to lead it toward its proper role as a service equal to the army and the navy.

Armies do not deal kindly with prophets. Exponents of new weapons find implacable opposition among old warriors who have spent decades becoming masters of old weapons. An army that still depended heavily on horses was not prepared to embrace airplanes overnight. And in peacetime these difficulties are multiplied; hardwon careers come into jeopardy, wartime budgets are radically reduced, and public apathy resumes. Billy Mitchell was met by all these obstacles and more. But he persisted, driven by an obstinate personality and demagogic vanity. He took his case to the public and to Congress, writing articles, making speeches, giving testimony, issuing challenges. He became so strident in his crusade that even when he eventually proved his case with his famous demonstrations of aerial bombing in the 1920s, opposition to him merely hardened. Finally, his caustic demagoguery won him a court-martial and ended his military career. He died a pariah just before his country adopted nearly all his recommendations.

The other officer rushing from the trenches of France to the corridors of Washington to do battle with the War Department, Col. Amos Fries, was practically a clone of Billy Mitchell.

When the American Expeditionary Forces had arrived in Europe unprepared for gas warfare in 1917, Gen. John J. Pershing had turned the problem over to Fries, then a lieutenant colonel on Pershing's staff. Fries had rallied his fellow officers and led the American gas warfare effort during the bitter last year of fighting, rising to the rank of colonel in the process. He had been catapulted out of obscurity to become head of the chemical warfare effort, and he was not about to put down his weapons just because the war was over.

As Mitchell had seen the future of warfare embodied in the airplane, Fries had seen it in clouds of toxic chemicals.

"No other invention since that of gunpowder has made so profound a change in warfare as gas is making, or will make, in the future," Fries declared. But he was dealing with the same War Department and the same political organism as Mitchell, and his cause was treated even more harshly by a country sick of war and in love with isolation.

Fries was told, he said, that "the Chief of Staff had ordered the complete demobilization of the Chemical Warfare Service and that no poisonous gas should be used, manufactured, or experimented with and no researches made, and that the defensive work and such research as might go on with it should be turned over to the Engineers." If that did not bury the issue deeply enough, a subsequent memorandum from the army's assistant Chief of Staff to the head of the Corps of Engineers did; it specified that "no funds or special personnel for chemical warfare will be authorized."

Such an attitude in the spring of 1919, toward a weapon that had dominated the battlefields only one year earlier, was intolerable to Fries. During the nineteen months that America had participated in World War I, the number of American gas warfare companies deployed for combat had jumped from six to fifty-four, and the productive might of the United States had been mobilized behind chemicals. Fries even went so far as to credit chemicals with bringing the war to an end. "No wonder the German quit," he said, "it was time, and he knew it."

If this was the overstatement of a chemical partisan, it was no more distorted than the attitudes of his opponents, who chose to ignore a weapon that had caused one-third of all casualties suffered by the American Expeditionary Forces in Europe and had been used in close to half the artillery rounds fired in the closing months of the war. Fries was able to draw only one conclusion for America: "The universal adoption of gas warfare on sea and land and in the air, combined with its persistent quality, will make that nation able to produce and use gas in the largest quantity superior in war to any other nation on the globe. The United States can reach that position and maintain it."

Fries made one last attempt to work within the army chain of command—a personal appeal to the Chief of Staff. He was coldly rebuffed. But he was far from defeated.

Fries was not a flashy dresser, a social butterfly, or a flambuoyant performer, as Billy Mitchell had been. But he had his friends in Congress, and he was prepared to use them to rescue his cause. The situation was desperate. By June 1919, chemical personnel in the army had been reduced to a meager 3 percent of the wartime level. The army engineers were taking over what people and facilities were left. Fries needed to stop—or suspend—the dismantling of the service long enough to give him a chance to change army policy.

In the first of several extraordinary accommodations he was able to win from Congress, an appropriations bill was amended to provide funds for the continuation of the Chemical Warfare Service. (The same amendment provided funds for the continuation of the air service, and gave Billy Mitchell maneuvering room in his parallel battle with the brass.)

The real battle now loomed. It took the form of a debate over the National Defense Act of 1920, which would reorganize the armed forces of the United States throughout the years of peace and for any future war. The fate of chemical warfare during this debate, it was clear to Fries, would influence the conduct of warfare for the rest of the century.

The issues during the debate, and the attitudes adopted by the participants, would persist through all the crucial international negotiations on gas warfare of the 1920s and would shape our own misconceptions half a century later.

The public climate in which the Congressional debate arose was curiously uncharged by passion or horror. This is surprising because the use of gas in World War I had produced apocalyptic visions of the end of the world only two years before the debate commenced. Many of these visions were provoked by the inflammatory propaganda the belligerents employed to undermine the morale and gas discipline of their enemies. The horror stories of propaganda were amplified by uninformed rumors on the battlefield and at home. But for a number of reasons, these terrible fears had lost their grip on the public consciousness the moment the war ended.

The most profound of these reasons was that American civilians were never threatened by chemicals during the war. So they did not react with as much real horror as did the people of England, France, Belgium, Holland, and Italy. The source of almost all public information about chemical warfare at the time was the propaganda of the warring countries. So while British propaganda stressed the horrors of poison gas in order to generate hatred of the Germans and sympathy with the Allied cause, the Americans were interested in other matters. The sinking of the *Lusitania* a few weeks after the first gas attack at Ypres had claimed the lives of 124 Americans. None had died at Ypres.

The War Department's studies in preparation for entry into the war had not so much as mentioned chemical weapons, thus the underlying American perception in 1919–20 was that poison gas was something nasty introduced by the unscrupulous Germans, to which Americans had simply responded—and the response had been adequate.

To those who stopped to consider the matter more thoughtfully, there were other issues involved: Were chemical weapons a proper instrument of war? Had they been an effective instrument of war? Would they be a necessary instrument in a future war? On each side of each question, there were vigorous and committed partisans backed by good and plentiful evidence.

Most senior military officers found themselves on unaccustomed common ground with pacifists in reviling poison gas as immoral. But what the pacifists perceived as immoral, the generals called immoral but meant unchivalrous. Poison gas violated military codes of conduct just as torture did. They were extremes to which soldiers resorted in moments of desperation. Victorious soldiers were not desperate, and could feel only contempt for those soldiers who were.

Furthermore, gas was indiscriminate—a gas cloud, once unleashed, would not stop killing when it moved on from the battlefield to the adjoining town (or, for that matter, when it moved on from the infantry to the commanders). There could be no front line with gas. There could be no such thing as cannonfodder. Everyone was equally vulnerable, even men on horseback. It was not wise to promote a weapon that failed to make distinctions according to rank.

Nonmilitary opponents of chemical weapons based their moral condemnation on the contention that chemicals were inhumane—for some reason more inhumane that other weapons. Moral opponents pointed to gruesome accounts of lingering death among gas casualties and noted that the survivors came home with racking coughs and ruined health. Opponents of the moral argument questioned whether there was a moral difference between being asphyxiated or disemboweled by shrapnel—a death that could also take hours of agony—and wondered whether it made much difference to come home without a lung or without a leg.

There were some who counterattacked, claiming that chemicals were in fact more humane than any other weapon. Col. H. L. Gilchrist, chief of the medical division of the Chemical Warfare Service, made an exhaustive analysis of casualties. He found that out of 37.5 million casualties in World War I (of whom 8.5 million died), only 1 million were gas casualties, and of those only 78,000 died. (These figures excluded Russia, which suffered the greatest proportion of gas casualties in the war, despite the fact that Russia had withdrawn from combat early because of the Revolution. It was left out of Gilchrist's figures because it was believed that the Russian statistics were unreliable. Of course, this proved to be a serious oversight.)

Gilchrist found that the mortality rate among those wounded by conventional weapons averaged 35 percent, while the mortality rate for gas victims was, on average, less than 3 percent. A soldier's chance of survival, he concluded, was ten times better if he was gassed than if he was wounded any other way.

Other gas advocates observed that chemicals were not unique in their threat to civilians. Changes had occurred in war itself, with terror bombings of London from across the Channel, and of villages in the Rhine. Modern war had become total war, involving noncombatants as well. Chemicals, they said, should not take the blame.

So far as morality was concerned, the international sanctions against chemicals as immoral, represented by the Hague Convention of 1899, were put to the lie by the fact that it was one of the Hague signatories that had first introduced gas at Ypres.

Finally, although the use of chemicals had been dramatic, and had occupied the strenuous efforts of all combatants to gain superiority, gas had been decisive in combat only when first used by Germany at Ypres, in 1915, and by the British at Loos the same year—when it had been a total surprise to unprotected troops. Perhaps a cunning general could find other opportunities for surprise, but if armies maintained an adequate chemical defense, such surprises could in theory be kept to a minimum. It was never worked out just what an adequate defense or an acceptable minimum of surprise was.

To most people in America, the most important argument was that the war was over.

Fries took on the formidable, self-appointed task of galvanizing American indifference into a national enthusiasm to maintain chemical weapons despite the specific opposition of his own army superiors.

As Billy Mitchell recruited aircraft manufacturers to his cause of a separate air force, so Fries made use of his natural allies, the chemical companies and their trade organizations and lobbyists. Displaying a remarkable gift for public relations, Fries even provided the trade groups with a sample resolution, which he suggested they endorse and pass on to the proper authorities:

"Be it resolved, that it is the opinion of _____ that chemical warfare is such a complete and distinct science in itself, as well as such a powerful weapon of war, that a strong Chemical Warfare Service should be maintained as a complete and independent department in the United States Army, as a prerequisite to any proper national defense of our country."

Fries also produced a glut of articles and speeches that were spread across the country by his partisan industry groups. He stayed in close touch with his two special friends at Congress, the chairmen of the House and the Senate Military Affairs committees. Fries even managed to fragment his opponents in the War Department by agitating the habitual competition between the general staff and the heads of the separate services. His campaign was brilliant and thorough. Its success was assured even before the hearings on the Army Reorganization Bill began.

On June 4, 1920, Congress completed action on a bill that preserved the Chemical Warfare Service, gave it the status of a separate department, and—in an unprecedented move—specified both the staffing levels and the duties of the service. Not only was the army forced to keep the chemical service, it had to structure it exactly as Fries wanted.

Unlike Billy Mitchell, Fries was able to achieve this rather remarkable victory without incurring the bitter personal hatred of his army opponents. Where Mitchell lost his temporary wartime rank of general and reverted to colonel, Fries was promptly on his victory promoted from colonel to brigadier general, and formally took command of the revitalized Chemical Warfare Service.

An admiring Maj. Victor Lefebure, the British liaison officer for chemical warfare during the war, visited the United States in the afterglow of the Fries victory.

"It was a striking contrast to land in America," he wrote, "and find New York plastered with recruiting posters setting forth the various reasons why Americans should join their Chemical Warfare Service. It was not only a sign of American methods but also one of their appreciation of the importance of the matter." The creation of a separate chemical arm, he said, "is very largely due to the creation of an intelligently informed political and public opinion." In fact, it had been General Fries who had done the creating. Virtually singlehanded, he had cleverly manipulated all the essential levers of power in government and private industry to jerk America out of one rut and into another.

Fortune had not been so kind to Fritz Haber. Immediately after the German defeat, Haber and the men of I.G. Farben had to fight for their survival and the preservation of their extraordinary cartel. Germany's prospects after the armistice were black. The crippled nation was in the grips of a workers' revolution. The Allies—especially the thoroughly ravaged and frequently gassed French—were discussing war crimes trials and the dismantling of the German dyestuffs industry.

But the I.G. was not without resourcefulness, and had never been short of will. Fritz Haber disguised himself with a beard and took up temporary residence in Switzerland, where he joined the president of I.G. Farben, Carl Duisberg, who had wisely chosen to take early retirement. Duisberg handed the reins of the cartel over to Carl Bosch, who had engineered the practical production method for the Haber process of fixing nitrogen, making Germany self-sufficient in explosives.

Bosch's first test as chief executive soon came. The French realized the critical role of one I.G. plant at Oppau to the German war machine when they discovered that the plant had produced during the last year of the war a total of 90,000 tons of synthetic nitrates. This was equal to 20 percent of world consumption of nitrates from Chile. The French accordingly demanded that the Oppau plant be started up so that they could learn its secrets. Bosch simply refused. When the direst of threats failed to move him, the French went to the Allied Control Commission for support. Incredible as it seems, the commission decided that the nitrate synthesis process was a commercial, rather than a military, matter and endorsed Bosch's refusal.

The French were determined to destroy Germany's capacity for chemical warfare. If they had lost the preliminary skirmish, they found more support from their allies in the peace conference at Versailles. The British supported the French demand that all Germany's armaments facilities, including the dyestuffs and nitrates plants, be destroyed. The British added a demand of their own— that the I.G.'s chemical secrets be confiscated and distributed among the Allies. This extraordinary proposition failed in the face of opposition from President Woodrow Wilson, who thought it was "unfair." The Americans concurred, however, with the need for destruction of the factories. Then, prodded by the duPont chemical establishment and the Chemical Foundation, the Americans asked approval to confiscate I.G. Farben patents and facilities in the United States, which had been seized at the time it declared war on Germany. Both provisions were incorporated into the peace treaty that the Germans were obliged to sign, and the doom of the I.G. appeared to be sealed.

Before leaving Versailles, where he had represented the cartel's interests in the peace negotiations, Bosch had set into motion certain murky arrangements, however, that resulted in a total about-face by the I.G.'s bitterest enemies—the French. As a direct result of secret arrangements made by Bosch involving a partnership agreement for the manufacture of synthetic nitrates in France, the French delegation agreed not to press for the implementation of the treaty clause shutting down the German chemical industry. Bosch had bought them off. To understand just how incredible the reversal was, it is necessary only to recall that as they retreated from Chaulny, the site of France's oldest and largest chemical factories and a factory town of 13,000, the Germans had carried away everything portable and had reduced all that remained—including the town—to rubble. All that was now conveniently forgotten in the postwar scramble for profit. The clumsy and ill-prepared Allied effort to prosecute war criminals, including the Kaiser and many of the chief executives of I.G. Farben, soon foundered on incompetence and disinterest. The remnants of the German army began to force the revolutionaries to heel, and the Allied occupation of the Rhine had the effect of bringing order and security to the German chemical industry. The Americans had been gleeful at their windfall of I.G. patents and facilities in the United States, but they soon found that they did not have the knowledge they needed to use them.

Only one year after the defeat, Carl Bosch was already planning a new, tighter, far more powerful organization for the I.G. and scanning the horizon for opportunities to return the cartel to its former dominance of the world dye industry.

It is doubtful that, in the midst of this preoccupation, the I.G. spent much time contemplating chemical weapons or other warlike materials. But it cannot be ruled out. In 1921 the nitrate factory at Oppau was devastated by a terrific explosion, killing more than six hundred workers and injuring two thousand others. According to Fritz Haber, the processes involved in nitrate manufacture could not have produced such a force. Then what did? "An investigation," Haber said in an oddly seductive statement, "may reveal new and terrible forces." There was no investigation.

The euphoria that came with the armistice indeed did not last long. By 1921 the world was again busy circumscribing its future behavior with treaties, protocols, and agreements, those magic circles that exist only to be broken, the houses of cards that can never shelter expectations.

Geneva was to become the catchword. In recent years, it has been fashionable to put the burden of chemical warfare restraint upon the Geneva Convention of 1925, as once it was upon the Hague Convention. At best it serves as a symbol. In fact it was a far from clear-cut, undying statement of principles. Political leaders point to it sagely. Politicians use it as a buzzword. Like so many other things endowed with magical properties, it is only what it is believed to be. And on that there is no consensus.

A far more germinal convention of chemical warfare, which set the international stage for Geneva, occurred four years earlier at the unlikely forum of the 1921 Conference on the Limitations of Naval Armaments in Washington. Poison gas had become such a burning issue that it was added to the agenda of a conference on naval forces—which had had little or no contact with poison gases during the war.

The United States convened the conference to consider the drain on the treasuries of the major world powers, and the potential threat to world peace, posed by the building of capital ships. The principal outcome was to be a five-power treaty limiting the capital shipbuilding of the United States, Great Britain, France, Italy, and Japan.

But the proposed agenda specified the control, also, of "new agencies of warfare." The specific question put before the conference was whether the use of chemicals against cities and against non-combatants should be prohibited. A simple yes or no would have done. But the American delegation, demonstrating the kind of anxiety lying just beneath the surface of the poison gas issue, spoke of "depopulation of large sections of the country" by the deployment of chemicals from airplanes, and said that the American people had been "profoundly shocked by the savage use of scientific discoveries for destruction." The American delegation then urged a resolution totally prohibiting chemical warfare among nations. This resolution was placed before the startled delegates for their approval.

The language of the resolution was taken from the Versailles Peace Treaty, which in turn had been based on the Hague Convention prohibiting the use of asphyxiating gases—which had been in effect, and supposedly binding on Germany, during World War I. Aware that they were doing nothing that had not proved utterly futile before, the compliant European delegates agreed to the resolution. However, because of objections it had to another provision covering submarines, France did not ratify the treaty and consequently it never took effect.

The Washington Naval Conference then disbanded, having provided yet another archetypical protocol—one that avoided meeting the issue squarely and employed false or emotional arguments to arrive at an artificial consensus that was promptly ignored.

Meanwhile, at the League of Nations, a two-year-long struggle to formulate some kind of international agreement on chemical warfare continued. The best the league could manage was an inconclusive report on the possible effects of such warfare. When it did finally address the subject in open forum at the renowned Geneva Conference of 1925, it was not squarely addressing chemical warfare but the issue of arms trade. The conference was fully termed the Conference for the Supervision of the International Trade in Arms and Ammunition and in Implements of War. Its real concern was private international arms dealing. Chemical weapons were not part of the agenda. It was the U.S. delegation that raised the subject of controlling the private international trade in poison chemicals.

It was well known to all parties at the time that most chemical weapons were also vital legitimate ingredients of the dye, pharmaceutical, and other chemical industries; how could the trade in one be stopped without crippling the other? Many benign chemicals can, in sufficient quantities, be deadly; how could war poisons be distinguished from those not yet used in war? If trade in toxic chemicals was ended, would not countries with large chemical industries have a military advantage over those with no such industry?

When it became impossible to resolve these ambiguities, the U.S. delegation in Geneva fell back on the device used at the Naval Conference in Washington. The delegation introduced a resolution using the language of the Naval Conference article on chemical warfare (borrowed in turn from Versailles and the Hague) calling for total prohibition of "asphyxiating, poisonous, or other gases, and all analogous liquids, materials or devices," and extending the prohibition this time to include biological weapons. The protocol—now known as the 1925 Geneva Protocol—was approved and signed by twenty-nine nations, including the United States.

However, before it became binding on the United States it had to be ratified by the Senate. The Senate had approved the virtually identical Naval Conference article without a dissenting vote. But there had been a significant change in the Senate's attitude since then. Supporters of the protocol were overconfident of the weight of public opinion against poison gas; little lobbying was done to prepare the Senate, on the assumption that there was adequate public sentiment against gas and that the Senate would reflect it. Nor was it felt necessary to press the case. Unfortunately, the Senate did not consider it until almost a year later, when Geneva was only a vague memory.

During that year, opposition to ratification of the protocol had been intense. Among the most vocal opponents, interestingly, were the various veterans' organizations, particularly the American Legion. The Chemical Foundation weighed in, as a matter of course. And General Fries applied his considerable skills. Ratification of the Geneva Protocol, Fries argued, would be a blow to military preparedness. It would also, of course, be a blow to his fiefdom. But it was an argument that drew many influential military lobbyists to his side.

When the Senate took up ratification late in 1926, it was with a far more skeptical attitude than had prevailed in 1922 when it had endorsed the Naval Conference article. "There was much of hysteria and much of misinformation concerning chemical warfare," said one Senator of the earlier ratification. This time, in 1926, he assured everyone within earshot, there was "complete information, with the result that a completely different picture is afforded." It was a self-serving remark. When new careers are at stake, reputations can be made by condemning previous actions.

The debate emphasized preparedness—the United States must not be allowed to fall behind its potential enemies, whoever they were.

"We know just about as certainly as we know we are sitting in this chamber," opined the Senator, "that it is against all human nature to expect a nation to deny itself the use of a weapon that will save it."

The Senate refused to ratify the Geneva Protocol.

Thus, in the midst of germinal international conferences at which hopes were raised of dealing squarely with the chemical warfare question, the United States led the way by agitating expectations, creating contradictions, then refusing to agree to the very things it had first proposed. Friends reeled.

American diplomats were rescued from the embarrassment of having to explain away this gratuitous exercise by the emergence of a new dominant figure on the scene whose ideas on chemical warfare were so firm and clear-cut that his appearance at that moment served to justify the policy reversal. He was the new Army Chief of Staff, Gen. Douglas MacArthur.

MacArthur had been asked by President Herbert Hoover to attend the World Disarmament Conference then clearing its throat in Geneva. MacArthur declined.

"The way to end war is to outlaw war," he said, "not to disarm." It was only one shoe, and MacArthur never dropped the other one. But if his statement left the matter in total suspense, it was nonetheless brief, terse, quotable, specific, and smacking of certainty. So it provided an excellent rallying point for diplomats and bureaucrats drowning in ambiguities.

MacArthur's attitude toward the thorny problems of chemical warfare was that a policy of prohibition was fine as long as nothing interfered with the ability of the United States to prepare for what was prohibited. This became the new American policy. The United States would continue to press for a total prohibition of chemical warfare, but reserved the right to make limitless preparations.

The Europeans decided that MacArthur's position contained its own contradiction, so they pressed at the World Disarmament Conference for the prohibition of not only the use of chemical weapons but also the preparation for their use. The delegates explored endless combinations of controls, sanctions, and reprisals—intended to stiffen the 1925 Geneva Protocol—but ended in deadlock. The result was a bland general prohibition of chemical, biological, and incendiary warfare—yet another toothless watchdog.

Appearing as it did in a world increasingly preoccupied with the expansive military aggressiveness of Germany and Japan, the resolution of the Disarmament Conference made no impression whatever.

The world of the mid-1930s was moving implacably toward war again, however imperfectly that was understood at the time. Given the fact that the previous war had ended in heavy and increasing use of chemical weapons, it was reasonable to expect the next war to begin where the last had ended. Two developments lent weight to that assumption: the Italian use of mustard gas when it invaded Ethiopia, and the development in Germany of a whole new generation of chemical weapons that made mustard gas seem nearly harmless.

Italy had signed and ratified both the Washington Naval Conference article on chemical warfare and the 1925 Geneva Protocol. When Benito Mussolini decided to resume the role of Imperial Rome by invading Ethiopia in 1935, and his troops became bogged down, the Italians used tear gas grenades, then introduced mustard gas bombs. It was the first use of aircraft in chemical warfare.

Pleading his case before the League of Nations, Ethiopia's Emperor Haile Selassie described how "special sprayers were installed on aircraft so that they could vaporize over vast areas of territory a fine death-dealing rain. Groups of nine, fifteen, and eighteen aircraft followed one another so that the fog issuing from them formed a continuous fog. It was thus that as from the end of January 1936 soldiers, women, children, cattle, rivers, lakes, and pastures were drenched continuously with this deadly rain." Soviet sources estimate that the Italians took 700 tons of tear gas, mustard gas, and possibly phosgene into Ethiopia, and that of 50,000 Ethiopian army casualties, 15,000 were caused by chemicals.

Italy told the League of Nations that the 1925 Geneva Protocol did not, in its view, prohibit the use of chemical weapons in reprisal against other illegal acts of war. A variety of colorful Ethiopian atrocities were described in order to create a balance of horror. The episode was in the end more instructive as an example of the inadequacy of international protocols than as a model of chemical warfare. It remained the most famous case of gas being used in international warfare after World War I—until the Soviet invasion of Afghanistan in 1979. Military observers in 1936 could discern little that was intriguing about the use of chemicals against totally unprepared, primitively equipped African defenders who were in no way capable of retaliating in kind. Furthermore, it was a situation unlikely to obtain again among the major powers of the world —so far as anyone could imagine at the time.

But a disproportionate advantage of another type was developing for Germany once again as World War II approached. It was an advantage that neither Germany nor its future adversaries were aware existed.

While the dye industry had spawned the first generation of chemical weapons, a new and far more deadly generation arose from the search for more effective pesticides. Dr. Gerhardt Schrader, working in the Bayer research laboratories of I.G. Farben, was testing the effectiveness of various organophosphorous compounds on insect pests when in December 1936 he chanced upon a compound that proved highly toxic to mammals. Under a German law requiring the reporting of all militarily significant discoveries, Schrader notified the War Ministry in Berlin, which clamped a lid of secrecy over the substance. It was called tabun.

Tabun was the first of the nerve gases, and represented an awesome leap in toxicity. The most potent chemical weapons then known—phosgene and mustard—killed in a matter of hours. Tabun killed in minutes. When tiny amounts—on the order of a particle of mist—were inhaled or absorbed through the skin, tabun affected the human nervous system in such a way as to cause almost immediate convulsions and death. It did this by interfering with the actions of an enzyme called acetylcholinesterase. Normally, nerve impulses would instruct a muscle to clench; then the clenching action would be halted by the cholinesterase enzyme instructing the muscle to relax. Tabun blocked the enzyme action so body muscles clenched and could not unclench, causing paralysis, spasms, and quick asphyxiation. Because of the way organophosphorous compounds worked, they were called anticholinesterases. Tabun was only the first, and slowest. Three years later, Bayer's Dr. Schrader isolated an even more potent nerve agent, sarin.

Germany was never able to produce significant quantities of sarin, but had tabun in full production early in World War II. The Nazi leaders failed to realize that they alone possessed a weapon that could change the course of the war radically. The reasons for this incredible failure lie in the confusion of claims and counterclaims about poison gases throughout the negotiations of the 1920s and 1930s and the vagaries of policy in America in particular. Nobody could be certain what secret advances had occurred in another country in chemical warfare research and development. Therefore, Germany assumed that America, and probably Britain as well, also had nerve gas.

The Germans were painfully conscious of the time they had lost in chemical research and development while their military apparatus had been prostrate in defeat, and military reorganization had to proceed surreptitiously to get around the dictates of the Treaty of Versailles. During the twenties and thirties, as a result, little time and few resources had been available to chemical warfare. It was 1936 before any organized development of chemical weapons got under way again. During the previous years, also, the chemists of I.G. Farben had been preoccupied, along with the executives of the cartel, with saving the I.G., reorganizing its operations, and re-establishing the preeminence of their global monopoly.

The rise of Nazi anti-Semitism ruptured the usual tight link between the I.G. and the leadership of Germany. There were many Jews among the cartel's executives and scientific staff—not the least of them the remarkable Fritz Haber.

Haber had ardently pursued his quest for gold from seawater because he was determined to pay off Germany's war debt through an act of scientific genius equal to his solution of the problem of synthetic nitrates. It had been speculated that the oceans contained upward of $8 billion in gold. If nitrates could be extracted from thin air, gold could be extracted from the oceans.

Haber succeeded in extracting some tiny amounts of gold at great cost, but his process was commercially untenable, and he abandoned it in 1928. Haber remained a devout German patriot and a dedicated scientist as head of the Kaiser Wilhelm Institute. But when Hitler came to power in 1933, Haber the patriot faced unexpected peril as Haber the Jew.

"One would have thought," observed a biographer, "that, having saved the German armies in World War I, having organized their gas attacks, having labored for years to pay off reparation, he might have been recognized as a German of Germans." Instead, Haber was forced to resign his post and flee Germany for England.

He detested England, and pined hopelessly for his homeland. Although he was given a prestigious post in the Cavendish Laboratory at Cambridge, and his responsibility for the gas attacks on British troops in World War I was ostensibly forgotten, Haber could not adjust himself to the accommodation. After only a few months he moved to Switzerland to be near Germany. On January 29, 1934, he died in Switzerland, brokenhearted.

When Carl Bosch, Haber's old colleague and now the chief executive officer of I.G. Farben, cautioned Hitler that if Jewish scientists were driven from Germany, physics and chemistry would be set back a hundred years, Hitler screamed, "Then we will work a hundred years without physics and chemistry." Hitler thereafter would not occupy the same room with Bosch.

Since the nature of both tabun and sarin had been predicted in technical journals as early as 1902 and their patents had been published before the Germans realized their military significance and tightened security, the Germans wrongly thought that their enemies had developed their own nerve agents. Years later, the officer who commanded the German chemical troops during World War II—Gen. Oschner—reviewed all the reasons why German authorities considered themselves to be fifteen years behind. "The realization was forced home," he said, "that it was of vital interest to Germany that chemical warfare agents should not be used in war."

But another factor, perhaps the most decisive in the end, was Hitler's personal abhorrence for gas. As a German army messenger during World War I, with the rank of corporal, Hitler had been on a courier mission along the western front not far from Ypres when he was suddenly enveloped by a chlorine cloud and was nearly asphyxiated by the fumes. He had ended the war as a casualty of a poison gas attack recovering in a hospital from the effects—a horrifying experience whose memory never left him. In a country whose leaders found that their very survival depended on sensing and reacting to the whims of a volatile leader, Hitler's revulsion for gas had a pervasive, if subliminal, effect on policy.

General MacArthur also had been gassed, in France in March 1918, but that did nothing to discourage him from helping to shape the following policy of the Joint Chiefs of Staff: "The United States will make all necessary preparations for the use of chemicals from the outbreak of war. The use of chemical warfare, including the use of toxic agents, from the inception of hostilities is authorized." There was no restriction to use only for defense or only for reprisal. Under MacArthur, Edgewood Arsenal's mustard gas manufacturing facility was partially rehabilitated.

But the momentum was short-lived. When MacArthur was replaced as Army Chief of Staff in 1935, the old hostility toward gas reasserted itself again in military circles. So often does this pattern recur that it is possible to conclude only that policy at any given time is more the result of the personal prejudice of a single leader than of any rationalized evolution of principles.

With the Depression ravaging the American economy, appropriations were scant in any case. When World War II began, the total chemical warfare stocks of the U.S. Army amounted to 500 tons of mustard gas. The German arsenal consisted of 12,000 tons, 80 percent of which was mustard. Tabun was in production, and other, deadlier nerve agents were on their way.

Britain had an arensal of roughly the same size as the United States, but had made considerable progress in delivery systems, particularly in a cooperative program with France. In France, where the chaos caused by gas in World War I was remembered, even the obsolete fortifications of the Maginot line were prepared for World War II with sophisticated antigas defenses.

Each nation was prepared for the worst; each group of political and military leaders expected the sudden outbreak of gas warfare. But when war came, it came so swiftly that there was no time for the use of the slow-acting first-generation chemical agents. Said General Oschner of the blitzkrieg against Russia: "The use of chemical agents could only have reduced the speed in operations of this nature. Further, it would have strained to the breaking point our supply service, which was difficult enough anyhow. Hence, under no circumstances did we dare commence the use of chemical agents."

So convinced were the British that chemicals would be used if the Germans invaded the British Isles that 38 million gas masks were distributed to civilians by the time of the Munich crisis. Within another year, every civilian in the country, excluding infants, had one. The Germans, contemplating such an invasion in 1940, expected equally to be met by British gas. General Oschner believed that "immediately after landing, our troops would come up against large-scale vesicant agent barriers and that they might be subjected to further gas attacks from the air and by gas shells fired by artillery and chemical projectors."

In Russia as well, the Germans expected to be met with gas. "The Russians," marveled Oschner, "did not even use gas in defense of their excellently prepared field fortifications within the rear defense lines, those for instance before Leningrad or in the middle sector in the so-called Stalin Line. We thought it possible that the Russians might use gas because, as masters in the construction of positions and in position fighting, they fully realized its value."

The Russians were indeed elaborately prepared to use gas, but were prevented from doing so by two developments. The first and most incredible was the destruction of the command leadership of the Red Army by Stalin's purges on the eve of war. The second development was a simple consequence of the first: Without a viable command structure, and with Stalin convinced that all the signals of an imminent German invasion were false, the Russian defenses collapsed as soon as the invasion began. During the rout that followed, most of the Soviet chemical warfare arsenal in the region facing Germany was captured.

When it became the Allies' turn to press the Germans on the Continent, with the opening of the Second Front, it was they who feared German chemical retaliation. Observed Gen. Omar Bradley: "While planning the Normandy invasion, we had weighed the possibility of enemy gas attack and for the first time during the war speculated on the possibility of his [the enemy's] resorting to it. For perhaps only then could persistent gases have forced a decision in one of history's climactic battles. Since Africa we had lugged our masks through each succeeding invasion, always rejecting the likelihood of gas but equally reluctant to chance an assault without defenses against it. When D day finally ended without a whiff of mustard, I was vastly relieved. For even a light sprinkling of persistent gas on Omaha Beach would have cost us our footing there."

It nearly cost that footing anyway. Never before in World War II had so much hung in the balance. Never before had Germany been in a position to alter the outcome of the war simply by spreading a few canisters of gas. At Stalingrad, gas would have changed defeat into victory, but it would have had less overall impact on the war. Normandy was the key. And there on Omaha Beach merely the fear of poison gas caused General Bradley to despair of success and to set in motion the decision to withdraw and attack elsewhere. We can conclude only that all the preparations of Gen. Amos Fries were of little use in the crunch. If the First Division had worn all its protective gear, it would have been secure from mustard or phosgene or chlorine, but that did not give the soldiers sufficient confidence in the heat of battle to keep them moving across Omaha

Beach. And even if they had worn all the protective gear that Amos Fries and his Chemical Corps had ever devised or dreamed of, the soldiers would not have been prepared for tabun.

The lesson is clear. It is wise to prepare for all the familiar war poisons, but impossible to prepare for the totally unexpected. Since the enemy cannot be counted on to be content with familiar agents, he can be expected to develop new poisons that are specifically designed to get around protective gear. The examples are legion: If gas masks protect troops from chlorine, use phosgene for its delayed action; if they learn to protect themselves from phosgene, use mustard to burn exposed parts of the body; if masks and garments are worn to block all of these, use an agent that interferes with the mask filtration chemicals, or a vomiting agent to force the soldiers to take off their masks. Then develop nerve agents that penetrate all protective gear and kill instantly in minute doses. When defenses against the nerve agents are perfected, find something unpredictable or more violent or both.

The other lesson to be drawn from Bradley's statement, and from Omaha Beach, is that these were the words and actions of generals and men committed to avoiding toxic chemicals at all cost. General Bradley was thoroughly prepared to have chemical weapons sprung on his troops at any moment in the campaign, and he was well equipped to retaliate in kind if called upon. But up to that time, poison gas was still something unconscionable that only the enemy used first.

After World War II, something of that wholesome righteousness went out of America—whether temporarily or permanently we have yet to see—and was replaced by a new and furtive mentality that thrust the nation onto a strange detour.

5.
Blue Skies and Ranch Hands

With the sophomoric perversity of military nomenclature, they called it "Operation Blue Skies." It was supported by the American Chemical Society, guided by civilian public relations experts, and promoted to the press across the nation in the late 1950s. The articles appeared everywhere in major newspapers and magazines, small-town gazettes, and on television news. The stories bore irresistible titles such as "War Without Death" (that ancient dream of mankind) or "Silent Weapons Aired" (a contrivance of a copy desk with an exhausted sense of humor).

Combing through a newspaper during a visit to Chicago in spring 1958, I found a short article beside a photograph of a calico cat cringing before a tiny white lab mouse in a cage. The gist of the story was that American science had discovered a way to end war forever by destroying the craving to be an aggressor and the will to resist. Like a carnival tout pushing snake oil from the back of a buckboard, a spokesman for the U.S. Army Chemical Corps showed everybody a cage filled with your ordinary, everyday hungry calico cat and another cage containing the white mouse. The cages were put close together, and the cat very obviously wanted to eat the mouse. Waving his magic aerosol dispenser of the new psychochemical called BZ, the Chemical Corps spokesman gave the cat a squirt, waited till the cat inhaled, then took out the mouse and dropped it into the cat's cage. The cat, blown away by a heavy dose of something similar to the potent hallucinogenic drug LSD, cringed desperately in the corner of his cage. The mouse went untouched.

Similar exhibits and traveling shows fanned out across America, featuring Chemical Corps speakers extolling the virtues of new chemical weapons. Many of the traveling shows had the unintended and decidedly unfortunate effect of horrifying the local inhabitants of some communities with displays of a prototype gas protector for infants. Operation Blue Skies soon stimulated angry opposition, forcing the corps to crawl back under its rock.

The management of the Chemical Corps has periodically gone through this cycle from obsessive secrecy to the need to win popular recognition. In the case of Operation Blue Skies, America was witnessing a remarkable airing of some of the corps's pet fantasies—that someday it will succeed in making war painless, effortless, deathless. It will do this by manipulating people's minds chemically—a very American ideal—while sparing their bodies. It will be always in the service of good. And in the event that its gentle chemicals do not have their effect upon everybody, there are about 400,000 tons of nerve agents standing by to handle emergencies.

The negative effect these fantasies have on the American public when they are periodically expressed—and their awful effect on Europeans at all times—seems difficult for the corps to comprehend.

Nonetheless, there were many bystanders taken in by Operation Blue Skies. *The Wall Street Journal,* setting aside its usual editorial judgment, published the following appreciation: "Chemical-biological warfare, long regarded as too barbaric for future use, may be edging toward comparative respectability. Exotic chemical sprays and powders, now under secrecy-wrapped development, hold promise of permitting relatively bloodless battles. They're designed to temporarily disable, but not permanently injure, masses of enemy troops and civilians. Some typically incapacitate a foe by casting him into a dream world of utter depression or witless euphoria."

The Washington Star also picked up that theme: "The latest and best, a gas called 'BZ' by the army, put a number of soldier guinea pigs out of action during tests at a Utah army base last November, and did it without harming a man."

Both articles were published long after the army had quietly given up on the psychochemicals in 1961, thus testifying to the momentum of propaganda.

Although the CIA has retained some specialized psychochemicals for use against individual enemy agents—to erase their memory, for example—the Army Chemical Corps finally gave up on Operation

Blue Skies and dropped all its psychochemicals except Agent BZ. Ultimately, when it was found that there was no way to predict its effect in combat in Vietnam, even Agent BZ was dropped, and its records were artfully submerged in security. Vietcong guerrillas who were sprayed with BZ like the calico cat were supposed to lay down their guns, greet their conquerors with open arms, or simply curl up into fetal positions. Instead, they had a disturbing tendency to run amok and perform astonishing stunts of violence and mayhem up to and including butchering the people who sprayed them. They did not act at all like the calico cat.

Indeed, Operation Blue Skies was based on very shaky foundations to start with. The psychochemicals, including marijuana, mescaline, LSD, peyotl, and a long list of more obscure and arcane roots, herbs, and marine toxins, attributed the most marvelous qualities by folklore, were believed to exert their effect and then leave the victim unharmed when the drug wore off. One drug tested, an herb used by witch doctors of Indian tribes in the upper Orinocco River of Venezuela, was actually believed capable of producing telepathy, and came under close scrutiny with the name Telepathine. The promise of these drugs was taken so seriously at the time that the CIA became involved with the army in tests on both voluntary and unsuspecting human guinea pigs, with dismaying consequences including suicides and permanent psychic damage. On August 8, 1979, for example, the government finally agreed to pay one of the largest private claims in history—$1.7 million—to former GI James Thornwell of Oakland, California. Thornwell's lawyers had proved that he had suffered psychiatric disorders ever since being given LSD without his knowledge in an army test in Europe in 1961. There are numerous other examples in the open literature, and presumably many more in the classified records.

Nevertheless, BZ did serve the purpose of awakening a few politicians to the promise of chemical weapons. Congress agreed to finance a number of expensive research projects into puffer fish poison, Colombian frog poison, newt poison, castor bean poison, the poisons of other harmless-looking household plants such as the croton, and assorted marine toxins including shellfish poison and soft coral poison.

Moscow in due course became alarmed at this sign of American acceleration in chemical and biological weapons. The staggering size of the American stockpile of World War II German nerve gas in Denver, although most American citizens were unaware of it, was not lost on Russia. It was at this time—1959–60—that the Soviet Union appeared to speed up its own already substantial program to train and equip its troops for chemical and biological warfare. It was also at this time that Moscow shifted from a program of merely stockpiling and laboratory-testing war poisons, which was the case through the 1950s, to the active field-testing of old and new chemicals as the opportunities arose under combat conditions in foreign countries. The first instance was the Yemen civil war in the Middle East from 1963–1967.

Perhaps these Russian field tests would have taken place without the drumbeating in America. Maybe any country possessing poisons will eventually use them. But England's Dr. Julian Perry Robinson, after observing the ebb and flow for years, is convinced of a direct cause-and-effect relationship in which chemical proponents in America and Russia fan each other to renewed exercises of zeal, without real benefit to their people.

During most of the 1960s Americans were unaware of their status as the proud possessor of a chemical monster. Virtually unnoticed by the public, the Chemical Corps had adopted one of the most frightening weapons the world had ever chanced upon—a weapon that even the Nazis had refused to use. In the bellicose atmosphere of the cold war, the corps played upon fear of Russia to obtain money to produce the German nerve agents, bungled the job at great cost to the taxpayers, and then in the end produced far more than they knew what to do with. The corps was then unable to induce the NATO allies to stock part of the nerve gas, so this unbelievable quantity of deadly poison was left in the suburbs of a major American city, under primitive precautions, exposed at all times to the hazard of airplane crashes at the adjacent airport.

In an effort to win public approval, the corps attempted to persuade the country that its new psychochemicals were humane and desirable, demonstrating a ludicrous misunderstanding of human nature. Its campaign to sell LSD and other mind-altering drugs as a solution to disputes between nations was evidence of such naiveté that it raises serious doubts about the corps's capacity to be trusted with 400,000 tons of nerve agents.

But then the whole history of America's postwar fascination with poisons is fraught with such adolescent judgment. The adoption of the German nerve agents in the first place is a case in point. For in the rubble of Germany's defeat both the victorious Americans and Russians were inclined to take home all the souvenirs they could find, regardless of consequences.

In 1945, the crippled German war machine had produced approximately 25,000 to 30,000 tons of nerve agents, mostly tabun. A factory had been built at Dyhrenfurth near Breslau (now called Wroclaw in Poland) in 1941, and produced 1,000 tons of tabun a month until 1945 when it was overrun by the Russians. There were 12,000 tons of tabun still at the factory. Once the Russians realized what they had stumbled upon, they spirited the captured tabun stocks off to the Soviet Union. By September 1946 they had the Dyhrenfurth plant operating again. It is believed by some authorities that they later dismantled the plant and moved it to the Urals, like so much of Russia's wartime industry, where again it resumed production.

A second nerve agent, even more toxic to mammals than tabun, had been christened sarin by the Germans. A factory for sarin was built at Falkenhagen, near Fürstenberg on the Oder River southeast of Berlin, and began production in 1943. It was supposed to produce five hundred tons of sarin a month, but due to delays and shortages, only about five hundred kilos of sarin were produced before this plant, also, was overrun by the Russians. It was apparently dismantled and removed to the Urals.

The third and deadliest German nerve agent, called soman, was discovered only in 1944, and never entered wartime production. But for reasons that are unclear, the Russians apparently chose soman eventually for their main stocks, while the Americans, British, and French chose sarin.

After World War II, the American government perceived the Soviet Union as its principal adversary, and in the hostility of the cold war that followed it became customary to exaggerate the Russian threat in ways that often lacked any justification. In time, many of these exaggerations hardened as basic truths. In chemical warfare, little was really known about what Russia was doing, and information was accumulated slowly over a period of years. But for their own purposes, the cold warriors chose to portray the Soviets as far ahead of America, making it necessary to catch up through urgent infusions of money from Congress. For example, they claimed that Russia achieved a strategic leap in chemical warfare by capturing the Dyhrenfurth tabun plant and the Falkenhagen sarin plant.

This does not appear to have been the case at all. Although figures do vary as to which country got precisely what from Germany, French officials have stated that 13,500 tons of nerve agents in all were captured by the American, British, and French forces in the parts of Germany that they conquered, the south and west. This, added to the 12,000 tons of tabun the Soviets seized at Dyhrenfurth, adds up to more than 25,000 tons—within the ball-park figure for the total quantity of nerve agents possessed by Germany then. Therefore, the Russians could not have obtained any significant advantage, as alleged.

Because of the *G* markings that were found on the German containers of tabun, the captured nerve agents came to be called "G" agents, with tabun as GA, sarin as GB, and soman as GD. These designations have stuck.

While the Russians were busy with their captured plants and captured German scientists, the Western Allies inherited the huge complex of chemical factories in the remainder of Germany that were part of the vast industrial cartel of the I.G. Farben, which had been the nucleus of German chemical weapons development since World War I. The Allies immediately began sifting through the captured research papers and interviewing captured German scientists.

None of the Allies was in a position to do much with the captured nerve agents at first. Contrary to cold-war propaganda, the Russians did not race off to the Urals and boil up great vats of soman. They were too busy picking up the pieces after the terrible damage inflicted by Germany deep inside the Soviet Union. Common sense dictates that if it took three years before basic elements of the Russian economy were again operating normally, a similar period passed before serious production of chemical warfare agents could get under way there, as was the case in the West.

A similar lag occurred in America as the nation caught its breath. In the meantime, Chemical Corps scientists at Edgewood studied the German processes. The nation was preoccupied with disarmament.

The German nerve agents might have remained a mere curiosity of the war at this point had it not been for a recurrence of the very situation that confronted Amos Fries after World War I. Thanks to Fries, the Chemical Corps had provided support to the American army throughout World War II, standing by with gas masks and protective garments, and heavy stocks of mustard gas.

But with the end of the war, there was no longer any need for a

Chemical Corps unless one assumed—as the cold warriors did—
that another war was about to begin, and that America needed to
remain vigilant and armed to the teeth. Men like Senator Joe
McCarthy were building careers on this hysteria. Even then, a reduced
corps would have sufficed. Faced by the prospect of imminent re-
trenchment and return to the tedium of civilian life, the Chemical
Corps picked up the one weapon it knew best how to use and directed
it against the Pentagon and Congress with all its might. That weapon
was fear. This time, fear of Russia. Amos Fries himself had long
since retired, but in this retirement he had become a rabid anti-
Communist, active in the Washington, D.C., school system; he once
led a campaign to prevent teachers from so much as mentioning
communism in the classroom, much less teaching students what it
was all about. Fries relented only to concede that teachers could
tell what the word meant but could not explain it or its historical
development. At this point it becomes difficult to distinguish between
the zealous hostility of Fries and the nationalistic fervor that drove
Fritz Haber to inflict large-scale chemical warfare on the world at
Ypres in the first place. They were men cut from the same patriotic
cloth—the flag. In their intemperance there is a great deal of the
bigotry and excess of the flagellants of the medieval church. In this
twentieth-century reincarnation, their scourge was poison gas.

Driven presumably by this same patriotic fervor, the successors
of Fries in the Chemical Corps in 1946 convinced the U.S. Army
that America had to go into the nerve gas business to rescue democracy from the Russians. Nuclear weapons were not enough. Tens of
thousands of gallons of mustard gas and other first-generation chemical agents—although they had never been needed against Nazi
Germany—were not sufficient to cope with Communist Russia.
Furthermore, it was not enough simply to go to the relatively sophisticated and undamaged American chemical industry to purchase the
necessary ingredients ready-made. And it was not enough to make
do with a few hundred tons of it. Security demanded that the corps
have a special plant built in Alabama, within the complex of the
Tennessee Valley Authority, at Muscle Shoals near Wilson Dam.
Of course the fearsome, first-stage brew called dichlor, already as
deadly as strychnine poison, would then have to be shipped in fragile,
ordinary railway tank cars all the way across the United States,
through countless cities and towns, across innumerable junctions and
through mazes of freight yards, up to Denver where it would be

given its final mixture at Rocky Mountain Arsenal and be loaded into munitions. This arguably insane scheme aroused no great outburst of astonishment and indignation in Congress, where it was proposed with all due secrecy behind closed doors. Years later, when the U.S. government commissioned the Midwest Research Institute (MRI) to undertake an exhaustive study of the whole process of America's nerve gas production, the report stated the following conclusions:

> Because of the apparent urgency of the situation, the Site operation was entered into without sufficient bench-scale or pilot plant data and experience. The cart, indeed, was put before the horse.
>
> Why it was essential to charge into the construction phase without adequate pilot plant back-up is not clear. But one can theorize that immediately following World War II military spending started to recede significantly. Previously, relatively unessential projects often had little difficulty in getting funded. But in the late 1940s this was no longer true. To get "big money" the purse holders had to be convinced that a program was absolutely essential to the preservation of democracy. The Chemical Corps convinced the War Department that (1) we had no adequate lethal CW capability, (2) we had to produce more agents quickly and in quantity, especially in view of the fact that the G agent capability developed by Germany had been taken over by the Russians, (3) that mass casualty weapons such as CW agents were essential for our defense, and (4) that we had the technical know-how to produce G agents.

In plain language, it was a boondoggle of the worst sort, hidden from public scrutiny by the convenience of secrecy and endorsed by Congress at a moment of cold-war paranoia. Even the fourth point—"that we had the technical know-how to produce G agents"—was simply not true. The manic drive to produce nerve agents was a technical disaster from the very beginning.

The Muscle Shoals plant was to produce the intermediate substance, called dichlor, for shipment to Denver, and Rocky Mountain Arsenal would add alcohol and pour the mess into weapons. The split process was ultimately known as a *binary* system, as it involved two parts. The original German process being copied was a five-step dimethyl hydrogen phosphite process, with the first three stages producing dichlor through the reaction of phosphorous trichloride and methyl alcohol. The contract to build the plant was given to the Vitro Corporation under management of the Army Corps of Engineers. The plant was to be operated by the TVA and a Chemical Corps technical and administrative staff. However, the corps proved technically incompetent to handle several of the chemical processes involved, and never was able to get some of them working. There were endless problems with management, administration, and personnel. The project was launched in 1950 for completion in 1951, but Muscle Shoals was not completed till 1953. Even then it could not operate at design capacity.

"Our initial effort at Muscle Shoals," groans the MRI report, "was a thorn in the side of at least three Chief Chemical Officers (Gens. McAuliffe, Bullens, and Creasy), and wasted hundreds of thousands of dollars."

The corps did manage, however, to produce a few big batches of dichlor before shutting down the plant in 1957—having spent a total of $80 million on the project.

At Rocky Mountain Arsenal, meanwhile, the final assembly and filling plant for sarin, or GB, was built and operated by the army and proved able to perform its design function. Although it was completed on schedule in 1952, however, it could not function without dichlor from Muscle Shoals, so it never operated at capacity either. In the end, when the tank cars finally started arriving from Alabama, Rocky Mountain Arsenal produced a total of 500,000 gallons of GB in 1954 alone, at a total cost of $30 million. Why so much was needed is beyond human comprehension. Over the following three years the army rushed a total of 15,000 tons of sarin through the arsenal and into weapons (or two-foot-by-eight-foot storage canisters). In 1957, with this staggering quantity of one single nerve agent ominously stashed in Denver, the army suddenly decided it had enough sarin, stopped production, and mothballed the Denver plant as well as Muscle Shoals.

This curious debacle was carried out in total secrecy of a sort that Americans were not acquainted with before World War II. No American private citizens were even aware of it. At the same time, the public was being buffeted by relentless sounding of alarms in Washington, fortified by the news media, over the rise of Maoist China, the growing strength of Russia, the implacable hostility of Stalinism and Maoism, the imminent threat of total nuclear holocaust, the urgent need to rescue Berlin from red hordes and South Korea from yellow hordes. In the midst of this national alarm, the Chemical Corps went about its business with much the same morality as a riverboat gambler shifting green peas around under walnut shells, while the rubes remain paralyzed with a fixed expression of glazed eyes and slack-jawed stupefaction. The net result was that nobody in America was ever in a position to know what was going on, and therefore could not protest.

During the Korean War, U.S. commanders were worried that the Russians might pass their chemical weapons to the Chinese and to the North Koreans. Partisans in Washington agitated for the use of American chemicals on North Korea, and there was even discussion of launching biological warfare on China. The Chinese became alarmed and charged that the United States had bombed North Korea with fleas and flies infected with foul diseases, and produced confessions from captured American pilots to support the allegations. Although such means of introducing biological poisons had been the subject of a dismaying amount of research in a surprising number of otherwise enlightened countries, there was no credence given to the Chinese charges even by liberal groups in third countries. The United States claimed that the pilots had been brainwashed. If disease-bearing insects—or "vectors"—were used, they did not work. No plagues occurred.

The Chinese Red Cross and an International Association of Democratic Lawyers (a suspicious name at the best of times) charged that U.S. forces had hit North Korean towns with chemical artillery and aerial bombardment. Because of the raving bombast and propaganda surrounding nearly every event on both sides of the Korean War, it remains impossible to tell if there was any substance whatever to the charges.

On one occasion when Americans did use chemicals—riot-control agents—to put down a disturbance by Chinese and North Korean prisoners in a United Nations prison compound, the canisters of chemicals were handled so foolishly that the prisoners were able to pick them up and hurl them back. There was, apparently, something of a gap existing between the aspirations of the Chemical Corps and the ability of soldiers to carry them out without bungling. Because of this demonstration of chemical incompetence, it is difficult to give credence to any of the Chinese charges.

The Korean War did establish a pattern for regional conflicts

in which chemical poisons would prove to be more and more tempting to field commanders, however. These new regional conflicts,
breaking out all over the world, came in various guises—independence movements designed to throw off foreign rule, civil wars to
replace old tyranny with new, and local aggressions by an energetic
despot against a weak or flaccid neighboring despot. The Chemical
Corps had long been frightening Congress with predictions of a
global cataclysm. What it got instead were these local conflicts in
which the major powers played their roles through proxies. With
few exceptions, Washington would support the established order,
while Moscow or Peking supported the upheaval. (In Hungary,
Czechoslovakia, Afghanistan, and Poland, the reverse applied.) According to the ground rules, nuclear weapons were proscribed. But
excesses of brutality were condoned within the broad limits established in World War II—including carpet bombing, firebombing,
and napalming. These were considered appropriate responses to
guerrilla terrorism until the midpoint of the Vietnam War. Long
before public protest began to exercise some restraints on these
so-called "conventional" weapons, U.S. commanders had begun to
realize that the weapons had little effect on the enemy except to
strengthen his resolve and hatred. Therefore, in frustration, the commanders began to look for more insidious weapons. If the enemy
could succeed with unconventional weapons, so could the Americans.
At this point, the chivalry that had been a substitute for morality
in warfare for a thousand years (albeit sometimes only as a talking
point) suddenly and totally vanished.

The same frustrations had beset the Italians during Mussolini's
invasion of Ethiopia in 1936 and caused them to turn to chemical
weapons, arousing widespread condemnation for Italy and sympathy
for the Ethiopians. In Vietnam, America turned to chemicals and
was widely condemned for doing so; sympathy was stirred up for
the Vietcong. Years later, after the Soviet invasion of Afghanistan
in December 1979, the Russians became similarly frustrated by the
unexpected resistance of the Afghans, turned to chemical weapons,
and were condemned for it, with sympathy again going to the rebel
cause. It is an interesting pattern that recurs, making no distinction
as to the politics of the attacker. The advantage of chemical weapons
in each case would appear to be outweighed by the bad publicity,
but in each case the generals seem to be surprised by the negative
reaction. The resulting stigma usually attaches to the country long

after the war ends, making it perfectly justified to wonder why chemicals are used in the first place, and why the politicians let themselves be persuaded by men like Fritz Haber and Amos Fries.

In the absence of chivalry, the Chemical Corps enjoyed a brief renaissance. Throughout the 1950s, the corps had been brooding henlike over its nest of nerve gas and older, first-generation agents. It was now ready, one presumes, to defend democracy. But it was not being given the chance. So its ability to be effective was unproven. The arguments in favor of having an American stockpile of nerve agents, although rather questionable, had been sanctified by the passage of time and were graven in stone. Most of the people responsible for the fiasco at Muscle Shoals—the people who had first urged the adoption of nerve gas—had long since retired to nursing homes in Saint Petersburg or Phoenix. The people they left behind to tend the rabbits guarding the canisters of sarin from leaks decided that the time had come to promote chemicals to the public again. And so they launched the ill-fated Operation Blue Skies. Although it was a resounding failure, the chastened corps was able to find consolation in the discovery of a grisly new nerve agent— one that America quickly adopted and added in staggering quantities to its already bulging arsenal.

The new agent, dubbed VX, was the deadliest yet. Not the least reason for this was the fact that it stuck to your skin so you could not wipe it off before it killed you. It was deadly no matter how small a droplet touched you. This new asset for the arsenal was developed more or less concurrently in Britain, Sweden, and Germany. Work was under way in all three countries on insecticides during the 1950s. The work in Germany was being headed by the redoubtable Dr. Gerhard Schrader, who had made the discoveries leading to tabun, sarin and soman, for the I.G. Farben. In Britain the work was headed by Dr. R. Ghosh, and in Sweden by Dr. Lars Eric Tammelin. Due to a sequence of patent applications, credit ultimately went to the British team. VX was just one of the new "V" agents, but it was the one selected by the U.S. Chemical Corps to add to its stockpiles. The primary military advantage offered by VX was its ability, because of its thickness, to persist for many weeks on the battleground without evaporating. This made it possible to "deny" areas of virtually any size to the enemy by spraying them with VX. This quality enabled the Chemical Corps to persuade Congress in 1958 to pay for the construction of yet another factory to produce nerve agents—the 15,000 tons of sarin already on hand not being sufficient. This time at least the plant was finished on schedule in 1961 and promptly went into production with few problems. The plant was built at Newport, Indiana. Five thousand tons of VX were produced during the initial operation, beginning in April 1961, and then the plant operated on a limited production schedule until 1968 when it was shut down.

The Russian response to VX was a new nerve agent of their own. They apparently did not adopt the V agents, but found a way of thickening their own soman nerve agent so that it would not evaporate so quickly. To all intents and purposes, this oily form of soman—which came to be known in the West as "thickened soman" or by the code name VR-55—was able to persist on the battlefield for a number of weeks, like VX. Thereafter, the American arsenal of nerve agents was composed primarily of sarin and oily VX, while the Soviet stocks apparently were primarily soman and oily VR-55. There appeared to be a balance stuck in chemicals and in quantities of munitions.

Up to this point, the dawn of the 1960s, the American and Russian chemical arsenals had not been loosed upon the world. All that was now about to change, with dismaying consequences.

It began at Fort Detrick, a peaceful-looking army camp made up mostly of cheap, one-story wooden barracks-style buildings, on the outskirts of Frederick, Maryland. Lying to the west of Washington about thirty miles, just over a few low hills, Frederick sits in a valley beneath the first ridge of the Catoctin Mountains. The setting is reminiscent of the lower hills of Bavaria. Many German immigrants have settled here and throughout the Catoctin Mountains farther west, at Hagerstown and Cumberland. The presidential retreat, Camp David, is hidden in these ridges. The quiet enjoyment of hillsides cultivated with apple orchards is broken frequently by anxious helicopters whopping past on urgent missions of state.

Frederick itself is a quiet town with roots in the American Revolution and the Civil War. The scientists and soldiers based at Fort Detrick enjoy a bucolic setting only forty-five minutes from the heart of Washington and busy themselves with what irreverent critics call "bugs and gas." Until President Nixon banned biological warfare in 1968, Fort Detrick was the center of research and development in germ warfare.

In the early 1960s, off in a corner of the 1,300 acres there was a cluster of greenhouses surrounded by high wire fences. The scientists working here were not concerned with gassing people, or with infecting flies and fleas with bubonic plague germs. They were concentrating on killing plants.

The problem that they were addressing came from Indochina. The Vietcong had totally infested the jungles, swamps, and rain forests of South Vietnam. Whenever they wished, they appeared out of the foliage to ambush U.S. convoys and patrols along highways and footpaths. Then they melted back into the foliage so quickly and thoroughly that you could not get a good honest shot at them. This was not a new military problem. The earnest patriots of the American Revolution had relied on woods for cover. Even before that, during the French and Indian War of 1755, Gen. Edward Braddock marched his Redcoats all the way from Virginia to Fort Duquesne at Pittsburgh, planning to wipe out the French in the Ohio River Valley. His Redcoats fought like true gentlemen, but the unscrupulous Indians ambushed them from the cover of woods and cut them down with guerrilla tactics. His forces decimated, Braddock himself was mortally wounded. Before he died he exclaimed, poignantly, "Who would have ever thought . . ."

To save Uncle Sam from similar embarrassment in South Vietnam, the scientists in the greenhouses at Fort Detrick were exploring the possibility of using ordinary agricultural herbicides to defoliate the jungles—at first perhaps only broad strips of jungle on both sides of highways, to deprive the Vietcong of ambush cover.

The tests were satisfactory, and in December 1961, President John Kennedy authorized operational trials along certain lines of communication in Vietnam. The result was "Operation Ranch Hand"—whose unofficial slogan soon became: "Only we can prevent forests." Three large twin-engine C-123 cargo aircraft were fitted with spray equipment and in January 1962 began operations in the Saigon area. Each aircraft carried ten thousand pounds of herbicide spray and was designed to apply it to three hundred acres of rain forest. It took only four minutes to discharge this amount at the recommended rate, but in an emergency (such as coming under attack by a ground-fired missile) the entire soup could be ejected in thirty seconds. Emergencies, it turned out, were frequent; the large aircraft lumbered along at the low altitudes necessary for effective spraying, putting themselves within range of small arms fire. In one eighteen-month period of operation after Ranch Hand got under way, four aircraft were reported to have been hit 900 times by rifle and machine gun fire.

Four agents were selected for use in Operation Ranch Hand, each designated by a color coding—Agents Orange, White, Purple, and Blue. Agent Orange was a brew of two commonly used weed killers, 2,4-D and 2,4,5-T. The fourth, Agent Blue, was an arsenic-based herbicide with cacodylic acid as its active ingredient and was recognized from the outset as being highly toxic, normally used to spray roadsides and powerline rights-of-way, but never crops. Agent Orange became the herbicide most frequently used, and the most notorious.

Encouraged by the Vietnam operational tests of summer 1962, the Pentagon authorized tactical defoliation missions in August of that year, and the first large-scale operation began in September. Its results were characterized by the chief of the Chemical Corps as "outstanding." From then on, Ranch Hand expanded rapidly until eighteen C-123s were equipped for spraying chemicals and fifty-five pilots were assigned full time. Vietnam was receiving its chemical baptism.

For several years, Ranch Hand received little attention from the press or the public. But immediately there was pressure from the South Vietnamese government to expand operations to include destruction of crops. President Ngo Dinh Diem argued forcefully that Ranch Hand should exterminate the crops that fed the Vietcong. The Americans at first believed there was a clear distinction that must be drawn between forests and crops (although they would later deny it), so they resisted. But under continued pressure they soon bent their convictions and began providing herbicides for the Vietnamese to spray on crops. Because of the equipment needed, this was done with U.S. aircraft repainted with Vietnamese air force markings. By 1963, according to modest Pentagon figures, one hundred square kilometers had been sprayed for deforestation in South Vietnam and one square kilometer for crop destruction, at a cost of $1.4 million. (By 1967, more than 6,000 square kilometers, roughly equal to a swath running along the U.S.-Canadian border from coast to coast, had been defoliated, and 900 square kilometers erased of crops, at a cost near $40 million. So much herbicide was used that the entire American industrial production of it was absorbed, and orders were placed for more overseas.)

In the same year, 1963, pressure mounted to put other chemicals into general use in Vietnam. The argument was put this way in the *National Review:* "A single helicopter equipped with a gas dispenser could flush out an entire band of guerrillas in a few minutes of work. Gas is also effective on rough terrain where guerrillas hide in caves and tall grass and where counter-guerrillas cannot go except at high cost in human life. A nation that has no qualms about training counter-guerrillas in the art of knifing guerrillas in night-time operations should have no objection to gas warfare, especially with gases that are nonlethal. Unless the United States is prepared to make use of its industrial and technical know-how, as in the case of chemical warfare, it will continue to fight at a disadvantage."

This is a tricky example of utterly specious reasoning. Contrary to what the author claims, there is no corollary whatever between knifing and gassing. But he builds his case on such deceptions and sleights of hand, and throws in the term "nonlethal," which has become meaningless. These arguments for gas warfare in Vietnam involved so-called riot-control agents and incapacitants, which the Chemical Corps protrayed as "nonlethal." This does not mean that they are harmless, as it implies, but that they do not kill when applied in very small doses in open areas. In large doses, nearly any strong chemical will kill. Their potency is also increased sharply when used in confined quarters like caves. It is true that there is little difference between gas warfare and *napalming* civilians. But it would not have served his purpose to make such a forthright comparison. At root his argument reduces to the question: If you are going to kill somebody, what difference does the choice of weapon make? To be sure, if all that sets the United States apart from its enemies is its industrial and technical know-how, then it definitely should have no compunction against making full use of these strengths. By the same reasoning, Hitler should have authorized the use of tabun at Stalingrad and Normandy. And Dr. Goebbels should have been elected pope.

A historical turning point had been reached. If it was all right to use agriculture herbicides for military purposes, then it was probably all right to use riot-control gases and incapacitants, especially when these same gases were being used to put down political rioting at home. Nobody drew attention to the fact that the Chemical Corps was always leaping into things without properly assessing the consequences; nobody pointed out that the excessive zeal of the corps had already yoked America with a great albatross of nerve gas that it did not know what to do with; nobody mentioned that the corps understood little about the ultimate effects from by-products such as dioxin that were known to be present when Agent Orange was sprayed around. Nobody questioned whether these "nonlethal" riot-control agents and incapacitants might also kill civilians if used recklessly.

The arguments in favor of gas seemed reasonable to the hard-pressed Department of Defense, so in 1964 it requested from the Department of State an opinion on the "legality" of using irritant gases in combat. Legality was an overprecise term for the highly amorphous question that was really being asked. Since 1956, the *U.S. Army Field Manual on the Law of Land Warfare* had stated that "the United States is not a party to any treaty, now in force, that prohibits the use in warfare of toxic or nontoxic gases. The Geneva Protocol for the prohibition in war of asphyxiating, poisonous, or other gases, and of bacteriological means of warfare, is not binding on this country." The question was not really whether the use of chemicals was legal, but whether it would provoke unacceptable international outcry.

The strength of international law is really based on the degree to which an infraction causes an international outcry. A treaty that when broken causes no outcry has no strength. Yet there are nonlegal sanctions on actions that have no relation to specific treaties but would cause outcries. This is often not considered by those with "legal" backgrounds.

The secondary question was whether using these chemicals would conform to U.S. policy. The last definite statement of that policy was in 1943 by President Franklin D. Roosevelt—that the United States would use poison gas only if an enemy used it first. In the end, the Pentagon took the position that herbicides and riot-control agents—although toxic gases by definition—were commercially available compounds, and not in the same category as the toxic gases referred to in the Geneva Protocol or the Roosevelt policy statement. Army commanders, accordingly, were authorized to use "certain chemical agents such as flame, incendiaries, riot-control agents and defoliants" at their own discretion.

A senior State Department official later recalled: "We're not overjoyed with the use of tear gas, but people have decided it represented a humane decision."

Three types of riot-control agent were then introduced to general combat in Vietnam. The mildest was CN, the standard tear gas developed during World War I. In ordinary field use it causes watering of the eyes and burning irritation of the skin and upper respiratory system. A stronger, or supertear gas called CS was favored because it produced these effects more rapidly and also caused nausea and dizziness. The most toxic was DM, or adamsite, an arsenic-based "vomiting" agent first deployed at the end of World War I. Army manuals prohibited its use except in situations where deaths were "acceptable." In riots, the use of CN, CS, and DM is restrained by public visibility; in Vietnam there was no restraint on dosage. In riots, people can run away from the gases. In Vietnam, children and elderly villagers alike took refuge in caves and bunkers with the Vietcong, and were trapped.

U.S. forces in Vietnam began using CN, CS, and DM in December 1964. Only three months later, the issue blew up in Washington.

Associated Press reporter Horst Faas, accompanying a combat mission near Saigon, noticed canisters of a chemical agent aboard the helicopter. He was told that they contained the arsenic agent DM, for use if the unit came in danger of being overrun by the Vietcong. The next day he filed a story that accurately specified that "nonlethal" gases were being used in certain tactical situations, but included an inflammatory phrase; the U.S. and Vietnamese forces were, he wrote, "experimenting with gas warfare." He quoted a U.S. spokesman as saying: "Even if it does work, there is a real problem in getting it accepted. The idea of it all brings back memories of World War I and mustard gas."

The sudden appearance of a rash of headlines saying "U.S. Using Gas Warfare in Vietnam" caused a furor. Members of Congress and the press, aroused by what appeared to be a major issue, challenged the White House, the State Department, and the Pentagon, which seemed to be taken by surprise. Lamely, the case was made that the use of these gases was not really out of the ordinary. Secretary of Defense Robert McNamara argued that the same chemicals were used by police everywhere. When it developed that DM was rarely, if ever, so used by police, McNamara's credibility was damaged. Secretary of State Dean Rusk claimed that the AP story's use of the word *experiment* was at fault. "It suggested that something new and weird might be involved here," he said. "That is not the case." Rusk claimed that the intention was to use the gases only in situations analogous to riot control, not in general combat. He said the purpose was to prevent Vietcong guerrillas from hiding among civilians; ordinarily soldiers would have to allow the guerrillas to slip away, or attack the civilians as well as the guerrillas among them; with gas instead of conventional weapons, the guerrillas could be flushed out without causing permanent injury to the civilians. Or so the administration chose to believe.

These explanations and rationalizations did not work. A *New York Times* editorial perceived a racial element in the use of gas by white men against Asians, and added: "No other country has employed such a weapon in recent warfare." A German cartoon depicted the Statue of Liberty wearing a gas mask. A Japanese cartoon showed the ghost of Hitler hovering over Vietnam.

The gas warfare dispute was only one part of a complicated agony through which America was passing in the 1960s, and which was reaching crisis proportions by 1965. Antiwar demonstrations and race riots were also eroding the national self-esteem. In this corrosive atmosphere, the uneasy suspicion began to grow that the United States might be employing more in Vietnam than herbicides and riot-control agents alone. The North Vietnamese had begun to charge that the U.S. military was employing "lethal asphyxiating gases," including nerve agents, and LSD. In the year 1965, Hanoi charged, 146,240 people had been "poisoned" to one extent or another by American herbicides, and 351 persons were killed by them. The figures are questionable, but under the circumstances no reliable figures are available.

Whatever the original intention for the riot agents, in practice in Vietnam they were used on a massive scale. In addition to grenades, artillery, or mortar rounds and bombs, the riot agents were dropped in bathtub quantities in canisters the size of oil drums to penetrate caves and bunkers. So popular did they become with the troops that procurement rose from 1.2 million pounds in fiscal 1967 to more than 6 million pounds in fiscal 1969.

Helicopters dispensed CS from the eighty-gallon drums, or from Mity Mite agricultural pesticide dispensers charged with ten-pound bags of CS. The Mity Mite could direct a heavy blast of CS into tunnels or bunkers. In those confined spaces, the concentrations built up, the victims were unable to escape, their mucous membranes became irritated and the lung tissues flooded. There was not sufficient oxygen exchange, causing pulmonary edema, permanently damaging the lungs. In some cases death apparently followed at once, particularly among the old or very young. It became customary for soldiers to use CS to flush people out of caves and bunkers into defoliated areas where they could be slaughtered with conventional weapons. The option was to die of automatic weapons fire or to die of suffocation. Many chose the latter.

More than 5 million acres of South Vietnam—an area larger than the entire state of Massachusetts—and another area nearly as large in adjacent Cambodia were drenched with more than 18 million gallons of herbicides during the ten years they were used there. The majority was sprayed with 2,4,5-T, roughly 50 million pounds of it, producing more than 300 pounds of the extremely deadly by-product dioxin. Broad reaches of Indochina, ranging from the South China Sea across to the Gulf of Thailand, were reduced to a wasteland which will require one hundred years or more to recover its plant life. The mangrove swamps that are characteristic of the coastline in Southeast Asia, and which produce the shellfish that are a vital part of the diet of the poorer people of the region, were particularly hard hit. In these areas as well, the dioxin poisoned all animal life that survived the herbicides.

In South Vietnam alone, 500,000 acres of cropland producing rice, manioc, beans, and other vegetables were eliminated. And the poison is still there, deep in the soil, percolating through the underground water table, waiting to kill again. The earth looks as if it had been trampled by a hastening giant, flattened by a meteor, leaving only stubble. This is defoliation damage from the summer of 1968. The forest had been sprayed repeatedly with Agent Orange by lumbering American C-123s. The trees and plants had been wildly stimulated into frantic growth—years of growth had taken place in a matter of hours—and the plants had all exhausted themselves and died practically overnight. Only then had the B-52s come, to leave their pockmarks to be filled with rainwater. Meanwhile the dioxin that had come with the Agent Orange had killed the birds and silenced even the beetles, then leeched into the soil to become a deadly permanent part of this landscape, ready to kill anything that tried to grow or to drink the water. In dioxin the world had accidentally found a true third-generation war poison, fifty times deadlier than the old German nerve gases.

Ironically, the spraying of Vietnam began the same year that Rachel Carson's book *Silent Spring* appeared. Under the circumstances, it is impossible to measure the damage to wildlife except that, due to the combined effects of B-52 bombing, extensive napalming, and defoliation, most wildlife has been exterminated from Indochina and can be seen in significant numbers only on the borders of Thailand and Burma.

In all, 100 million pounds of herbicides of all types were expended. By 1969, the consequences of Agent Orange alone became more ominous with the emergence of reports that individuals exposed to it were developing acne, skin rashes, nausea, numbness of the hands and feet, and were giving birth to deformed children. Stillbirths and a high incidence of liver cancer soon were added.

The culprit was dioxin. One kilogram of dioxin (2.2 pounds) will kill one billion guinea pigs. It is far deadlier than any known nerve agent and is considered the most lethal synthetic chemical ever produced. The only poisons that are stronger are biotoxins produced by biological organisms, such as botulin. An ever increasing number of these biotoxins are being synthesized.

Dioxin is a powerful carcinogen and teratogen—it causes cancer and deformations. It may also be a mutagen—causing genetic mutations. It causes cows to give birth to stillborn calves, chickens and ducks become sterile, women cease ovulating. Dioxin attacks the lymph glands, damages the sweat and thymus glands, generates skin disease including extreme acne pustules, causes liver cancer and edema of the eyes, alters chromosomes as it attacks the DNA chain, and produces birth defects including cleft palate, deformed kidneys, and paralysis of the body's immune system.

There can be no doubt that the Defense Department was aware of the presence of dioxin as a by-product of 2,4,5-T before it approved the use of Agent Orange in Vietnam. As early as 1957, a German scientific journal reported the toxicity of dioxin to humans. In 1962, the *Journal of Investigative Dermatology* discussed methods of testing the harmful effects of dioxin by using the skin from the ears of laboratory rabbits. In 1963, a pharmaceutical subsidiary of the Philips company of the Netherlands, Philips Duphar, had an explosion at its Amsterdam plant that released upward of 200 grams of dioxin. Twenty workers, plus the inspectors who investigated the damage, developed severe acne. So did nine of the workmen who came to clean up. Three of these men, and a Philips employee, died within two years. The plant was sealed off for ten years, then was dismantled brick by brick, the rubble embedded in concrete and dumped into the Atlantic near the Azores. Similar accidents occurred in other countries, causing alarm in the industry and bringing about extreme industrial security precautions during the processes that produced dioxin.

In spite of this, on July 10, 1976, a factory belonging to the Hoffmann-La Roche Corporation at Seveso just north of Milan, Italy, lost control of a steam-heated reaction process and a vessel exploded, releasing more than 2.5 kilograms of dioxin over nearly a thousand acres of densely populated countryside. Birds dropped out of the sky, animals fell over, 1,500 people were evacuated, and another 5,000 have been affected. All farm animals had to be slaughtered, and therapeutic abortions (in stringently Catholic Italy) were made permissible. The land was sealed off by barbed wire and soldiers. The extent to which the damage may proceed is impossible to measure because of the limits of knowledge about dioxin and the fact that it degrades so slowly. The entire aquifer in the Seveso region has been defiled, jeopardizing the water supplies of the greater Milan area. Although emergency measures were taken by the Italian government, they were too late and hopelessly inadequate. The factory, called Icmesa, continues to function. The overall effect of the industrial effluents of the Milan-Turin-Florence triangle has been to produce pollution probably worse than anywhere else on the planet, of which the dioxin from Seveso is only a part.

What was documented at Seveso went undocumented in Vietnam. Only six pounds of dioxin were involved at Seveso, while at least three hundred pounds of dioxin were dumped on South Vietnam. So many years passed before the impact of dioxin on Vietnam came under study, and there was so much upheaval and dislocation of the civilian population during that time, that it may never be possible to measure the human tragedy brought about by Agent Orange alone. That the Pentagon, and certainly the Chemical Corps, were aware of at least the potential danger involved before becoming committed to the defoliation program does not mean, of course, that any serious consideration was given. That would be uncharacteristic of the entire history of the corps. It does not generate unqualified optimism about its judgment in any future activity, including the proposed production of new binary weapons.

Two lawsuits grew out of the tragedy. Long Island lawyer Victor Yannacone, who earlier had fought for the ban of DDT, launched a class-action suit in behalf of thousands of American soldiers who believe that they have been permanently damaged by exposure to dioxin, including genetic damage resulting in deformed children. The other suit, by the National Veterans Law Center at American University in Washington, D.C., sought to force the Veterans Administration to go through formal public rule-making procedures to establish policies for veterans claiming Agent Orange disabilities. In 1979 the air force, under pressure, began a six-year study of the 1,200 American males who were members of Operation Ranch Hand, compared to a control group of men never exposed to Agent Orange, to see if genetic mutations could be transmitted by fathers. The North Vietnamese scientist Ton That Tung, who has conducted a detailed study of the aftereffects of Agent Orange in his country, reported that there were no direct indications that mutations were transmitted by fathers, only by mothers; the GIs contend that it is transmitted by fathers. There is at least a plausibility the dioxin deformations are transmittable by men because of the high incidence of chromosome abnormalities, which are linked to mutations. But extensive study, and years of complex court proceedings, may be required to establish this. The legal implications are almost as staggering as the humanitarian questions. For example, if the American government was obliged to pay more than $1 million in damages to a GI injured as an LSD guinea pig, what will be the ultimate legal consequences if Agent Orange is determined to have caused genetic damage to thousands of GIs?

Against this gruesome litany, the uncertain reports from Vietnam of nerve agents and biological weapons become almost an anticlimax. But there were such reports, and it is difficult not to give them some credence. As they were impossible to verify at the time, and are now even more inaccessible, we can only review the barest outlines for the record:

According to soldiers who participated, both GB and VX nerve agents were tested secretly in 1966 and 1967 at the Vietnam training location on the island of Hawaii. Stocks of VX, according to both soldiers and medical officers, were stored in South Vietnam at Da Nang and Tuy Hoa air bases, apparently for use if the bases were about to be overrun by the Vietcong. GIs also claimed that GB nerve agents were stocked at Bien Hoa air base. There were rumors of these nerve agents being used, but the only report that included specific details was carried on August 8, 1970 by the Swedish newspaper *Dagens Nyheter*:

"A military source in Saigon says that a deadly nerve gas has been used against North Vietnamese troops in Cambodia last year. It was part of an experiment called 'Project Waterfall'—a top-secret experimental program headed by the U.S. Department of Defense. The gas, with the code name VX, was dropped from airplanes over an area chosen by the American Special Forces. . . ."

The story was originally reported by Tom Marlowe of the Dispatch News Service in Saigon. According to Marlowe, his sources said two one-hundred-pound containers of oily VX were spread over an area of Cambodia believed by the Special Forces to be massed with North Vietnamese troops. This phase of Operation Waterfall, which took place during 1969, was called Operation Redcap. There was no indication what results were achieved.

There were also reports of American biological weapons being stocked at bases in Thailand, accompanied by the suggestion that their presence was confirmed by officials of the Navy Department. In this instance, reported by *The Sunday Times* of London, on April 28, 1968, an official of the Office of Naval Research allegedly told Indian journalists that the biological weapons were in Thailand and complained that they were being supervised in an incompetent manner. Just what the biologicals were remains unclear, but other reports suggested that "special crash programs" were underway to determine the most effective means of hitting North Vietnam with bubonic plague and tularemia (rabbit fever). Nothing more certain is known, although some observers claim that there were sharp increases in the incidences of these and other diseases in North Vietnam during the war that would not be accountable by normal rates of infection.

If nerve agents or biologicals were ever used in Vietnam, the results were not sufficiently spectacular to draw attention in themselves, as was the case with Agent Orange and dioxin. If dioxin had been dispensed deliberately, the results could not have been much more spectacular than they were from what we presume to be its accidental application—accidental, that is, insofar as it was coincidental to the use of Agent Orange.

The disastrous results of dioxin in Vietnam might lead a cynic to conclude that the U.S. Chemical Corps has achieved significant results only when it has blundered grotesquely and tragically. This conclusion is reinforced by events in the United States during the Vietnam War that—because of their greater visibility—ultimately contributed to a mass public outpouring of revulsion. The production of nerve agents at Rocky Mountain Arsenal in Denver had been so ill-conceived that waste disposal was contaminating ground water in the area. The wastes at first were pumped into ponds simply to evaporate, leading to pollution of the Denver aquifer and the destruction of livestock and crops. Early in 1962, the army tried to rectify the situation by pumping the wastes into a 12,000-foot well dug for the purpose. This triggered a series of earthquakes that shook Denver and its environs—some of them reaching a magnitude of four on the Richter scale. Residents of Denver were becoming increasingly hostile to the presence of the nerve gas stocks at the arsenal. Political pressure mounted.

Then on March 13, 1968, an air force jet conducting an experimental spray of VX at the Dugway Proving Grounds in the Utah salt flats failed to close its dispenser valve after a spraying run. The nozzle continued to spray as the plane turned. A cloud of VX droplets was carried more than halfway to Salt Lake City, eighty miles away, leading to the death of 6,300 sheep on nearby grazing land. The Pentagon totally denied responsibility for more than a year, and then did a complete about-face and grudgingly admitted guilt.

In an effort to pacify its critics, the army in 1968 decided to ship 27,000 tons of weapons loaded with nerve gas and mustard gas by train across the country to South Carolina, where it would be loaded on old ships and then scuttled 125 miles at sea. This proved to be too much for even the tolerant and permissive American public. Government investigations were demanded, and the army found itself stuck with its chemical arsenal and no immediate solution to disposing of it. Not that it really wanted to.

The political crisis over Vietnam had already claimed President Lyndon Johnson, who had announced that he would not seek reelection in 1968, and the new Nixon administration took office in January 1969 in an atmosphere of rampant civil disorder, scathing criticism of the government, and serious questions about whether the nation had not been led by Fries and his successors in the corps down a detour from which it needed urgently to retrieve itself.

While some people worried about the ethics, not to mention the sanity, of using or stockpiling deadly poisons, a few officers were beginning to wonder whether chemical weapons had really lived up to their advance billing. Even the defoliants had not defoliated the way they were supposed to. Certainly they had not brought about the magical nakedness of all hidden Vietcong and North Vietnamese strongholds the way the generals had been led to believe they would. And crop destruction had done nothing to stop food from reaching the enemy. The Vietcong always helped themselves to foodstuffs first, no matter what, so if agriculture was reduced by half, the Vietcong still took their rations and only the rural civilian population starved.

Although there were a number of incidences where the use of riot agents may have helped to rescue American troops from disaster, or may have flushed hard-core enemy units into the open, one is hard pressed to find many factual or documented stories of such successes. In Vietnam in the end, as with most other episodes involving the Chemical Corps, wishful thinking ran afoul of reality.

Under mounting public pressure, the saurian Congress was at last prodded into motion. One quarter of its members signed as sponsors of a bill calling for ratification (a half century after the fact) of the oft-violated 1925 Geneva Protocol; the Senate Foreign Relations Committee scheduled hearings on the use of chemicals in Vietnam; and the United Nations, reflecting a general European condemnation of American chemicals in Vietnam, moved toward a resolution specifically including riot agents and herbicides in the prohibitions of chemical weapons.

The pressure on President Richard Nixon to make a dramatic gesture and defuse the popular revolt was extreme. The Vietnam War was rapidly being lost anyway. It became possible, therefore, for Nixon to take what appeared to be a bold and impressive step in public relations while having virtually no consequence on the war whatever. On November 25, 1969, Nixon announced a unilateral ban:

"Soon after taking office," he said, "I directed a comprehensive study of our chemical and biological defense policies and programs. There had been no such review in over fifteen years. As a result, objectives and policies in this field were unclear and programs lacked definition and direction."

Nixon then announced that the United States henceforth unilaterally renounced the use of biological weapons and the first use of lethal chemical weapons. He extended this renunciation to include "incapacitating chemicals." He limited future U.S. research in biological weapons to "defensive measures such as immunization and safety measures," and directed the Defense Department to make recommendations on the disposal of all existing biological weapons in the American stockpiles.

He promised, also, to submit the 1925 Geneva Protocol at last to the Senate for ratification "to reinforce our continuing advocacy of international constraints on the use of these weapons."

Although he continued to maintain that riot agents and herbicides were not chemical weapons, Nixon one month later ordered a sharp curtailment and rapid phaseout of all defoliation and crop-killing operations in Vietnam.

Finally, in February 1970, Nixon extended his renunciation of biological weapons to include all biotoxins, "whether produced by bacteriological or any other biological method or by chemical synthesis."

To all intents and purposes, America was going to stop using chemical weapons unless attacked with them by an enemy first. It would stop preparing biological weapons including biotoxins, and would at last ratify the Geneva Protocol. The Pentagon would find a sensible way to dispose of its increasingly leaky stocks of war poisons. This sounded like a great historic decision. Opponents of chemical warfare stopped protesting and went back to their normal pursuits.

In Moscow, the Politburo must have had a good belly laugh.

The Kremlin had begun its own field tests of war poisons more than two years earlier. Hardly anyone had noticed because of the uproar over Vietnam and a score of other crises, including the Six Day War between Israel and Egypt. Some experts contend that the Soviets were spurred on by their observation of America's obsessive use of chemicals in Indochina. Whatever the motivations, as America tried to patch together its lost virtue, Russia unnoticed began a very strange program of deadly experiments that would lead in a new and disturbing direction. It began in a dusty, wretched backwater of the Middle East called Yemen.

6.

A Political Nonevent

The dogs cry with dusty barks in Yemen. It is a dismal place of dried mud and broken stones on the heel of the Arabian boot. Shattered mountains rise above the Red Sea to heights of 11,000 feet. In the cooler highlands, I found green patches nourished meagerly by the southwest monsoon. Mocha coffee grows on the bushy slopes and takes its name from the port of Al-Mukhā down the coast at one end of the Bab el Mandab Strait, which guards the entrance to the Suez Canal a thousand miles to the northwest at the other end of the Red Sea. Perversely, the best land in Yemen is given over to the cultivation of a narcotic called *qat;* its boat-shaped leaves are brewed as a tea or are chewed and kept for hours as a wad in the cheek. The leaves are exported throughout the Moslem world by airplane to reach buyers while it is still green. Even in bleak Somalia, across the Red Sea, at the end of 1980 a rich merchant offered me a sprig to while away the afternoon. In Yemen itself, *qat* is chewed in copious quantities every day to ward off reality. And for good reason. Once this mountain fastness was considered prosperous. Its name comes from the Arab root *ymn,* meaning prosperity. It also means "on the right hand of Mecca," for it does guard the southern approach to the sacred city. In medieval times, Yemen was referred to as Arabia *felix*—happy Arabia. These happy times are gone. For centuries Yemen has moldered in decay, ruled by warring sheiks. Their feuds were tolerated by the powerful bedouin princes of Saudi Arabia because Yemen was a useful buffer against the outside world. Its decay and corruption could be ignored. Currents of history swept past, leaving Yemen populated by human debris neglected in the crevices of hills above the Red Sea. In their isolation, the Yemenis indulged in tribal vendettas, murder, treachery, and made a national pursuit of venality. The men—dressed in loose turbans, shiny, ill-fitting Western suit jackets, and dingy midi-length skirts—developed what struck me as a degenerate skulk and an intense, askew stare, the result—I concluded—of a diet of *qat* and little else. The women hardly existed, like feudal ragbags moving in sullen, odious silence from wretched birth to wretched death. It was a perfect place for a war. But war swirled instead in the countries adjoining Yemen.

Down the coast at the mouth of the strait, Britain seized a foothold and turned the barren coastal village of Aden into a mighty naval fortress. After World War II, the rest of Arabia grew rich on oil and became strategically vital to world power interests. In the mountains of North Yemen, nothing changed except the price of *qat,* which inflated. The British protectorate of South Yemen enjoyed the same civil liberties as England; under Labour governments in London, radical movements were tolerated in Aden, and they plotted to throw the British out. Up the Red Sea, other revolutionaries rose up and overthrew Egypt's King Farouk in July 1952, bringing Col. Gamel Abdel Nasser to power.

President Nasser accepted massive military aid from the Soviet Union and commenced plotting against Israel. It is unlikely that Nasser ever considered the possibility that his military ambitions might founder on the bare slopes of Yemen. But in his effort to become the champion of Islam against Israel, he squandered vital advantages in North Yemen, allowed himself to become a pawn in a much greater Soviet game, and began a series of bungles that in time cost him dearly. Decades later, my search for clues to the new generation of chemical warfare agents would lead back to Nasser and to the desolate landscape of Yemen, where Russia first began testing its chemical compounds and spread poisons deadlier than any in Vietnam.

It began with the death of Imam Ahmad in September 1962. He was succeeded as North Yemen's king by Imam Mohammed el Badr. One week later, the new king was overthrown by young pro-Nasser Yemeni army officers. The deposed king and his royalist followers took to the hills where they rallied loyal tribes and began a civil war, backed by Saudi Arabia. The new republican army regime that replaced the monarchy was backed by Egypt. Nasser sent Egyptian troops and warplanes to reinforce the new regime and to bomb and strafe royalist hideouts in desolate villages and mountain caves.

In a seemingly unrelated incident, in March 1963, Israel's Foreign Minister Golda Meir charged that Egypt was developing unspecified armaments "banned in international law" with the help of West German scientists employed by Cairo. The Egyptian government admitted that there were German scientists working for it, but specifically denied that they were engaged in projects having to do with chemical or biological warfare. Egypt's UN delegate Mahmoud Riad charged that Israel itself was doing research on biological warfare at the Weizmann Institute. At the time I was on the staff of *The Washington Post* and kept up with the counter charges on the wire services.

Several weeks later, a small group of French mercenaries who had been hired to fight for the royalists were brought as casualties to a hospital in Saudi Arabia. They had been felled by vapors that had blinded them and attacked their lungs. Reports then reached Beirut that Egyptian planes had gassed several Yemeni villages. One of the villages, called el Kawma, was said to have been gassed on June 8, 1963. Out of a population of about one hundred, the gas had reportedly killed seven people and seriously damaged the eyes and lungs of twenty-five others, inflicting painful blisters that peeled away into raw open wounds. It seemed likely to me at first that it was mustard.

There were three kinds of foreign observers present in Yemen: members of the United Nations Yemen Observer Mission (UNYOM); medical and bureaucratic representatives of the International Committee of the Red Cross (ICRC) in Geneva; and a variety of journalists, ranging from professionals to poseurs, and including some who openly served as propagandists for the royalist cause and others (like Britain's Col. David Smiley) who doubled as military advisers and informal agents of their secret service.

Here are the personal observations of Colonel Smiley, which I have obtained through diplomatic channels: "The Imam was not sure who had been piloting these bombers, though they were supposed to be Egyptian, but the royalists had recently shot down a Yak recce [reconnaisance] plane and the pilot, who spoke a few words before he died, was alleged from both his speech and appearance to be a Russian."

Smiley went to el Kawma where he talked to the survivors and dug in one of the gas bomb craters for fragments.

> The story they told me was that when the bombs dropped they did not explode in the usual way of high-explosive bombs, but gave off a dense cloud of smoke variously described as brown, grey, and black. They stated that six children had died of what I could only conclude was injuries to the lungs, as the chief symptoms were vomiting and coughing blood, common to all cases. . . . They also added that the bombs had caused some form of skin contamination, for people who had handled pieces of the bomb had come out in septic sores about two inches in diameter, and any body or animal they touched also came out in these sores.
>
> I spent some time digging in the bomb craters, and I found a number of fragments. While digging, even after a month during which rain had fallen, I noticed a distinct smell, something like geranium, and twice I had to sit down and rest after spells of dizziness when I almost blacked out.

"I must admit," said Smiley, "that, at the time, I thought that the truth was being suppressed for political reasons." He concluded, with others, that "the use of gas was experimental, using the Yemenis as guinea pigs (rather in the same way as various countries tested their arms and equipment in the Spanish Civil War)."

One of the royalists' advisers, Lt. Col. Neil McLean, a British member of Parliament and an old comrade-in-arms of Smiley, was also sent by Imam el Badr to investigate the gassings. McLean found "a peculiar odor of putrefaction hanging over the area." From el Kawma the investigators visited six other villages that also had been reported hit by gas bombs.

The first detailed public account of el Kawma came from one of the legitimate journalists who had accompanied McLean, Richard Beeston of the *London Daily Telegraph*. The *Telegraph* is distinguished by its sobriety and by an inclination to reflect the conservative point of view of the old-school British military establishment. It ran Richard Beeston's report on July 8, 1963:

> I reached el Kawma after a three-day journey in a lorry, on a donkey and on foot from the Saudi Arabian border. The village is perched on top of a high rugged mountain in the

unmapped part of northern Yemen. I approached the village late at night. From more than a hundred yards away I could hear the coughing of the gassed villagers, which went on ceaselessly.

In the morning villagers crowded me, pleading with me to send medicines and doctors to cure their coughs and blisters. The face of one woman had turned a vivid yellow.

Another woman was blinded by rubbing her eyes with contaminated fingers. One of the worst-affected villagers I saw was Mohamed Nassr, 12, who had a perpetual cough and deep open wounds on his body, the size of a half-crown, from gas blisters.

The gas bomb was dropped on the village during the evening early last month and six people, including a five-year-old girl, Hadia Rashid, died in agony within four days. Last Monday the seventh death took place. It was a boy of 13.

The population of the village of el Kawma is about 100, a third of whom have been gassed. The village headman told me that when the bomb fell it gave off a cloud of brown smoke and had a "dirty smell."

"We thought it was just smoke, because nobody had ever heard of poison gas," he said. "Soon after, people began coughing up blood. Some bled from the nose."

I was shown the remains of what the villagers stated had been the gas bomb. It consisted of two circular bands of metal about two feet across. Into each were screwed fifteen canisters about the size of a car's carburetor.

It was obviously a complicated piece of machinery, probably beyond the engineering capabilities of the Egyptians. Since the Russian bloc supplies all military equipment for Egypt, it is likely that the bomb was manufactured in Russia or Czechoslovakia.

Beeston's descriptions are noteworthy for more than their caution. In light of what followed—confusion, contradiction, and official obfuscation—the journalist had hit upon some essential truths. First, the gas reports were true; the Yemenis had not lied. In the events to follow, the royalists might attempt to capitalize on sympathy, and their Saudi backers might seek to publicize the gassings, but they both demonstrated a surprising naiveté and forthrightness about the chemical agents and their effects. Whenever it was physically possible for on-the-spot investigation to be conducted, it was discovered that the circumstances of a gassing were virtually as represented. The deception, when it came, was originated not by the Moslem participants in the Yemen war but by the international agencies (from the United Nations to the International Red Cross) to whom the world turned for judgment. In Yemen they revealed a predilection to evade unpleasant realities. The case was straightforward, but the jury was corrupt.

Second, Beeston, although he did not claim to know the exact agent, had narrated a perfectly clear description of the medical signs and symptoms of ordinary mustard gas, which presumably caused the burning of the eyes and lungs and the painful blisters that peeled away into open wounds—unless something new could do precisely that. The delay between bomb detonation and the onset of symptoms, described by the villagers, also was typical of mustard. And, finally, it could have been the garlic smell of mustard that had produced the smell described by the village headman as "dirty." But what was it in the bomb crater that Smiley thought smelled like geraniums and made him get tight in the chest and dizzy? Certainly not mustard or slow-acting phosgene.

The amount of bleeding described was not really extraordinary. It might have been caused by a severe dose of mustard burning holes in the mucous membrane of the nose and throat. Later in the Yemen war, the flow of blood would change surprisingly (but by the time bleeding became astonishing in itself, everyone directly involved had lost the capacity to be surprised, and the amazing hemorrhages passed with only the most desultory notice).

Once it had been established by direct observation that the gassing had taken place, it was surprising that both the United Nations and the International Red Cross took the position that the gassings had never occurred.

Fragments of the gas bomb had been delivered to the UNYOM, and (at the urging of the British government) UN Secretary General U Thant had ordered the UNYOM to collect any other evidence at hand. On July 16, one week after Beeston's story appeared and two weeks after the foreign observers had visited el Kawma, the office of the secretary general announced that there was "no evidence" of the use of gas in Yemen. It was a political nonevent.

The day after Beeston's story was published, a representative of the International Red Cross in Jeddah, Saudi Arabia, Dr. Beretta, stated that he had been receiving reports of gas warfare for more than a month, but had no way to check them. Therefore, so far as the ICRC was concerned, the reports remained mere allegations.

In Israel, Golda Meir speculated that President Nasser, having demonstrated that he was prepared to use poison gas against fellow Arabs, would not hesitate to use it against Israel.

Both the U.S. State Department and the British Foreign Office said they had told Cairo that they took "a serious view" of the gas reports. We can presume that Nasser pleaded with Moscow to stop the experiments, for the gassings ceased as suddenly as they had begun. Throughout the rest of 1963 and 1964, the Yemen war went on. The number of Egyptian troops involved grew to 50,000, supported by 30 Tupolev Tu-16 medium bombers, 40 Ilyushin Il-28 light bombers, and 150 MIG-15 and MIG-17 fighter-bombers. The major buildup of Soviet military equipment in Egypt was concentrated along the Suez Canal and in the Sinai Peninsula facing Israel, but this Russian-equipped Egyptian air force was therefore only a few minutes flying time from the mountains of Yemen.

Along with the Soviet hardware buildup in Egypt came large numbers of Soviet advisers. At *The Washington Post* foreign desk we ran a story from Cairo about Egyptian field officers complaining that Soviet SAM surface-to-air missile installations remained under strict, direct control of Russian officers. The same was true of the air force. Soviet aircraft were never "given"—only "loaned." So when Ilyushin bombers were prepped for sorties over Yemen, the loading of bombs, rockets, and other armaments was carried out under the watchful eyes of Soviet officers.

In autumn 1966—after an interruption of three years—the gas attacks in Yemen abruptly resumed. But the villages were so inaccessible that it was January 1967 before a target was hit where the report could be confirmed. Until then an effort seems to have been made to avoid the publicity aroused by el Kawma in 1963. But this attack hit the town of el Kitaf, only two miles from the cave headquarters of the royalist prime minister, Prince Hassan bin Yahya.

Colonel Smiley was well acquainted with some British mercenaries who were with Emir Hassan and witnessed the attack on el Kitaf. This is what they told Smiley:

At 0730 hours on January 5, 1967, two MIGs circled the area and each dropped a smoke bomb—presumably to mark the village and to enable the pilots to judge the speed and direction of the wind. They were followed by nine Ilyushin 28 bombers which then dropped their bombs, three aircraft at a time dropping three bombs at each run. They all made three runs, thus 27 bombs in all were dropped. The bombs each made a black crater 3 feet deep and 6 feet wide—I saw these myself —and released the gas in a grey-green cloud which drifted with the wind over the village of Kitaf. All but 5% of the people within 2 kilometers downwind of the bombs' impact point died or were seriously injured. About 120 died within 10 to 15 minutes of the attack, and a further 80 later on. Nearly all animals in the area died, mainly camels, goats, sheep, chickens, and dogs. Crops and vegetation in the area turned brown. Those who died did so with blood emerging from the mouth and nose, but they had no marks on the skin. Those who survived stated that the smell compared with fresh fruit or yeast. It affected their breathing and made them cough continuously.

The absence of blisters ruled out mustard.

From the speed of its action, the deadly gray green specter that descended on el Kitaf could only have been a compound of chemical agents *including* a nerve gas, or a new chemical compound involving unknown third-generation agents that worked as fast as a nerve agent. Whichever it was, the cloud at Kitaf was deadlier than any chemical ever actually used in combat before.

As soon as he heard about the attack, a young American oil company employee named Bushrod Howard jumped into his Land Rover and roared off through the wadis to Kitaf, where he scribbled down firsthand accounts of the few survivors and persuaded them to load the carcasses of some of the dead animals onto the back of a truck, which he drove across the Saudi border to Najran, where there was a field hospital. Howard did not get contaminated, indicating that the killing agent was nonpersisting. He turned the carcasses over to Saudi doctors in Najran for examination, and immediately organized twenty journalists at the Saudi capital of Jeddah to go together to Kitaf. On January 22, 1967, sixteen days after the gas attack, they flew to Najran. In the group were NBC's Robert Conley and Rushan Arikan, UPI's John Lawton, AP's David Lancashire, John Cooley of *The Christian Science Monitor,* and Andrew Borowiec of *The Washington Star,* all Americans. The two British correspondents were Nicholas Herbert of *The Times of London* and Richard Beeston of the *Daily Telegraph.* Borowiec described the next stage of their journey:

> The unwieldy caravan set out from Najran on donkeys with a guard of some 60 Yemeni warriors who fired their rifles signalling our approach to lookouts perching on mountainsides. Camels carried the baggage, including television equipment. One collapsed under his burden and the convoy halted until a replacement was found.
>
> Tripping on rocks, falling from their animals, quarreling, swearing, complaining, threatening to go back, the caravan of exhausted newsmen reached Kitaf after a 27-hour march.
>
> All correspondents participating in the trip agreed that evidence strongly pointed to the use of poison gas.
>
> Terrified survivors were still telling of a brown, windwhipped, "sweet-smelling" cloud that caused foaming at the mouth, vomiting, nose-bleeding, and death from one to 24 hours after the attack. Bodies of killed animals were strewn through Kitaf's dusty alleys without any visible trace of wounds. In Najran, local doctors who treated 118 patients said all symptoms pointed to gas.

The newsmen were certainly in no position to judge exactly what chemicals had been used or precisely which medical clues might be more revealing than others. But they were in a position to establish beyond doubt that a lethal attack had taken place, and to describe the characteristics of an agent or combination of agents far more powerful than mustard, phosgene, or prussic acid, none of which would have produced the smell universally described as "fruity"—this is associated only with the nerve agents tabun and soman. Heavy concentrations of "harassing" agents like adamsite, which is an arsenic-based compound, can produce fatalities, but would not kill as suddenly as the gray green cloud at Kitaf.

Some signs pointed clearly to a second-generation nerve agent: the fruity smell, the suddenness of death to between 200 and 300 people, and such symptoms among survivors as a tight chest and shortness of breath—all things Smiley noted three years earlier. But the physical symptoms recorded by the earliest observers were not sufficiently detailed to draw more specific conclusions. We do not know, for example, whether there was twitching, drooling, vomiting, violent convulsions, and involuntary urination and defecation, which would confirm a nerve agent. The survivors were not programmed to observe such fine distinctions. Death throes are death throes. By the time outsiders arrived, the villagers had repeated their accounts so often that a consensus had developed. A decade would pass before it occurred to anyone—myself included—that there was a third generation of killing agents loose in the world, and that these might explain what happened at Kitaf. In 1967, the most likely candidate was tabun or soman, and even then the observers present— including the Red Cross doctors in the area—had no real grasp of how nerve agents work and what signs and symptoms they produce.

The Red Cross doctors in Yemen fled to Saudi Arabia immediately after the Kitaf air strike because other gas attacks made it appear that a disastrous chemical offensive was under way. The day before Kitaf, Ilyushins had struck Hadda with chemical agents of similar lethal potency as the gray green cloud at Kitaf. On January 6 two other towns were hit, but the only fatalities were livestock because the towns were not occupied by humans at the time of the strikes.

On January 7, 1967, the third day of the blitz, twelve Il-28s struck the town of Katar, causing 125 sudden deaths and 225 casualties.

There was a precision about the attacks that was not characteristic of the Egyptian air force. In each instance, as at Kitaf, the Ilyushin bombers were preceded by MIGs dropping smoke bombs that revealed the wind direction. The Ilyushin pilots then altered their target accordingly and carried out precision bombing of such accuracy that the toxic chemicals were laid upwind and the aerosol clouds folded precisely over the strike zone. In view of this remarkable flying and expert disposition of aerosols over the target, Cairo's denial that Egyptian pilots ever carried out such raids takes on a new credibility.

Reaching safety in Najran, the Red Cross doctors demanded gas masks before they would return to Yemen. But André Rochat, head of the Red Cross Yemen mission, convinced them that it was folly to be so equipped when no one else was. If the gas masks were not immediately stolen, he argued, the doctors would certainly be mobbed in the first panic. Two of the doctors then went back to Kitaf where they took samples of clothing, contaminated soil, and parts of lungs from dead animals.

If the doctors had better understood the characteristics of nerve agents, they would have realized that they would be exposed to death from tiny aerosol droplets on the skin, even if they were wearing gas masks. They were the only people on the scene who were in a position to record the crucial medical signs visible immediately after the attack among the dead and the casualties—and they had no real idea what to look for. If they missed many of the most revealing details, they could hardly be blamed. Ordinary people in the 1960s had no way of knowing much about nerve gas except the name.

They demanded the gas masks anyway, in a direct appeal by cable to headquarters in Geneva:

> The members of Yemen Unit 2 of ICRC reply to your cable of 14 January 1967 as follows: (1) You were at Cairo from 2 to 7 January. The gas bombs were dropped while you were there. (2) We continue to maintain that Dr. L—— was not at the scene and that the team which remained at the scene for the longest time was not consulted at all. (3) The assurance from the highest quarter and your assumption of responsibility are no guarantee for our safety, when the Geneva Convention has been violated previously. (4) The only realistic protection is masks, which we therefore suggest should be awaited. (5) In view of what we have observed, our remarks are not based on fear. Najran, 14 January 1967.

The cable was signed by nine Red Cross field staffers.

In spite of the fact that they were too ill informed to note more clearly the medical signs that might have better characterized the nerve agents, the Red Cross doctors, with considerable courage, did make clinical observations of casualties, performed autopsies on animals, and gathered specimens of vegetation and sand for analysis. On January 31, 1967, the Geneva headquarters of the ICRC produced the following curious statement:

"In the interests of the persons in need of its assistance" in the war zone in Yemen, the Red Cross drew attention to the need for restraint in disclosing "the observations made by its delegates" of the "alleged use of poison gas." The ICRC made an urgent appeal "to all authorities involved in this conflict for respect in all circumstances of the universally recognized humanitarian rules of international morality and law."

In other words, the Red Cross had drawn certain conclusions regarding the use of poison gas in Yemen but could not reveal these conclusions without risking forfeiture of the right to provide medical assistance and other humanitarian aid to victims on both sides of the conflict. The implication was not only that the republican military regime in Yemen might close down the Red Cross operations in zones that they controlled if the ICRC revealed what it had discovered but—far more seriously—that Egypt, and particularly the Soviet Union, might exercise sanctions against the Red Cross in many of its other humanitarian enterprises elsewhere in the world.

Rarely is political rhetoric more brutally effective than when it is used in arguments involving chemical warfare. People who spoke out against gassing in Yemen had been ridiculed as royalist flunkies or sophomoric romantics. Realizing the vulnerability of their targets, politicians opposed to discussion of chemical warfare often indulged in stupefying excesses. The most typical device is to charge "lack of evidence," otherwise known as the smoking gun tactic. Users of the smoking gun tactic are aware that even direct witnesses of a gas attack are not in a position to provide tangible evidence—given the intangible nature of chemical vapor.

Even if a witness is standing a few feet from a deliberate attack with a violently toxic agent, whether the attack is administered by fighter aircraft launching rockets, propeller planes releasing vapor clouds, tanks spraying from nozzles, or individuals with hand-held aerosols, the witness cannot then provide tangible evidence of the attack to somebody who was not at the scene. Even if the witness possesses a test kit designed specifically for the agent being used, he or she may be upwind and unable to employ the test kit without personal hazard. All descriptions of the attack therefore are by definition suspect if not actually circumstantial.

A witness standing at a traffic intersection in the middle of an empty desert, for example, can observe an automobile running over a person at the intersection. But after the automobile has driven away over the horizon, the only proof of the instrument of death, aside from the claims of the witness, exists in the tire tracks on the body, bits of car paint or chrome, and other residue. If such traces cannot be found, then the observations of the only witness can easily be questioned, and it may be concluded that the victim died elsewhere and was brought to the intersection, or perhaps did not die from being struck by a vehicle at all.

With chemical warfare, there is rarely any trace. There are few equivalents to the smoking gun or the tire tracks. Although traces of chemicals may be found in clothing or skin tissue, in vital organs through autopsy, or in the suppression of certain enzymes, these clues may just as easily be missing, dissipated by wind or rain, metabolized by the body, or diminished by the passage of minutes or hours. The special appeal of the new third-generation killing agents is that they leave no detectable traces at all.

Throughout the Yemen war, from el Kawma in 1963 to el Kitaf in 1967, reports of gas attacks had been received by the outside world with disbelief at best, and at worst with ridicule and demands for the smoking gun. In the weeks immediately following Kitaf, this continued. In Washington, the administration was obsessively preoccupied with Vietnam, and protests growing over the spraying of Agent Orange, so the atmosphere did not exist for a frank discussion of chemical attacks in Yemen. In any case, Washington had chosen to recognize the republican regime in Yemen, so it could not show interest in any atrocities reported by the royalists. In London, the Foreign Office was attempting to reestablish diplomatic relations with Cairo, broken since Egypt nationalized the Suez Canal in 1956, so nothing could be said publicly against Egypt or, for that matter, against the Soviet role in Egyptian military adventures. There was an increase, however, in the number of members of Parliament who believed that something very disturbing was being done with chemicals in Yemen, and who were not to be written off as "royalist sympathizers." Britain therefore tactfully deferred to the UN Security Council on the matter. But not before Prime Minister Harold Wilson told the House of Commons on January 31, 1967, that he had evidence strongly suggesting that poison gas had been used in Yemen.

Egypt's response was to declare once again that "the U.A.R. has not used poisonous gas at any time and did not resort to using such gas even when there were military operations in Yemen." This assertion is probably quite true. Egypt said that it, too, would defer to the United Nations on the matter. On March 1, 1967, UN Secretary General U Thant announced that he was "powerless" to deal with the issue. "The facts are in sharp dispute," U Thant said, "and I have no means of ascertaining the truth."

I had known U Thant quite well all my life, since growing up in Burma, and had last talked with him privately at the United Nations in 1965. There is no question that he knew exactly what was happening in Yemen. But for him there were overriding issues. I concluded that he particularly did not wish to annoy the Soviets.

A Red Cross doctor in Yemen told a journalist: "We are convinced, like you, but we cannot play politics." The issue of what was true or false in Yemen had to be considered in two contexts: that of objective reality and that of political reality. The two are entirely different; what is true in one context may be false in the other. What happens in one may not happen in the other.

There was another political nonevent on January 17, 1967, at Jabal Iyal Yazid (four five-hundred-pound gas bombs failed to explode, so there were no casualties); another nonevent on February 9 at Beni Salamah (seventy dead); again on May 4 at Bassi (no body count available); and on May 7 at Arhab (where two hundred died). There were abundant outside witnesses to the nonevent on May 10 at Gahar (seventy-nine dead) and nearby Gadafa (twenty-four dead), just two miles from the headquarters of Prince Mohammed bin Mohsin. Many of the victims were huddled in caves when eight Ilyushin light bombers appeared and dropped gas bombs that spread a greenish brown cloud.

Comments Colonel Smiley:

> This attack was witnessed by two British and one French mercenary who were attached to the royalist HQ in Wadi Hirran, about two miles away from the villages. They later told me that they saw the Ilyushins dropping bombs, and saw the usual greenish to brown smoke drifting up after they were dropped. They went to the village to give medical help, approaching from upwind, and said that those casualties that were not dead were either vomiting blood or suffering from blindness. Most of the dead had died in the caves where they usually went to take shelter when the bombers came over.

> At the time of the bombing two bombs had failed to explode, and one of the British who saw them said he saw Russian markings on the bombs. The news of these bombs was immedi-

ately signalled back by radio, and steps were put in hand to recover these bombs as direct evidence and for analysis. Experts were on their way to Wadi Hirran—a three-day drive from Najran—when the Egyptians carried out a very heavy attack with HE [high explosive] bombs on the area, and both the dud bombs were destroyed. It is almost certain that they intercepted the radio message about these bombs—Yemeni wireless security was notoriously bad—and took immediate steps to destroy any evidence before the bombs were recovered. In this they were successful.

A Red Cross team set out for Gahar three days after the attack, led by André Rochat, accompanied by ICRC representative Jacques Ruff, Dr. Willy Brutschin, Dr. Raymond Janin, male nurse René Vuille, and Yemeni male nurse Yahya bin Saleh. Italian journalist Claudio Cesaretti went along and recorded their harrowing adventure:

At 3 A.M. the first night out, the convoy of two vehicles came to a small stream where one truck got stuck in the mud. There was nothing to do but wait till dawn. Rochat ordered all medical supplies removed from the truck and stacked 150 yards away on a nearby hillside. There the group bedded down while the truck was guarded by Yahya bin Saleh. As usual, the ICRC had routinely notified all parties in the conflict that its team was setting out for Gahar by this route. But as a precaution, Rochat had the party spread on the ground by the truck a Red Cross flag twelve yards long.

At 7:45 A.M., with the sun already high in the east, three Ilyushin bombers with Egyptian markings appeared, circled once over the flag, then commenced a bombing run.

"As we rushed to cover," said Cesaretti, "the first bomb fell. In seconds the area was transformed into a landscape of craters. We sought shelter in a grotto. But already the bombs were there again. Three enormous explosions shook the air."

Two MIGs then appeared to observe the damage, then the Ilyushins returned and dropped three more bombs for good measure. The bedouin guards shouted that one of the Red Cross party had been hit. It was Yahya bin Saleh. He was lying under a bush. A bomb fragment had been driven through his body past his kidneys to lodge in his lungs. His left arm was broken and there was a deep wound in his left leg.

Gathering what was undamaged from their supplies, the Red Cross team attended to the injured man and moved on to Gahar.

Three gas bombs had been dropped at the foot of a hill beneath Gahar. The brownish gas had drifted up the slope to reach the village, killing seventy villagers immediately. Others were severely injured; two hundred head of livestock were killed. The circumstances of the attack were curious for several reasons, which emerge from details gathered by Rochat, the head of the Red Cross mission:

> The bombers circled the village for some time, then dropped three bombs on the hillside, east of and below the village, two or three hundred yards away to windward (wind direction east to west). No houses were damaged. The explosions were relatively mild. The bomb craters were about 8 feet in diameter and 20 inches deep, smaller than the usual craters. Twenty minutes after dropping the three gas bombs, the planes dropped four or five high-explosive bombs on the village and the western flank of the hill. Only one of these bombs caused any damage; this was sustained by a house in the center of the village.
>
> The 75 gas casualties were either within range of the gas when it was released or were in its path as it was blown by the wind. Some of the victims were found dead in their homes, as if they had died in their sleep. Other inhabitants, working in the fields or watching over the livestock, were eastward of the area where the gas bombs fell, some of them very near to the spot, and none of them were affected. The four survivors who were in the contaminated area are all in pain from the affected eyes and almost blind. All have pain in the chest and none has any wound. Many animals, including almost 200 cattle, sheep, goats, donkeys, and numerous birds were also killed. The villagers, who were not contaminated, buried the dead animals in a large pit west of the village, whilst the 75 humans killed were buried in four large communal graves.
>
> The ICRC delegates, for their part, observed the following: They inspected the village for several hours, checking, whenever possible, the accuracy of the information mentioned above. The doctors examined the four surviving gas casualties. Their medical report is attached hereto. The head of the mission had

one of the four communal graves opened. There were 15 corpses in it. An immediate autopsy by Dr. Brutschin and Dr. Janin left no doubt that death was due to pulmonary edema [the lungs filled with blood]. The doctors cannot testify to an air raid with gas bombs of which they were not personally witness. On the other hand, they stress that all the evidence leads to the conclusion that edema was caused by the breathing of poison gas. The delegates were later informed that on May 17 and 18 the villages of Gabas, Nofal, Gadr, and, for the second time, Gadafa were raided with gas bombs and that as a result 243 persons were killed.

This is only the first of three striking reports by the Red Cross growing out of the Gahar attack, but it deserves to be examined closely for its very curious aspects before proceeding to the others.

The aircraft first circled for some time, presumably attempting to establish wind direction from such signs as village cooking smoke. The pilots had perhaps not been provided with smoke bombs for some reason, had forgotten to load them, or had wasted them. They may have been duds. Only after considerable delay did they drop the gas bombs upwind of the village. Judging from the unusual craters, the bombs were canisters that did not detonate like high explosives, but released their aerosol contents slowly after impact. They were clearly the product of advanced technology.

Twenty minutes later, the planes came back and dropped what the doctors described as high-explosive bombs on the village (hitting only one house, however) and on the western flank of the hill— all of them, therefore, hit downwind of the original strike zone. If the bombs were napalm, the purpose would have been clear—to burn off any gas residue—a technique later employed routinely in Afghanistan. The bombs actually might have been napalm rather than HE, the distinction lost in translation or deemed unimportant by the villagers at the time. It is only since 1980 that the use of napalm to eradicate gas residue has become a widely recognized technique. But even if the bombs were HE, the purpose at that early stage might have been the same, given the way they were laid downwind, away from the dwellings.

Although it was concluded from the reports that the agent used was mustard gas, the lethal effect of mustard is delayed by hours, and is preceded by the onset of terrible burning and the eruption of large blisters. At Gahar "some of the victims were found dead in their homes, as if they had died in their sleep." Death had come suddenly, with little if any warning. The two most pronounced symptoms of the four strike-zone survivors were damage to the eyes and pain in the chest—but no blisters.

This was not the first incident in Yemen in which nerve gas signs had been noted, mixed with the effects of what people assumed were first-generation agents, primarily burning mustard and choking phosgene. But phosgene has a long-delayed effect of up to twenty-four hours, while mustard can take four to six hours. Given the apparent effort to eradicate the chemical residue by bombing downwind twenty minutes after a gas attack, could it have been that mustard gas was used to overlay and thereby disguise a more deadly agent?

On June 2, 1967, the Red Cross in Geneva—having carried out a detailed analysis of samples sent from Gahar—took its firmest public stand yet on the Yemen gassings. Given the ICRC's anxiety about forfeiting its humanitarian access to areas of conflict, the statement was striking. In part it read: "Extremely disturbed and concerned by these methods of warfare which are absolutely forbidden by codified international and customary law, the International Committee at once communicated its delegates' reports to all authorities concerned in the Yemen conflict, requesting them to take the solemn engagement not to resort in any circumstance whatsoever to the use of asphyxiating gases or any other similar toxic substances." The latter part of the phrase *or any other similar toxic substances* was perhaps an indication that the ICRC then considered the possibility that something a great deal more powerful than mustard or phosgene was being used. But the ICRC was still sticking to its determination to avoid direct confrontation with the Soviet Union— covered by the phrase *all authorities concerned.*

It was not the intention of the ICRC that the two analytical reports should be made public, but copies were obtained by the magazine *U.S. News & World Report,* which published them in its issue dated July 3, 1967.

Provocative details from the reports include the symptoms: shortness of breath, coughing, pink foaming at the mouth, internal thorax pain, and extreme fatigue. Opening the mass grave released the garlic stink of mustard, but the corpses showed no blisters. The lungs were reddish brown throughout with hemorrhagic pulmonary edema—that is, they were full of blood. There was, in short, a remarkable amount of hemorrhaging in the lungs and beneath the skin. There were no blisters because everyone was dead long before a mustard gas could take effect.

Professor Lauppi of the University of Bern Institute of Forensic Medicine concluded that in his opinion a nerve agent was not involved, and that mustard gas, adamsite, or lewisite were the most likely candidates. He reached this conclusion in spite of the absence of mustard blisters. None of these agents was capable of producing some of the more peculiar effects noted.

The presence of so much bleeding was also extraordinary in the January attack on el Kitaf. Casualties of that attack, and of other attacks during the January gas onslaught on various Yemeni towns, had been trucked to the Saudi Arabian field hospital across the border from Yemen at Najran, where there were both Saudi and Red Cross doctors. Aside from the repeated indications of nerve agents in Yemen, the inexplicable bleeding was the most remarkable aspect of what the hospital recorded.

This was apparent to nobody at the time. More than a decade passed before Dr. Charles Lewis examined the Hmong refugees from Laos and established that exceptional bleeding was the one characteristic that could not be explained by any known first- or second-generation agent. So it was only then that I began searching for incidents in other countries where massive hemorrhage was a major factor in a poison gas death. Within several months after Dr. Lewis drew the conclusion, I had obtained enough background material on the forgotten war in Yemen to realize that there was an amazing amount of blood everywhere. So I started searching for the original medical reports, the firsthand narratives of witnesses, and the descriptions in Arabic of patients who arrived at Najran field hospital after the raid on Kitaf. These were translated into English at the time of the incident, and therefore the translations are not colored by later developments.

When these original observations were made, nobody knew exactly what to look for, so naturally they looked for familiar details that they could recognize as significant. For example, if something burned and caused blisters, it was presumed to be mustard gas. If it choked the victim and made his lungs fill with liquid, it must be phosgene. If the victim died very suddenly, then it had to be nerve gas, which was the only agent everybody had heard of that could kill so quickly. If the details did not exactly fit any one of these agents, the witness or the observer was unable to make a connection to any more advanced agent, because nobody then knew such third-generation agents existed.

This effort to force the shoe to fit produced some silly confusion. Metal fragments of a gas canister from Kitaf were sent to a laboratory in Jeddah, Saudi Arabia, for tests by Saudi government chemists. Included with the metal bits and pieces were some fragments of a sort of cloth wadding from the canister. The purpose of this wadding or fusing is not known. But the Saudi chemists proceeded to subject the fragments to a number of tests. In the course of these tests, the chemists looked for phosphorous content which could have existed independently of nerve gas. They apparently assumed, wrongly, that they were looking for nerve gas, which is an organo-phosphorous compound and therefore would leave some unusual residue of phosphorous. They did find unusual phosphorous residue, but when they reported this as evidence of nerve gas, European scientists ridiculed their naiveté, and thereafter refused to take Yemen seriously.

Here is the report from Najran Hospital describing the survivors of Kitaf and other towns attacked early in January 1967:

A medical examination has been given to approximately 200 Yemenis in the town of Najran who are suffering from gas poisoning following the dropping of poison gas bombs by enemy aircraft on Yemeni territory. They were taken for first aid treatment to Najran Hospital, where the symptoms of the gas poisoning were diagnosed as follows: (1) Difficulty in breathing, with acute coughing; (2) Vomiting and the issuing of blood-flecked foam from the mouth; (3) Hemorrhage from nose and mouth; (4) Congestion of the face and eyes; (5) Hemorrhage of the conjunctiva [the mucous membrane lining the inside of the eyelids]; (6) Lowering of the blood pressure; (7) In some cases incapacity to walk or move; (8) In some cases total unconsciousness; (9) In some cases swelling around the neck and chest; (10) In some cases blood in the urine; (11) In some cases subcutaneous hemorrhage; (12) In some cases bloody stools.

Whatever was sprayed in Laos also caused death in minutes like nerve gas, burned but left blisters unlike mustard or adamsite, choked and gagged like phosgene, and also made everybody spew blood in every direction—unlike any known agent. So, it could have been some combination of nerve agent, mustard, phosgene, adamsite—plus the mysterious bleeding agent—or it could have been a totally new agent that produced many of the same effects as those older agents. I had no idea at the time which it was. But I did know from going through the raw data from Yemen that whatever it was, it was used there first, in the 1960s.

Twelve days before the outbreak of the Six-Day War in June 1967, Israeli intelligence reportedly discovered the existence of a stockpile of Soviet nerve gas in the Egyptian-held Sinai Peninsula. The gas was in artillery shells ready for use. Pending the outcome of emergency efforts to destroy the stockpile and to locate any others, Israel launched a frantic effort to buy gas masks. Twenty thousand gas masks were purchased in the United States with the secret assistance of the U.S. government. They were flown to Tel Aviv in a chartered 707 jet. Israel sought to buy others in West Germany. With the help of Chancellor Kurt Georg Kiesinger, 50,000 more masks were obtained and flown to Israel.

Meanwhile, an American laboratory that produces nerve gas antidote provided Israel with its entire stock of injectors with attached hypodermic needles for use by Israeli soldiers in the event of an attack. In Israel, the government secretly made arrangements for the mass funeral of up to 40,000 potential victims. The details of the Israeli discovery, and subsequent actions, were first reported by Marquis W. Childs, the Washington bureau chief of the *St. Louis Post-Dispatch,* in a story printed on June 18, 1967, after the lightning Israeli victory in the Six-Day War. The details were reconfirmed two years later by investigative reporter Seymour M. Hersh of *The New York Times.*

Childs had learned that the American intelligence community was excited about the discovery that one of the lethal agents in Yemen was not ordinary soman but the modified or "thickened" soman only recently developed by the Soviet Union, called VR-55. Childs referred to it only as a "V" agent. VR-55 stands for "Russian V agent—1955," the year it was apparently first identified.

Bomb fragments from Kitaf and Hadda were sent to Edgewood Arsenal where they were subjected to elaborate tests early in 1967. Along with the bomb fragments went grains of sand from the strike sites. Two Edgewood scientists analyzing the sand—unlike the Saudi chemists—had taken the precaution of monitoring their own cholinestarase levels. The chemical residue in the sand grains, sixteen weeks after the attacks in question, soon began to suppress their cholinesterase levels. Without knowing exactly what they were going to find in the Yemen evidence, the two scientists had discovered Soviet VR-55 residue.

They made their discovery in May 1967, just as the Israelis were discovering the nerve gas cache in the Sinai.

Just why the artillery shells loaded with VR-55, and other bombs filled with whatever compound was being used in Yemen, were not employed by Egypt during the Six-Day War is subject to speculation. The most acceptable explanation may be that Israel, after its startling discovery of the depot and its frantic efforts to obtain 100,000 gas masks and thousands of ampules of antitoxin, took the extreme action of informing Moscow of the steps it had taken, making clear exactly what kind of direct retaliation Israel would take against the Soviet Union or Soviet interests if Moscow permitted the nerve gas to be used by Egypt. Such last-minute diplomatic crisis maneuvers have been effective on other occasions, among them the Cuban missile crisis in 1962.

It would have been lunacy for the Soviets to place the nerve agent under Egyptian control, so it would have required Soviet action to release the nerve weapons. Since they were not used by Egypt even in the hour of its most humiliating defeat, in spite of repeated prior use in Yemen, it can only be concluded that Moscow had reasons of overriding importance to let Egypt down.

There were, of course, many other indicators pointing to the presence of nerve agents in Yemen: otherwise inexplicable medical signs demonstrated by casualties; the rapidity of death (less than ten minutes); the instances of a "fruity" or "geranium" smell, before all attacks became overlaid with the cloak of mustard gas; and the efforts to burn off gas residue after strikes by using napalm and explosives downwind. There was also the uneasiness of the ICRC, its unending equivocation, the obvious dread of its field doctors, and its choice of the evasive phrasing that typifies ICRC statements whenever the Soviet Union might take umbrage. The reluctance of Western intellectual circles for years afterward to accept anything more specific than the statement that "lethal gases" were used is merely a case of being scientifically fastidious in the absence of smoking gun evidence. Such smoking gun evidence, where it has existed in the form of residues on bomb fragments or sand particles, has not been made available to the general scientific community.

But the use of a nerve agent can hardly explain all the more bizarre chemical effects in Yemen any more than in Laos. Even if one does accept VR-55 as being employed in Yemen by Soviet pilots flying Soviet aircraft painted with Egyptian markings—and accepts that the Soviets were taking advantage of the situation to test experimental chemical warfare agents—some nagging questions remain.

An oily agent such as VR-55 persists for many weeks, so it could not have been used without leaving conspicuous residues. Even if VR-55 had been mixed in a compound with mustard and phosgene (producing the smell, the burning and occasional blistering effects, and the choking so widely reported), this would still not account for the extraordinary bleeding. In Yemen, as in Laos, victims were bleeding from all body openings in a matter of three minutes— many of them dying this way as rapidly as they could have been killed by VR-55. Even days later, survivors were still hemorrhaging from all their orifices, under their skin, and into their internal organs. What produced such bleeding?

While I was poring over the Yemen archives, beginning to realize the broad outlines of this mystery agent, the Russians invaded Afghanistan. It was December 1979. By the middle of January it looked like they were going to be in Afghanistan a long time. There was strong resistance to the occupation. In towns and mountains, the Afghans began a classic guerrilla war against the invaders. It was Vietnam all over again, but with the shoe on the other political foot. It was also Mussolini invading Ethiopia all over again. I wondered how long it would be before the Russians started using gas to flush out the Moslem guerrillas. And when gas was used, would the reports contain anything unusual?

I did not have long to wait, and I was not disappointed.

7.
A Visit to the Hindu Kush

Afghanistan was a spectacular frustration for the Russians. The Soviet invasion on December 24, 1979, came as a surprise because nobody expected Moscow to let itself be so thoroughly sucked into the affairs of a squalid South Asian buffer state. Although there was then a great show of bravado, of Slavic muscle flexing, showing off heavy weapons and brandishing Kalashnikovs in the face of unwashed Moslem rabble, you could tell at once that the Russians really regretted that they had ever come to Kabul. A joke made the embassy rounds in Washington about how the Soviets drank too much vodka one night, woke up in an Afghan brothel, and went home with the clap; now they were back in force to cure the disease once and for all by injecting all Afghans with lead.

I figured that it was only a matter of time till poison gas stories started trickling out of the Hindu Kush. The object then was to look closely and see what medical symptoms were described. After Laos, and after digging back into the Yemen war, the serious issue here was not whether Moscow would dare to use chemicals to eliminate Afghan opposition—that seemed inevitable to me—but exactly what poisons were used. It is illuminating that the gas reports began immediately, demonstrating that the Russians saw no need to wait like Mussolini in Ethiopia until the situation turned against them—which it soon did.

In the countryside, the Moslem rebels—the Mujahideen—fought with surprising effect. It took them only a short time to discover that a Soviet helicopter was heavily armored on the bottom, but it had no armor at all on its top. So Moslem snipers with geriatric Lee-Enfield rifles sat on rocky ledges high above the passing choppers and fired down at them, causing more than one to explode in midair. In the month of July 1980, thirteen Soviet helicopters were destroyed—millions of rubles worth of hardware. Among them were eleven Mi-8 Hip troop transports and two giant Mi-6 Hook skycranes.

On the ground, advanced Soviet equipment fared little better. The Afghan rebels discovered an ingenious method for knocking out the Soviet T-55 tanks. Baiting the tanks up narrow, rocky mountain defiles, the Mujahideen would lurk on an overhanging ledge till a tank passed underneath, then drop down on its top and smear a handful of excrement—there was no mud available in those dry, rocky ridges—over its periscope, blocking the driver's vision and bringing the tank to an abrupt halt. The moment a hatch opened, the Afghans would shoot the emerging tankman in the head, then drop a grenade down the hatch.

In the cities the Russians were equally frustrated. Kabul became a city of terror. In February 1980, civil servants and shopkeepers called a strike in protest of the Soviet occupation. Screaming "God is great," demonstrators stormed three police stations and seized their arsenals. Other demonstrators attacked a column of BTR-60PB armored personnel carriers and a T-55 tank. In the crackdown that followed, Soviet MIGs strafed crowds of demonstrators while Mi-24 Hind helicopter gunships fired rockets into the mobs. The battle raged for six hours, until the streets were swept by masses of Soviet troops.

But far from being subdued, the urban rebellion simply moved underground, taking advantage of the arabesque of narrow alleys and the maze construction of the old quarter, coming out at night to assassinate Soviet officers and members of the puppet government of Babrak Karmal. The Soviet occupation force in Kabul soon found it impossible even to go shopping for fresh vegetables and Levis without taking along their machine guns. Russian wives toting shopping baskets arrived with husbands wielding AK-47 automatic rifles.

It was a war that degenerated quickly to the most extreme methods. There was no question of military issues being confused by the sort of temporizing and moralizing typical of the Vietnam War. If the question of lethal chemicals involved any second thoughts, they were concerned only with avoiding attention. So from the outset, there was a conspicuous pattern: Tear gas and incapacitants could be used anywhere in Afghanistan—including psychochemicals of the BZ type and the new Soviet Blue-X gas, which knocked victims out harmlessly for eight to twelve hours, allowing them to be disarmed and captured. Lethal agents could be used only in remote Badakhshan—where it was unlikely that reports or witnesses would reach the outside world and, on a severely restricted basis, in Konarha and Paktia provinces. In these two provinces, the Moslem rebels were especially strong and were energetically supported from nearby Pakistan.

This pattern emerges from a scrutiny of the reports reaching Peshawar, Pakistan, and from a careful cross-checking of the location where each attack was said to have taken place. There were scattered reports of lethal and nonlethal gas attacks from various parts of Paktia and Konarha, usually coinciding with known Soviet military operations. But the predominance of lethal cases came from the impossibly rugged Hindu Kush mountain range that blocks Badakhshan Province from prying eyes. Despite the obstacles there, word still got out.

This is all the more remarkable because high valleys in Badakhshan are separated by sheer mountain ridges, making it unlikely that witnesses of one attack could compare notes with those of another only a few miles away. Passage out through the mountains is so arduous that only the very healthy can make it, cutting down the number of refugees from Badakhshan compared to other provinces. So when a report did come from Badakhshan, it deserved to be taken seriously. The disproportionate number of lethal cases held all the greater significance.

The reports themselves did not have shape or order at first. They were a remarkable jumble of perceptions crammed with local color and characteristic of the tales of seminomadic mountain folk, emerging with their goats and rifles from a desolate, lunar landscape. To make greater sense out of them, I had to go in myself.

Up to this point, a few newsmen and soldiers of fortune had ventured into Konarha, Nangarhar, Paktia, and Qandahar far to the south—all provinces with fairly direct access from populated areas of Pakistan. The Soviets had then mined the border and sprinkled little green plastic booby traps among the rock debris. Crossing anywhere became extremely dangerous. On the other hand, nobody had been to remote Badakhshan except the CIA, which had been running agents into the Hindu Kush to gather intelligence and to work with the rebels. This is the roof of the world. To reach it on horseback would take a week or more from Chitral or Gilgit—if you were extremely lucky. But there was another way, if I could prevail on some very old friends in the Pakistan army.

The air was very cold. From the top of the ridge on the Afghan side of the border the mountains of the Hindu Kush spread out to the horizon in row upon jagged row. Far below me in an alpine valley spotted with flowering rhododendrons and laced by a white mountain stream there was a whooshing chop-chop-chop as a Russian Hind helicopter fluttered into view, followed by two others, and tracked the stream up the next ridge toward a snowy pass. The sky, a deep Mongolian blue, outlined every detail of landscape in stark relief. To the east, toward China, loomed the first great snow peaks of the Tibetan Himalayas. To the north, only twenty-five or fifty miles by chopper, across this narrow neck of Afghanistan, stood the white peaks of the Pamir range in Soviet Tadzhikistan. To the west of my ridge, in the direction of Zibak and Feyzabad in Badakhshan, the Red Army's 860th Brigade artillery was pounding a rebel stronghold. A procession of Mujahideen insurgents passed below me, trailing puffs of white breath as they shouldered their captured AK-47 assault rifles and an RPG-16 antitank weapon and made their way down a footpath until I could no longer make out their baggy pantaloons and dingy turbans, vanishing toward the distant combat.

We had talked through an interpreter at the tiny border garrison on the ridge a few hundred yards to my right. Time was limited because the helicopter was returning soon to pick me up. The guerrillas had been wary, but they seemed to be on good terms with the garrison commander, so they soon began to tell him—rather than me—the answers to my questions.

It was here, they said, in the narrow mountain valleys of the Kush in autumn 1980, that the Mujahideen in their alpine hideouts were being exterminated by an evil weapon—a dirty yellow brown cloud spawned by the squatting helicopters, a cloud that brought the freedom fighters writhing from their caves to dance and squirm, spew blood, and die in spasms on the bare rock reaches, like earthworms wriggling in a lethal spray of insecticide. Their agonies signaled success to the gunships darting and swooping overhead. The helicopters withdrew together like dragonflies chasing off through the peaks, only to be replaced by MIG-21 jet fighters laying napalm. The jellied gasoline burned off the yellow cloud and any yellow powder residues on the scorched rock. Inside the cave hideouts, nobody lived. Outside, even close witnesses were not certain what they had seen. When they crossed into Pakistan for supplies and told their stories to me on the ridge, they fit similar tales that I heard from Konarha, and from Paktia—south of the Khyber Pass.

Since the armies of Darius the Great marched through these desolate mountains in the fifth century B.C., a pall of death has hung over the Khyber Pass, but it has always been a figurative one. Now the pall was real, a yellow brown aerosol of soft, talcky powders.

Here was the proof that vanished from Yemen. The similarities were striking: Moslem guerrillas fighting from mountain redoubts and caves hit with chemicals from Soviet aircraft using precision attack techniques, producing virtually identical symptoms—if anything more violent in dosage—provoking the same bitter resistance.

"On the first day of the attack," an Afghan told me there on the high ridge, "the helicopters fired rockets at the village we were defending. There was a dirty colored cloud, yellowish brown. Our fighters died quickly. They were vomiting blood and fouling their clothes and began to act like crazy people falling down and jerking about. This was the only time I personally saw the *Schurawi* [Russians] attack this way, although I know of other times when I was not there. Twice more I saw Mujahideen die like this, very fast. But not with rockets. One time the dirty cloud came from a bomb, and the other time from artillery. But both times, yes, our fighters were throwing up blood—as if they had been drinking blood and could not hold any more. There was also blood in their eyes, like tears, and from the nose. At first I thought it was from the concussion of the bomb, but the bomb did not make a big explosion. And our fighters did not have any marks on them. The rest of us ran from the cloud. We left our fighters there. They were lying on the ground jerking like dogs with broken backs."

The other Afghan had a white beard and a nose gnarled like a tree stump. "When I have seen it, the cloud is blue. The aggressor planes came and dropped sticks. Many sticks. When they struck the ground, they made a blue cloud and everyone went to sleep. When we woke up the sun was setting and there were aggressors everywhere. They had come to capture us while we were sleeping."

The sticks he described were twelve-inch metal cylinders, tubes containing a chemical agent that was ejected as an aerosol when the tubes landed. The chemical, dubbed "Blue-X" by some observers because of its gray blue color and unknown composition, proved remarkably effective in tactical use and was soon being described in use over much of Afghanistan. By autumn 1980, after seven months of occupation, Blue-X was proving to be the most popular CW weapon in the Soviet arsenal.

But the lethal agent was harder to be certain about. Because of the suddenness of death and the convulsions, it appeared to most observers to be nerve agent. But that would not explain the blood. At different refugee camps and at Khyber hospital in Peshawar, refugees and Afghan rebels described basically the same symptoms: first blinding and choking with terrible burning, then nausea with vomiting of blood, and blood issuing from eyes, nose, and ears. After a few minutes, the skin changed color to a deep yellow, then turned black either just before or just after death. Death was violent, involving twitching and jerking and retching blood.

Sometimes witnesses reported hemorrhage, sometimes they did not. Sometimes they reported muscular spasms, sometimes just sudden death. Sometimes they described burning and blistering, sometimes just choking.

They might have been describing the same episodes in slightly different ways, as if one witness had noticed one set of signs, another a different set—but both sets converging quickly in death.

Or else they were describing the effects of quite different compounds, in which the chemical mixture was altered for tactical or experimental purposes. Both possibilities were significant in light of the reports from Laos. In both countries, simple mountain people were describing elaborate chemical effects in almost exactly the same patterns. A description from an Afghan in Badakhshan could just as well have been narrated by a Hmong from Phu Bia Mountain.

In each instance there were certain provocative signs of nerve gas, mixed with signs of choking or burning agents, mixed with some powerful agent, producing violent hemorrhage. The effects might vary, or they might be perceived differently by onlookers, and the dosages might be different from case to case, from victim to victim—but the net result was the same. Quick, violent chemical death.

The Soviets seemed to employ these chemicals as a basic part of an overall attack. On January 13, 1980, during a Soviet assault on rebel forces near Feyzabad, the compound was dropped in aerial bombs that exploded in midair, dispensing the chemicals in a vapor that caused vomiting, constriction of the chest, blindness, paralysis, and quick death. On January 29 near Beharak in Badakhshan, Soviet forces crossed the Oxus River and assaulted rebels in a village with chemical mortars, killing eighty villagers including women and children. On February 3 not far away, near Sebak, a Soviet tank column was pinned down by rebels until helicopter gunships arrived and fired rockets that spread a lethal brown cloud. At other points, MIGs dropped canisters of chemicals or cluster bombs resembling oil drums, each MIG carrying three but able to drop only one on each pass. The cluster bombs contained concentric rows of chemical powders in bags. In most cases in which Soviet ground troops were involved, aircraft returned minutes later to follow the gas attack with napalm, burning off the agents once they had killed or incapacitated the rebels. In several instances in forested areas, fire sticks were used instead of napalm; the fire sticks resembled Oriental incense joss sticks and were scattered by the thousands from cluster bombs detonated in the air. Once the fire sticks were scattered through the woods or over a village, they were ignited by a single rocket or a burst of incendiary rounds. An area twice the size of a football field could be destroyed with each batch of fire sticks. Another curious Soviet innovation in Afghanistan was what appeared to be thickened soman spread on the ground in cold weather. Any rebels passing through got the agent on their feet—with or without shoes. The agent was released by warmth and perspiration, killing in minutes.

Although it was impossible to be absolutely certain of exact details in any of these cases, the overall pattern was clear. If the Afghans had been making up the reports, they could never have been so consistent from so many different incidents. And if they had been making it all up, the lies would have surfaced from all over Afghanistan; they would not have been concentrated in certain areas. These areas were the most difficult terrain in Afghanistan, the logical place to conduct chemical operations with minimum risk to Soviet personnel and equipment or of exposure to the outside world. The same was true of Laos and Yemen. In Yemen, on-the-spot investigation had borne out the stories told by the survivors. There was every reason to believe that on-the-spot investigation in Laos and Afghanistan, had it been possible, would also have confirmed the accuracy of the reports.

Foreign diplomats listened impatiently, then added the gas stories to their refugee reports and sent them along to their embassies in Islamabad where they were bundled into diplomatic pouches and flown to Western capitals. There they were sifted apprehensively by intelligence officers. Given Afghanistan's primitive circumstances and the initial lack of confirmation, the chemicals used could have been simply tear gas and incapacitants—but a disturbing number of deaths were reported. Many of the descriptions included peculiar technical details that raised eyebrows because they fit certain specific toxic chemicals, and could not have been imagined in exactly the right sequence by so many narrators.

It made no sense, unless you had access to the recent reports from Laos, thousands of miles away. Or unless you had just gone back over the original reports from Yemen, more than ten years earlier. Nobody thought to connect the three incidents until late February 1980, three months after the Soviet invasion. The analysts responsible for Laos were not the same as those concerned with Afghanistan. Those who had studied Yemen in 1967 had mostly drifted away to other jobs or retired from government service.

So the reports piled up and nothing was done while everyone waited for irrefutable confirmation.

On a hunch, I telephoned one analyst who I knew had access to the latest cables from Afghanistan. He insisted that no patterns were yet emerging in the gas accounts. I asked him if he had looked to see if there was any unusual bleeding. If there was, perhaps it would be fruitful to compare the medical symptoms in the Afghan reports with the medical symptoms from Laos. He said he would dig out the files and have a look for any blood.

The next day I got a call. "My God," he said, "there's blood all over the place—but only in three provinces. Most of it's in Badakhshan. Absolutely no blood—no unusual bleeding—anywhere else. Like you said, it's coming out everywhere, all over the body. Not just the sort of bleeding that you'd get from a broken nose, or ruptured lungs, or from any of the vesicant agents. I was so surprised that I lined up all the reports from Afghanistan next to all the reports from Laos and compared them symptom for symptom and they match perfectly."

"As if they all came from the same place?" I asked.

"Like different people describing the same thing," he said.

I suggested that he compare both sets to the medical reports from the Yemen war. "You have your confirmation now," I said.

"What do you mean?"

"The coincidence is too great. Massive internal hemorrhage with blood coming out all the orifices is a detail so strange and so unlike any known CW effect that nobody would invent it over and over again thousands of miles apart. Even the time factors are the same. The most devoted liars could never make it appear the same every time."

How could something so bizarre be happening in exactly the same sequences thousands of miles apart unless the same chemical compound, producing massive hemorrhage, was being used in both places? But if it was being sprayed by the Vietnamese in Laos and by the Soviets in Afghanistan, what was it and who was responsible for its development?

There was no doubt that the Soviets had come to Afghanistan with substantial chemical forces. Photographs and eyewitnesses provided elaborate verification of Soviet chemical corps equipment accompanying the five divisions of the Red Army—the 5th, the 54th, the 201st, and the 360th Motorized Rifle Divisions, and the 103d Guards Airborne Division. Included in their equipment were TMS-65 decontamination vehicles mounted with detergent vats and aircraft turbine engines that sprayed the detergents at high temperature and great velocity over passing tanks to remove all contaminants in minutes. There were also personnel decontamination chambers called AGV-3s consisting of three tents in which soldiers stripped, decontaminated, and dressed in fresh uniforms—each tent carefully sealed from the step before. It was well known that the Red Army was better equipped for chemical defense than any other military force, so it was not necessarily unusual for these standard vehicles and chambers to be in the inventory during the invasion—even though primitive Moslem rebels in Afghanistan were hardly likely to pose a chemical threat against which the Red Army would have to defend itself.

It would have been normal, that is, if the chemical equipment had remained in place at the divisional hard bases, where their presence would indeed have seemed routine. But by March 1980, satellites had photographed the TMS-65 decon vehicles and the AGV-3 detox chambers moving up to the most forward combat areas, in terrain so rough that they had to be there for a specific purpose. Other satellite pictures then showed the TMS-65s being used to decontaminate battle tanks, and showed Soviet combat troops lining up to enter the AGV-3 tents. Could they have been using the tents for delousing? The TMS-65s had, on occasion, been used to suppress mosquitoes around the division hard bases. Could they have been sent on remote guerrilla operations for pest control?

The sheer size of the Soviet chemical corps and the ubiquity of its equipment makes it tempting to assume that it is responsible for offensive chemical warfare. But in the USSR, the chemical corps is only a defensive organization not directly involved in the offensive use of chemical weapons. This is a responsibility of the Red Army's operational units, and of similar operational units of the KGB, or Ministry of State Security, which maintains its own paramilitary forces. These operational chemical attack units are under field officers following a command chain leading straight up to the minister of defense and the Politburo.

If the Soviets were using lethal agents in the Afghan war, this was a decision made by the minister of defense in concert with the Politburo—and had nothing directly to do with the Soviet chemical corps defensive units being in Afghanistan. The question at hand was really whether the highest levels in Moscow had approved the offensive use of lethal chemicals by regular troops to suppress opposition.

To answer that, we need to understand a bit about Soviet military psychology and how it is different—if it is—from the Western experience. Has the Soviet Union, for example, a history of being reluctant to use poison gas on its enemies? That means a look back toward the Bolshevik Revolution. I found many of the answers scattered through the military archives in Washington and London.

No country in World War I suffered as many casualties from gas warfare as Russia. Half a million Russians were stricken, and 50,000 of them died. Although Russia withdrew from the war before it ended, because of the Revolution, the Russian army suffered twice the gas casualties and five times the gas deaths of any other combatant. These terrible losses were largely the result of poor chemical warfare training and poor discipline in the ranks. There was virtually no protective equipment, and hardly any chemical stocks could be rallied for retaliation. The Russians were not prepared to defend or to attack.

When the new Soviet government took over after the Bolsheviks seized power, these memories were painfully fresh. As soon as the Red Army was organized in 1918, chemical troops were included. Two years later, in 1920, a Higher Military Chemical School was established to train officers for the chemical corps. In the spring of that year, while the Red Army fought to secure all of Russia in the face of numerous counterrevolutions, three thousand balloonlike containers of chlorine gas were set up near Kakhovka on the southern front in an effort to exterminate the White Russian forces led by the Czarist general Pyotr Nikolayavich Wrangel. The White Army had regrouped in the Crimea and was about to launch a new campaign in the Ukraine. The early stages of Baron Wrangel's onslaught were so successful that the Bolsheviks fell back at Kakhovka, and the poison gas they had so carefully prepared was never used.

By the following year, 1921, Wrangel's army had been defeated and the baron had gone into exile in Europe. But the hardships imposed by the Bolsheviks during the civil war had been so severe that urban workers in Petrograd and elsewhere rose up in strikes and demonstrations calling for an end to the dictatorship of the Communist party and for "soviets without Bolsheviks"—a precursor of the rebellion in Poland in the 1980s. Sailors at the Kronstadt Naval Base in the Gulf of Finland overlooking Petrograd (now Leningrad) had played a crucial role in the October Revolution. Now they took the side of the workers against the Bolsheviks, demanding political freedom, civil rights, and economic relief. Leon Trotsky and Mikhail N. Tukhachevsky prepared a Red Army assault to crush the Kronstadt rebels. In the event that a straight military attack on the naval base failed, an alternate plan was devised by the chief of artillery of the Red Army, Comrade Sheideman, to attack the forts at Kronstadt with poison gas in artillery shells and balloons. Details of the gas attack were worked out by officers at the Higher Chemical School and were sanctioned by Trotsky, who was commissar for war, and Kamenev, chairman of the Moscow Soviet and one of the more cautious Old Bolsheviks.

Trotsky's ground assault succeeded in overwhelming the Kronstadt forts, and all the survivors were either shot or imprisoned, making it unnecessary to carry out the poison gas attack. But a pattern was becoming apparent in which both Red Army commanders and senior members of the Politburo endorsed the use of poison gas to kill not wartime enemies but fellow Russians in circumstances of civil unrest.

It could be argued that since neither of these planned poison gas attacks was carried out, the endorsement or use of gas by the Politburo and the high command was never demonstrated in the field. Not so. During the 1920s, as Stalin tightened his grip on power, exactly such an incident occurred when the Soviet government forced peasants into collective farms. Already the countryside was in chaos from the upheaval of the Revolution and the civil war. It was also ravaged by the drought and famine of 1920–21. The peasants were becoming accustomed to the terror of the Bolshevik secret police. The greatest resistance to collectivization came from peasant farmers who despite the chaos had been moderately successful in growing crops and raising livestock and so were often in a position to employ other peasants as hired hands. To overcome their resistance and to cause them to be ostracized, the government labeled them "kulaks"—implying that they were wealthy landowners.

Other peasants who were barely self-sufficient also resisted. They, too, were labeled kulaks, deserving only "liquidation as a class," meaning extermination, imprisonment, or deportation to Siberia.

The peasants in the northern Caucasus Mountains, like those in the soil-rich Ukraine and the black-dirt farmers of the Volga, were better off than most. The Soviet government wanted their grain for distribution. When they resisted, the Red Army moved in to crush them. Whole villages defied the army. Poison gas artillery rounds were fired into the villages, and entire communities were killed. Although the deaths were apparently in the thousands, there are no precise figures, and what figures did exist were lost among the accounts of millions of kulaks killed, jailed, or sent to Siberian slave camps in the late 1920s. Although we do not know how many thousands died, the fact that many villages in the Caucasus were exterminated with poison gas fired by fellow Russians is attested to by members of the officer corps from the Higher Military Chemical School. Apparently, phosgene, mustard gas, and chlorine were the agents used.

In the years immediately following the purge of the kulaks, other groups rose against the extension of Soviet oppression across the vast reaches of the USSR. The rebels included the Basmatch tribesmen of Central Asia, who were decimated by mustard gas sprayed from Red Army aircraft, according to members of the chemical corps units involved.

The Basmatch were not ethnic Russians. They were more closely related to Afghans.

So there does not appear to have been any innate reluctance on the part of the Kremlin or the Red Army to employ any and all of the most lethal gases then known to exist against fellow Russian revolutionaries, fellow Russian peasant farmers, or Soviet Asians. At this point, the Red Army had not yet been put in the position of having to use poison gas on a foreign enemy.

In Russia, a massive chemical warfare establishment grew. The Soviet regime set up a Military-Chemical Administration for the Red Army in 1924 in Moscow, and in 1927 began providing the entire population with civil defense instruction—including chemical warfare protection. As the defensive chemical corps expanded, the Soviet chemical industry struggled to build a stockpile of offensive chemical weapons.

A proving ground was set aside in 1928 at Shihkany, near the town of Volsk. It was called the TsVKhP (for Central Army Chemical Range). Each military district in the nation had its own chemical battalion except Moscow, which had the First Chemical Regiment.

"The chemical weapon was recognized as powerful and effective both in trench warfare and in mobile warfare," according to Col. V. Pozdnyakov, an officer in the Red Army chemical corps. "It was intended to be used by the various branches of the armed forces and in all kinds of military actions. Its military value—because of the extensive area it affected, the suddenness of its action, its lasting effect, its capacity to inflict mass casualties, and its comparative low cost—was regarded as being beyond doubt."

In the 1930s, a large factory was built in the Karakum desert, about 150 miles from Ashkabad, to process sulfur deposits there for the manufacture of mustard gas and other chemicals. The mines at Ozinki on the Volga also contributed sulfur for the purpose. Colonel Pozdnyakov listed the principal factories in the Soviet military-chemical industry as: the Bandyuzhsky chlorine works on the Kama River; the Chapayevsk works near Kuibyshev, which produced basic toxic materials; the Beresniki works, which produced chlorosulphonic acid; the Khibinogorsk works, which produced phosphorus; the Karaganda works, which produced hydrocyanic acid. By midcentury their production capacity was the equal of anything in Western Europe besides Germany, the colonel boasted.

The chemical weapons included persistent, semipersistent, and nonpersistent agents, among them the asphyxiating agents phosgene, diphosgene, and chloropicrin; blood poisons such as cyanogen chloride and hydrocyanic acid; lethal vesicants like mustard and trichlorotriethylamine; milder eye irritants like chloroacetophenone; nose irritants including the sometimes lethal adamsite and diphenyl-chloroarsine.

New poisons were being developed by scientists at the chemical faculty of the Leningrad Artillery Academy, Moscow's Higher Military School for Chemistry, the Kalinin Military Chemical School, and the Moscow Military Academy for Chemical Defense. Like other major powers, the military assigned chemical warfare research projects to the laboratories of its Academy of Sciences, the universities, and the factories of the chemical industry.

"Work was done on substances which could break up under the catalytic action of activated carbon within the gas mask and produce carbon monoxide," Colonel Pozdnyakov said. "In particular much effort was put into devising agents or mixtures of agents suitable for use under both summer and winter conditions."

The lethal mixtures were tested on the Kuzminki range near Moscow, at the Gorokhovetsky camp near Gorky, and at TsVKhP, where factories were built to develop production processes.

"One can state with assurance," said the good colonel, "that the research work on military poisonous substances is on a modern level in the Soviet Union, and is not behind similar work in other countries."

Russian aircraft weapons included the RRAB cluster bomb—grandfather of the one used in Afghanistan—aerosol spray canisters, and thin-walled bombs charged with lethal agents—like those dropped on Yemeni towns. Red Army units were equipped with chemical artillery shells and mines charged with persistent and non-persistent agents, and similarly charged mortar rounds, toxic smoke candles, and toxic smoke generators. Hand and rifle grenades filled with toxic agents were tested, along with aerosol spray nozzle dispensers for battle tanks.

Not without accidents. Once, during an exercise in the steppe near Astrakhan, a deadly cloud rose above a forest, traveled fifty kilometers, and only then, thanks to cold air currents, descended—with what results to the local population the colonel did not tell us.

Troops were trained to use poison gas on enemy positions during an attack and to contaminate the path of enemy advances.

If the Red Army made a poor showing at the outbreak of World War II, it was not from lack of preparedness in poisons. Chemical defense companies were included in all Soviet rifle divisions. Each company had a chemical reconnaissance platoon that could field three or four teams and was responsible for locating enemy chemical weapons depots. Field labs capable of analyzing soil, water, and plants to identify chemical agents were attached to each reconnaissance element.

None of this was any use, as it turned out, because political misjudgments on the part of the Kremlin enabled the Germans to rout the Red Army totally. In the chaos, all chemical offensive stocks and munitions at the front were lost, and virtually all defensive equipment was abandoned. It was some time before the Red Army recovered sufficiently to counterattack with conventional means, much less with exotic chemicals.

After World War II, the picture become smudged. Allegiances had changed, and it was no longer possible to know what was going on in Russia with any clarity. The archives are of little help; everything known or guessed is too new. So when I passed through England on my way back from the Afghan border, I placed a call from London's Gatwick airport to Edinburgh—to the Defense Studies Center at the university—and soon heard the crisp, percolating voice of Dr. John Erickson, probably the leading Western expert on Soviet chemical forces and strategy. We arranged to meet for lunch at the faculty club. Fortunately, there was a shuttle from Gatwick about to take off.

The cool green hills of Scotland were a welcome relief after the Hindu Kush, and Edinburgh seemed tidy and inviting. As my taxi pulled up before a massive stone facade in the university complex, I recognized Erickson instantly. He resembled a peregrine falcon, lean and intense, the energy spinning off him like heat waves, and his movements quick and nonstop. At his office later, beyond the medical buildings, we talked on while he bundled together some of his recent studies outlining the composition of the Red Army chemical units and their astonishing diversity of equipment. We were talking about the specter of the blood agent, wondering whether it might be a certain marine poison that makes the arteries and veins contract, squirting blood out wherever the tissues burst. I was locked into tight plane schedules back in London, so in a flurry of Soviet military tracts in Cyrillic lettering, Erickson saw me off to the airport again, armed this time with a small mound of documents.

From then on I encountered Erickson everywhere I dug. He was either busy working on the same subject—China for example —or had already drawn some provocative conclusions about what the Russians were up to there. He seemed to be miles ahead of the pack, nosing through clues about mysterious clashes along the Sino-Soviet border or piecing the Afghan quandary together.

By the eve of the invasion of Afghanistan, I learned from John Erickson, the Red Army had between 80,000 and 100,000 chemical warfare specialists in its Chemical Corps, commanded by Col. Gen. V. K. Pikolov. Their responsibility, distinct from that of combat troops, was to deal with the contamination produced by nuclear, biological, and chemical (NBC) warfare. They were also to provide battlefield support with smoke, flame-throwing, and incendiary operations. Each division in the Red Army maintained its own chemical defense battalion, drawn from the Chemical Corps. There was a separate Civil Defense organization within the Red Army, commanded by Colonel General Altunin, with elements at all levels of the armed forces, but its responsibilities were defense, for the civilian population, not combat support.

The Chemical Corps, on the other hand, provided impressive, grueling training exercises for regular Red Army troops, using lethal chemical agents, including nerve gas, at more than one thousand ranges across the Soviet Union. Some training was conducted with nonlethal agents like tear gas and riot-control incapacitants such as chloroacetophenone and benzenesulfonyl, sprayed out of East German-made R-2 and S-2 atomizers. During these regular training drills, live agents such as diluted soman were also used, each year apparently killing a dozen or more soldiers who were careless about their protective gear. The lesson to other soldiers was presumably considered worth the fatalities.

In these drills, soldiers learned to use elaborate protective gear, keeping it on through strenuous field operations for up to twelve hours. Each soldier was issued a gas mask, gloves, leggings, boots, and a thin cape that converted quickly into coveralls—all of a rubberized material resistant to all known chemical and biological agents. The gas mask standard in the Red Army—the SbM—had certain failings. It protected adequately against cyanide-type blood poisoning agents and phosgene-type choking agents (neither of which is prominent in NATO arsenals), but was not equipped with corrective lenses, nor with openings for eating and drinking. It was also heavy and uncomfortable, and ill served any foot soldier who had to wear one for long periods. Possibly the Soviets expected only short-duration contamination with nonpersistent agents, which would allow Red Army soldiers to remove their masks periodically.

For any soldier exposed to agents without a mask, or to lethal poisons that could penetrate the SbM, there was the MSP-18 treatment kit, packed neatly with the Soviet equivalent of Western antidote injectors, called *shprits-tyubik*. It was a folding plastic case with five syringes on one side for treatment of nerve agents. The injectors contained atropine. In the other half of the kit there were six tablets for lung irritants like phosgene, an injector with a general painkiller, a blue injector for hydrogen cyanide blood poisoning, and ampules of amyl nitrate to break and sniff to expand the arteries and ensure free passage of blood when hit with cyanide.

Since Soviet combat strategy envisioned a high-speed offensive through battlefields heavily contaminated with nuclear, biological, and chemical agents, this elaborate protective gear was to be augmented by the constant measurement of contamination levels.

"Our troops," boasted General Pikalov, "are armed with special vehicles and armored transporters protected against radioactivity, and with automatic and semiautomatic instruments to detect and pinpoint in a few seconds contamination in the air and on the ground." He explained that special aircraft and helicopters were equipped to make fast surveys of combat areas, feeding data to computers that analyzed the exact types of agents present, their dosages, and the size of the area contaminated. Pikolov added that his troops received special training in mathematics, physics, and chemistry to carry out these complex calculations.

In addition to being supported by airborne hardware and

special detection vehicles, the Soviet foot soldier was issued the miniaturized detection kit designated the VPKhR (weight 2.3 kilograms), which used only three indicator tubes and yet was capable of detecting mustard, phosgene, diphosgene, hydrogen cyanide, cyanogen chloride, G-type nerve agents, V-type nerve agents, and possibly some as-yet-unknown agents as well. This indicated that Moscow believed these agents would be used in combat. But why the Red Army should be prepared against some agents that are in only the Soviet arsenal, not in Western stocks, can be explained only if the Soviets fully intend to employ these agents themselves and need to protect their own troops against their own poisons.

During the Arab-Israeli War of 1973, the Israelis captured Soviet battle tanks that had been provided to Egypt just prior to the war. Inside was found a novel Soviet antigas device—an automatic antidote injector that was designed for use against soman—a nerve gas that only the Soviet Union stocks.

Moscow must have foreseen certain circumstances in which its own nerve gas would be employed against Israel at that time, so tanks sent to Egypt were prepared for that contingency. Otherwise, the instruments could have been removed. This curious fact lends further substance to the episode in the earlier Six Day War of 1967 in which the Israelis said they discovered a cache of Soviet nerve gas in the Sinai.

John Erickson estimated that by the early 1980s up to 10 percent of all Soviet artillery projectiles, mortar shells, land mines, and aerial bombs were filled with chemical agents—an impressive figure. In the Warsaw Pact area facing NATO, the concentration of chemical loads as opposed to conventional munitions in rockets, artillery rounds, mortar shells, and aerial bombs might have been as high as 50 percent. Calculating the total tonnage involving chemical loads led to figures that varied widely from 400,000 to 700,000 tons.

In the same region of numerical guesswork, it is believed that the Soviets have more than 2,000 tactical missiles filled with chemicals. These include SCUD and FROG missiles with warheads that would burst over selected targets, such as airfields, command posts, or nuclear sites, releasing persisting V-type nerve agents. On a tactical level, where it would be vital to permit Soviet troops to enter an area soon after it was hit with gas, nonpersistent agents would be dispersed with extraordinary effect by the remarkable

BM-21 Multiple Rocket Launcher—called the Stalin Organ—a device not unlike a Gatling gun in its firepower. The BM-21 employed twenty launchers in a battery and was able to fire 480 rockets in thirty seconds to blanket an area of twenty square kilometers with an active nonpersistent nerve agent or hydrogen cyanide.

Clearly, the Soviet Union—after fumbling about during the years from 1918 to 1945—began the 1980s and the invasion of Afghanistan with the best-equipped chemical attack and defense forces of any modern army. Although there might be areas in which Western equipment was better, particularly gas mask design and some detection kits, this was more than compensated by the Soviets' very serious attitude toward training and execution of routine procedures. The inability of many front-line U.S. Army units serving with NATO to get their gas masks on correctly in the few seconds available before they would be killed by the gas triggering their alarms is most dismaying. The seriousness of the Red Army demonstrates a military psychology that makes it possible to use war poisons without hesitation, as simply another weapon.

Any country that has chosen to use lethal chemical agents to force its own population into line is unlikely to feel great remorse over a decision to wield chemicals against Moslem guerrillas holed up in mountain caves.

Laos had revealed that deadly poisons were now being used by Hanoi to wipe out dissent. Yemen had revealed that the same poisons were in use a decade earlier, probably by the Soviet Union, and helped define what were the basic characteristics of death. Afghanistan was a clear, blunt demonstration of the Red Army actively employing precisely the same killers. There was no longer any question *who* was wielding poison gas, just the bewildering question: *what?* While everybody else was looking for confirmation of Russian nerve agents, could it be that the Soviets had simply developed something new, something that we could not recognize because we had no idea what to look for? Maybe there was a clue that I had missed among the more exotic poisons. Maybe what we were dealing with here was some sort of mass weapon developed from the weird, nasty potions brewed up for one-on-one assassinations.

8.

Eye of Newt, Toe of Frog

Bogdan Stashinsky was the very incarnation of an antihero secret agent from the fiction of John Le Carré. He was born in the Ukraine, in the village of Borshovitsy. His parents were members of the Ukrainian nationalist movement that had been struggling hopelessly for decades against domination by Austria, Poland, Germany, and Russia. While he was still in his teens, Stashinsky was picked up by the police on a minor charge of riding a train without a ticket. He had no affection for his parents, so when the police asked questions about his family, Stashinsky ingratiated himself with the officers by informing on his father and mother's underground connections. For this he was honored by enlistment into the KGB. He served first as a petty thug in a gang called a *spetsgruppa* used to intimidate Ukrainian workers. By 1952 he was twenty years old and was graduated to a two-year training program to prepare him for service in Poland. In 1954 he was sent to East Germany with a false identity to serve as a minor contact between other KGB agents.

In East Berlin he met a girl named Inge Pohl at the Tanz Casino. She was a twenty-one-year-old hairdresser, unkempt and plain, but soon utterly devoted to him. It was at this emotional juncture in his otherwise sterile existence that Stashinsky was given the kind of KGB assignment from which novels are drawn.

It was the fateful spring of 1957 when he reported to the Karlshorst compound in East Berlin, the headquarters of the KGB for East Germany. There had been riots and uprisings in Hungary and Poland, and nationalist groups elsewhere in the Eastern Bloc were plotting to capitalize on these setbacks for the Soviets to spread the rebellion elsewhere. The Ukrainians were especially active, spurred on by their leaders in exile.

Later that year, Stashinsky was given his mission: He was to track down and assassinate two top Ukrainian emigrés—Lev Rebet and Stefan Bandera. Both were operating out of underground headquarters in Munich. It would take many months to set up the murders.

Lev Rebet was a Ukrainian intellectual and literary figure who had written such effective anti-Soviet propaganda for Ukrainians that he was thoroughly despised by the Kremlin and marked for death. He was a familiar sight in Munich emigré circles, a powerfully built man of medium height who always wore a beret to cover his shaved head. Stashinsky flew to Munich and took a room in a hotel near one of the emigré offices. He began following Rebet around the city, from the emigré office to the underground newspaper *Suchasny Ukraina*, to establish Rebet's pattern of movements. When he was ready, the assassin contacted his superiors. A KGB armorer was dispatched from Moscow to the Karlshorst compound with a secret weapon, an aluminum cylinder weighing no more than half a pound, only three-quarters of an inch in diameter and six inches long. It was a one-shot device, designed to fire an aerosol spray of a liquid poison, potassium cyanide, which was contained in a plastic ampule inside the cylinder. When it was fired, the tube shot a spray of colorless, odorless poison as a mist up to eighteen inches. Inhaled by the victim, the vapor would almost instantly paralyze the arteries carrying blood to the brain, causing a form of coronary thrombosis. Death could come in as little as ninety seconds. The drug would ordinarily wear off before an autopsy could be performed, so no trace could be found. Although the assassin was safe from the effect of the spray because it was pointed away from him, the Moscow armorer gave Stashinsky several tablets of antidote to take beforehand. They would cause his arteries to be enlarged so that blood could flow unimpeded if he did breathe some of the cyanide vapors. Stashinsky tried the weapon on a dog tied to a tree in the outskirts of East Berlin, while his KGB control and the armorer both watched approvingly. When Stashinsky sprayed the dog in the face, it collapsed without a sound, writhed in agony for three minutes, then died. A bit sloppy, considering the advanced billing by the KGB, but effective.

Stashinsky was given a sausage container in which to hide his poison weapon, and flew back to Munich. He had decided that the newspaper offices of the *Suchasny Ukraina* would be where he would strike. It was an old masonry building on Karlsplatz, next to one of the city's medieval gates. On the advice of the KGB armorer, Stashinsky would try to catch his victim coming up the stairs, so that it would be simpler to direct the spray into his face.

Stashinsky arrived in Munich at 9:30 A.M. one October morning in 1959. He went directly to Karlsplatz. In his hand he held a rolled newspaper with the murder weapon snug inside, its safety catch off. He watched Lev Rebet in his familiar beret get off the streetcar and walk toward the newspaper offices. Stashinsky reached the door first and quickly mounted the stairs. On the first floor landing, he heard footsteps and turned to descend, staying on the right side to keep Rebet on his left.

Letting his right arm swing forward with the newspaper, Stashinsky fired the poison mist directly into Rebet's unsuspecting face. The assassin continued down the stairs without looking back, heard Rebet stumble, and kept walking away from the building. Half a mile away, he dropped the tube into the Koeglmuehlbach Canal and strolled back toward his hotel and the Karlsplatz. An ambulance and a police car were at the door of the newspaper office.

Stashinsky checked out of his hotel, caught the train to Frankfurt, then flew to Berlin. There he was informed that his mission had been a success. The Ukrainian press was reporting that Lev Rebet had died "of a natural heart attack."

Two weeks later Stashinsky obtained a new tube weapon for the second part of his mission.

Stefan Bandera was quite different from Lev Rebet. He was an angry, fanatical cold warrior. The son of a Ukrainian Catholic priest, he had joined the underground in his teens and had remained a fighter with it ever since, becoming one of its most prominent leaders. In 1934, Bandera was sentenced to death by the Polish government for the assassination of Polish Interior Minister Bronislav Pieracki, but the sentence was commuted to life in prison in order to avoid provoking a riot by Ukrainians in eastern Poland. The German army released Bandera in 1939, and he was encouraged to slip across the border to organize anti-Soviet sabotage. When

Germany attacked Russia two years later, Bandera's hard-bitten partisans fought the Russians as they retreated from the Ukraine, then turned on the Nazis. Bandera was captured by the Gestapo in 1941 and was sent to Sachsenhausen concentration camp. He was released by Hitler in 1944 in the hope that he would rouse the Ukraine against the resurgent Red Army. Bandera set up headquarters in Berlin, but when the city collapsed he fled to Munich to escape Soviet agents. He continued to funnel international funds and support to the Ukrainian underground from Munich. His partisan army became known as the "Banderovtsy" in the Soviet press. The Banderovtsy was finally stifled by the Soviet army and secret police, under the direct guidance of Nikita Khrushchev.

Bandera continued to live in Munich, using the name Stefan Popel, working toward the day he would stir the Banderovtsy to life once again. That time seemed close in the ferment of the late fifties. With his wife and three children, Bandera lived in a small flat in an apartment building. On Sundays he went to a Ukrainian emigré church. He had a mistress as well, and visited her regularly. He had tough bodyguards with him around the clock.

At 1:00 P.M. on the afternoon of October 15, 1959, Stashinsky was waiting when the fifty-year-old Bandera drove up to his apartment house in his Opel with a bag of groceries, left his bodyguard waiting in the car, and started for the front door. The assassin went first, entering the building with a KGB passkey and moving quickly up the stairs. In his right hand he held a tightly rolled newspaper. He loitered on the first landing and became nervous when he heard women's voices above him. He pushed the elevator button. A woman came down the stairs just as the elevator arrived and its door opened. The woman entered the elevator. At that moment Stashinsky saw Bandera at the front door, juggling his grocery bag and his door key.

Stashinsky stepped quickly to the door. Bandera had got his key in the lock and opened it, holding it with his foot so that Stashinsky could exit first. He did not seem to be able to get his key out of the lock.

As he passed through the door, Stashinsky said in German: "It does not work?"

Bandera had at last extracted his key.

"Yes, it's all right."

Stashinsky raised his newspaper and fired the spray of potassium cyanide directly into Bandera's face. The warrior tried to lunge to one side but was caught full by the mist.

Stashinsky walked away quickly, dropped his passkey down a man hole, then reached the Koeglmuehlbach Canal and once again let his weapon vanish into its depths. He caught the next train to Frankfurt and flew with Pan Am to Berlin. His KGB superiors were so pleased that they met him at the Cafe Warsaw for a celebration while he gave his report.

In Munich, Bandera had screamed, then struggled valiantly up the stairs toward his family. He had apparently fallen several times along the way, because his face was covered with bruises and black and blue welts when they found him there, the bag of groceries beside him unspilled. He died in an ambulance on the way to the hospital. His family buried him at Munich's Waldfriedhof. While 1,500 Eastern European exiles watched silently, Bandera's coffin, draped with the Ukrainian independence banner of blue and yellow, was lowered into a grave and sprinkled with an urnful of Ukrainian soil.

This time the emigrés were not fooled. The autopsy had shown Bandera's death to be from potassium cyanide. His funeral announcement was printed with the epitaph "Died a hero's death at the Bolshevist's hands."

Stashinsky was also a hero, to the KGB. He was decorated in Moscow with the Order of the Red Banner at the recommendation of the Presidium of the Supreme Soviet. The citation referred to his "extraordinarily difficult mission" in assassinating two enemies of the state with poison. Stashinsky took the occasion to announce that he was marrying Inge Pohl. The KGB was not happy about that. They offered him his choice of KGB professional companions, who normally posed as the wives of agents abroad. Stashinsky persevered, even when he met the head of the KGB, Alexandr Shelepin, who was then chief of the secret police Moscow headquarters. At last permission came to return to East Berlin and marry. When he told Inge about his duties for the KGB, she was shocked. It was the beginning of a disenchantment that escalated as soon as she arrived with him to live in Moscow. She pressed him to realize that he was being used. She urged him to break away, so that they could escape to the West and start life over. She became pregnant and argued more firmly. They discovered that their one-room flat in

Moscow was bugged and kept under surveillance. Stashinsky naively complained to the KGB and was told that the flat was normally used for other purposes, that he was not the target of the bugging. He was not convinced.

At last Inge could bear it no longer and insisted on returning to East Berlin. There, her baby could be born as an East German citizen. She left Moscow in January 1961. Stashinsky was told that he could not follow, and was restricted to Russia for seven years without travel privileges. He was no longer a hero, just a nuisance.

In August 1961, while Inge was running an errand and the baby was with a neighbor, it choked to death during feeding. Stricken with grief, Inge cabled her husband. The KGB gave Stashinsky special permission to go to East Berlin for the funeral.

On August 12, he and Inge were driven by a KGB car to the East Berlin suburb of Dallgow to make final preparations for the funeral at the home of her parents. At four that afternoon, Stashinsky and Inge slipped out the back door, walked three miles to the town of Falkensee, and caught a taxi for the Friedrichstrasse in East Berlin. En route they used Stashinsky's old false papers and were waved through the checkpoint on the outskirts of the city. In East Berlin they boarded the S-bahn and rode to West Berlin, getting off at the first stop, Gesundbrunnen. Then they walked into police headquarters to tell everything. The next day the Berlin Wall went up.

It was the clumsiness of Bandera's killing and the resulting publicity, as much as anything else, that inspired the Soviets to look harder for a poison that the West could not detect. Stashinsky's defection and his embarrassing revelation of details about KGB assassination operations added urgency to that need.

Of all the earth's natural poisons, few are as deadly as botulin toxin, the chemical secretion of the *Clostridium botulinum* bacteria. These bacteria live in soil and produce spores. The spores constantly contaminate food of all types. If the food is not cooked properly before canning, to kill the spores, they survive inside the can or bottle. There they germinate and release the bacteria, which multiply rapidly and secrete their lethal toxin. Whoever eats the food becomes dizzy, tired, and develops severe headaches. Vision is blurred. The toxin damages the autonomic nervous system by blocking the transmission of nerve impulses. Soon the respiratory muscles begin to clench. If a tracheotomy is not performed quickly to open the victim's windpipe, death occurs by asphyxiation after only an hour or two as the respiratory muscles become paralyzed.

Ordinarily, botulin bacteria are considered weapons of biological or bacteriological warfare, along with anthrax and other living organisms that reproduce. But death is caused by the chemical poisons that the organisms secrete. These poisons are not living organisms. They cannot reproduce. Therefore they occupy a vacuum between treaties on biological warfare and treaties on chemical warfare. Biotoxins fall between the cracks.

Anthrax and botulin are only two of the more famous biological killers. There are literally thousands of others. Even the most innocent of decorative houseplants—such as the colorful croton—can be a deadly killer. All that is necessary is to place these basically innocent natural products in the right hands. For the purpose of torture, anything will suffice, including pouring holy water up the victim's nose. For the purpose of murder, secret murder, the world is a cornucopia of poisons waiting to be used.

To come to the attention of assassins, however, poisons must be able to kill in tiny quantities, preferably leaving no trace. For the lover scorned, the ambitious tyrant, or the psychopath, the ideal poison is one that will do the job, then be metabolized so that nothing shows in an autopsy.

To rank as a textbook poison, I found, the amount needed to kill is by definition less than fifty grams for an adult human. That is about as subtle as an express train. In that category fall killers such as too much bad whisky.

On a more sophisticated level, a useful poison is one that can kill in doses as small as cobra venom, strychnine, or curare. Even these are rather clumsy killers. The poison produced by certain frogs, known as betrachotoxin and used by Colombian Indians to tip blowgun darts, is twenty-five times deadlier than cobra venom. Ricin, the poison produced by castor beans, is nearly one hundred times as deadly as cobra venom. It is in the category of ricin that poisons cross the threshold into the category of supertoxins, and become ingeniously useful weapons.

In selecting a poison today, the choice is between synthetic poisons—like a nerve agent—and natural toxins—like ricin. Synthetic poisons are chemical products of our highly industrialized, technical society, and include by-products of the dyestuffs industry such as chlorine and phosgene and by-products of the pesticide industry such as organophosphates, which are the nerve agents. These are the first- and second-generation chemical killing agents.

The natural toxins—or biotoxins—and modified or synthetic analogues of them are the newest war poisons, the third-generation killing agents. But they are new only because they have just recently been structurally analyzed, and it is only in the past few years that it has become possible to modify and to synthesize them in the laboratory, to produce them in vast quantities, and to engineer even more deadly chemical analogues. They are in themselves ancient— the antithesis of the industrial age.

At a time when there is public debate about industrial pollution, when public fear of decaying chemical warfare stockpiles lies just beneath the surface, and when public recognition of such terms as "mustard gas" and "nerve gas" is high, what would be more cunning than to bypass these conspicuous killers and delve instead deep into the cupboard of ancient herbal folk poisons, for the arcane potions of the witches and witchdoctors, of Chinese imperial eunuchs and rival Renaissance princes. To seek out eye of newt and toe of frog. Witches who dabbled in potions made from the two amphibians were not as barmy as they are portrayed. Not only does a lowly frog produce the violently poisonous betrachotoxin, but the newt produces tetrodotoxin—a superpoison of awesome potency. A brew made from eye of newt and toe of frog, properly devised by a well-informed old crone, could quickly dim the roving eye of a feudal swain or forever alter the destiny of a medieval prince.

Primitive man gained his knowledge of poisons simply by observing the casualties from eating certain animals and plants, or their roots, nuts, berries, or juices. They extracted these substances to stun or kill fish, or to tip their arrows before hunting, as in the cases of curare in the Amazon and betrachotoxin in Colombia. Many of these primitive concoctions for hunting, combat, or ritual use have not yet given up their secrets to laboratory analysis. Some have. A synthetic form of curare has long been in use in modern medicine. A large dose paralyzes the muscles, but it was found that a smaller amount relaxes the muscular system without damage. Other natural poisons were found by ancient societies to be handy in producing intoxication, visions, or abortion when applied in controlled quantities; opium, strychnine, caffeine, cocaine, atropine, digitalis, and ergotamine are just a few. For magical visions, pain-killing stupors, or group therapy, there was a choice of nightshade, henbane, mandrake, thorn apple, marijuana, spanish fly, betel nut, peyotl, and assorted mushrooms. Other nuts, berries, leaves, and roots were especially useful for suicide, murder, and ritual trial (the accused was forced to swallow a potion or chew a twig, and guilt or innocence was determined by whether he or she died).

Knowledge of these drugs, and the plants, animals, ponds, or coral reefs where they were obtained, was extremely valuable. In some cultures the poison master was venerated openly in cults of sorcerers, witchdoctors, or high priestesses. In others he was condemned in public but celebrated in secret. In seventeenth-century France, during the reign of Louis XIV, the famous "Affair of the Poisons" became a scandal embarrassing even the king when it was revealed that nobles, rich bourgeoisie, and commoners alike had been buying drugs and poisons from fortune-tellers to stage black masses, arrange sexual debauches, and eliminate rivals. In April 1679, a special tribunal handed down 319 writs of arrest resulting in thirty-four persons being executed, four being doomed to the galleys, and thirty-four being banished. The principal poisoner, Catherin Deshayes, Madame Monvoisin—known to all of Paris by then as La Voisin—was burned in the Place de Greve on February 22, 1680. The involvement of several nieces of Cardinal Mazarin, assorted countesses, princesses, dukes, and marquesses was scandalous enough. But the exposure of the Marquise de Montespan for having purchased love philters from La Voisin to win the love of Louis Quatorze himself—philters that apparently worked with spectacular effect—caused the king to squelch the public trial and continue proceedings *in camera.*

In Czarist Russia the aristocracy, boyars, and commoners alike indulged in poisons to such an extent that a controversial figure at court was well advised to immunize himself from certain popular poisons by taking progressively larger doses to acclimate his system or to build up antibodies.

Such a figure, the "Mad Monk" Rasputin, probably took this precaution, for when Prince Felix Yussupov and other conspirators set out to murder him on December 29, 1916, he resisted massive doses of poison. Finally the assassins had to shoot him repeatedly before dumping his body into the frozen River Neva.

This knowledge of poisons was power. It was guarded jealously and was transmitted secretly generation after generation through the lines of succession within a cult or a family. The need for secrecy was sometimes so obsessive that it interfered with the sensible transfer of this knowledge. It was not at all unusual as a consequence for the power of poisons to end with village idiots as often as with enlightened scholars. The withered crone who lived down the forest path did for the locals what Merlin did for King Arthur.

At one time—and not very long ago (perhaps eighty years, or less in some areas)—everyone was familiar with folk poisons to some extent, or knew somebody who was. If someone died a mysterious death, if he did not break his neck or fall out of a tree or get cannonballed on a battlefield, it was commonly concluded that death came by poisoning. Little effort was exerted to do any technical analysis of the corpse because poisons were almost always beyond detection. Instead, it was customary to look for motives. Whoever had a strong motive was likely to be the poisoner.

So commonplace was this state of mind that every time a nobleman or high official of the Catholic Church died in Renaissance Italy, it was believed to be the work of poison by a rival. The powerful Borgias were believed to have liquidated literally scores of their rivals. One of them poisoned his way to become Pope Alexander. Then, according to the official chronicler of the popes, Onofrio Panvinio, Pope Alexander poisoned three cardinals and numerous other church notables to keep them from interfering with the succession of his son, Cesare Borgia, as the next pope.

When Pope Alexander died, his flock concluded that he had quaffed some of his own poisoned wine, intended for a rival at a dinner party on a country estate. Modern critics are divided about the case. There are those who conclude that it may well have been poison, because poison was everywhere—one Italian poisoner of the period is credited with killing more than seven hundred people, often employing poisoned cosmetics or poisoned perfume. Others maintain that Pope Alexander was simply bitten by mosquitoes during the country feast and died of malaria.

As Western societies have become more urbanized, people have been estranged from their traditional close association with plants, except as prepackaged groceries and ornamental shrubs or flowers. Only five years before the turn of the twentieth century, the fourth edition of John Reese's *Text-book of Medical Jurisprudence and Toxicology* revealed that poisoning was still "probably the most frequent of all the causes of violent death, the casualties of war excepted."

Only a few years later, thanks to the rapid population shift to the cities and the advent of the industrial age, poisoning was replaced by bludgeoning—in all its forms—as the leading cause of violent death. When synthetic poisons produced by industry put in their brief appearance in the trenches of World War I, society was appalled by what it took to be a throwback to the Dark Ages. It was one thing to smash people to death from the outside in with bombs, guns, ack-ack, speeding trucks, trains, planes, and cars— but it was another matter entirely to kill them from the inside out with poison gas. Death by poison seemed to imply a violation of the human spirit as well as destruction of the physical body, and this was something unacceptable in the Western world of the twentieth century. People pushed poisons as far from their minds as possible. Industrial poisons slowly crept around the environment and were tolerated as a sickening background smog. But poisons produced by herbs, fungi, reptiles, amphibians, and marine creatures lived on only in murder mysteries (such as the laburnum seeds employed as a device by Daphne du Maurier in *My Cousin Rachel*).

Synthetic drugs replaced herbal medications in medicine, and it came to be the popular Western notion that hideous natural poisons were the stuff of fairy tales, the province of Disney Studios. The Brothers Grimm were sanitized for the modern reader by pious censors.

This was not the case, however, in Asia, Africa, Latin America, and much of Eastern Europe. Countries such as Poland, Czechoslovakia, Hungary, Rumania, and Bulgaria have been devastated so thoroughly by war in this century that their industrial and material development has been only a thin veneer upon a medieval base.

The Soviet Union, although now highly technological and heavily industrialized, has emerged from the dark ages of Czarist Russia so recently that those circumstances are still within the memory of many of its rulers and citizens. The societies of both the Soviet Union and Eastern Europe rest on a foundation of rural, agrarian, peasant life steeped in folk traditions and alchemical lore. The Eastern Bloc assassin may hold a stainless steel automatic in his right hand, but in his left he clutches a wad of wolfsbane.

Nowhere is this contrast better demonstrated than in the necklaces of polished beads that have become popular in the United States since the start of the back-to-nature fad. Strung together in the necklaces are various combinations of coffee beans, the diamond-shaped seeds of the poisonous yellow oleander, and castor beans. Shops that sell the "folk" necklaces tout them as strings of "lucky beans" and suggest that they will bring good fortune to the wearer, who should stroke the beans when nervous. The term "lucky beans" comes from the oleander seeds, which are commonly called "lucky nuts" in the tropics. However, their name in Sanskrit means "horse killer," and the seeds are ordinarily used to commit murder or suicide all the way from backwoods Brazil to back-alley India. The seeds of the castor bean, of course, are the source of the super-poison ricin. The necklaces appear to have originated hundreds of years ago as items made for sale by gypsies, who surely were aware of their deadly contents, and presumably assembled the strings with malicious glee before taking them out to sell to unsuspecting burghers and their children. In Miami, strands of the beads have been popular with the tourist trade, as part of going native. The fad spread around the country. A University of Wisconsin coed who adopted the fashion rubbed her Mexican bead necklace nervously in class, then rubbed her eyes. A few hours later she was unable to see and was violently ill. It appeared that she had crumbled one of the ricin seeds in her fingers, and a tiny bit of powder got into her eyes. She had been stricken by an ancient poison ordinarily worn centuries earlier by gypsies who carried the seeds that way to keep them handy for use on their enemies.

The source of ricin, the castor plant, is an attractive household ornamental, which can grow up to thirty or forty feet in height. Its leaves are maroon and silky when young, dark green or dark red when mature. The fruit are up to one inch long, spiny green or red before they dry and turn brown, spitting their three seeds up to twenty-five feet. The seeds are smooth ovals about three-quarters of an inch long, sometimes black, sometimes red, sometimes mottled light and dark brown. They are perfect for peashooters and necklaces. The entire plant is poisonous, particularly the seeds. But when they are pressed to produce castor oil, the poison—ricin—remains in the press cake. When eaten by a human, the seeds have a delayed effect of up to ten hours (allowing time for a murderer or assassin to get away or to establish an alibi). The symptoms and signs are severe burning in the mouth, throat, and stomach, nausea, vomiting (sometimes bloody), cramps, delirium, convulsions, jaundice, and death after ten or twelve days.

However, there are many sicknesses that can cause symptoms such as these. Unless a doctor knows, or suspects, that ricin was the cause, there is no way he can tell from an autopsy because the poison is so thoroughly metabolized by the body. This makes ricin a beautifully disguised violent killer, a perfect weapon for an assassin.

Something like a gourmet menu, an East German military manual entitled *Chemical Agents and Defense Against Chemical Agents* contains a list of "Sabotage Poisons." From this shopping list, the Soviet or Eastern Bloc assassin may select the poison of his choice.

There is a similar list of supertoxins available to American agents. The top-secret development program began in 1952 under the CIA code name M. K. Naomi. The object was to produce a small but lethal arsenal of superpoisons that could be used against KGB agents and, while at it, perfect antidotes for each of the toxins so that American agents could be protected from foreign agents using the same poisons.

The CIA also wanted to find a better suicide pill for its agents to swallow when captured. The suicide pill developed during World War II, a capsule of potassium cyanide—the same poison sprayed by Stashinsky—takes up to fifteen minutes to work, and causes an agonizing death by asphyxiation. It was not very popular with agents.

Researchers at Fort Detrick suggested saxitoxin, a mollusk poison produced by a tiny marine plankton known as a dino-flagellate. It is also responsible for red tides, the unpredictable, sporadic red-colored murk spreading over large stretches of ocean in warmer zones and referred to in Exodus 7, 20–21: ". . . and all the water changed into blood. The fish died and the river stank." During red tides, shellfish become toxic and cause paralysis if eaten. Red tides also occur in the north Atlantic, but involve slightly different toxins, related to saxitoxin. The name saxitoxin is taken from the Alaskan butter clam, which is one of the hosts of the poison, along with a variety of other mollusks. It is a supertoxin, although not as potent as ricin. Its appeal lies in its awesome speed.

After swallowing the toxin, or receiving it in a pinprick, the victim feels a tingling sensation in the fingers and lips, then dies within ten seconds. Its virtue is that it does the job extremely quickly. In this sense it is more dramatic as a poison than ricin, although it takes a smaller dose of ricin to do the job over ten days. Sometimes an assassin could find it embarrassing or inconvenient if the victim dropped dead too quickly. In this way biotoxins are tailor-made for different jobs.

U-2 pilot Francis Gary Powers carried saxitoxin on his historic flight over the Soviet Union. It was contained in the grooves of a tiny drill bit concealed in a silver dollar in his clothing. When he was shot down by the Russians, he decided not to use it, much to the despair of his employers.

By 1970, after President Nixon had ordered the destruction of all biological weapons in the possession of government agencies, $3 million had been spent on Project M. K. Naomi. A secret memorandum was circulated within the CIA suggesting that the director could salvage these elegant supertoxins before the army began destroying the biotoxin stocks at Fort Detrick. Its closing paragraph reads:

> If the Director wishes to continue this special capability, it is recommended that if the above DoD decision is made (to destroy their stocks), the existing agency stockpile at SO Division, Ft. Detrick be transferred to the Huntington Research Center, Becton-Dickinson Company, Baltimore, Maryland. Arrangements have been made for this contingency and assurances have been given by the potential contractor to store and maintain the agency's stockpile at a cost no greater than $75,000 per annum.

CIA Director Richard Helms claimed later that he had never seen this memo, and insisted that he had given a verbal order to destroy the toxins. Dr. Nathan Gordon, a bushy-browed chemist in charge of the biological materials program for the CIA's technical services division—who claimed that he never received any such order —decided not to destroy the toxins because of their great potential value. He believed that these stocks were not covered in the presidential order—presumably because they were not intended for military use. William Colby, who succeeded Helms as director of the CIA, later observed: "I think that it was done by people who were so completely enmeshed in the subject and the difficulty of production that they simply couldn't bear to see the stuff destroyed."

Indeed, it had taken one hundred pounds of shellfish to produce only one gram of toxin. The CIA had eleven grams in its stocks.

Gordon transferred the eleven grams of saxitoxin, enough to kill tens of thousands of KGB agents and to permit tens of thousands of CIA agents to commit suicide, to a special storage room at CIA headquarters in Langley, Virginia. Along with it he took eight milligrams of cobra venom. The storeroom was special because it was where technical services kept eight supertoxins in all and twenty-seven other substances for use against enemy agents. These included colchicine, which paralyzes muscles, causing asphyxiation; strychnine, an ingredient of rat poison, which kills by causing convulsions and failure of the central nervous system; M-246, a substance that causes paralysis; halothane, a fast-acting anesthetic useful for knocking out enemy spies; and 2-4 pyrolo, a substance that causes amnesia. None of these were destroyed because they were all synthetic.

When the biological stocks became known outside CIA and the evasion was revealed before a congressional committee investigating the agency, the special weapons designed for use with the toxins also came on view. One was a Colt .45 mounted with a special telescopic sight, which almost silently fired a poison-tipped dart up to 250 feet. The dart, the width of a human hair and one-quarter inch long, would be hardly visible in the victim's body. There was another version of this dart gun contained in a fountain pen for close-range work. Other variations, developed by an engineer for the Defense Department named Charles Senseney, included dart launchers in walking sticks.

Naturally these CIA weapons could make use of more than one poison. In addition to saxitoxin, cobra venom, and ricin, project M. K. Naomi had developed quantities of tetrodotoxin from the sex organs and livers of the Japanese *fugu,* or puffer fish. The fish is eaten in Japan, and I have enjoyed it on several occasions; it is particularly good when smoke-cured, and washed down with Suntory whisky. Japanese chefs who prepare *fugu* for eating must be licensed to ensure that they know how to remove the sex glands.

The list of superpoisons by no means stops there. These are simply some of the exotic biotoxins that we know have been developed by the CIA. Probably there are many others, some even more bizarre. Since these are all included on the East German list of sabotage poisons, we can assume that they were also the subject of considerable study in Eastern Europe and the Soviet Union as candidates for ideal assassination weapons, to improve on the clumsy and obvious cyanide used by Stashinsky. When these elegant biotoxins were at last ready for use in the field, Eastern Bloc assassins could be forgiven if they felt like boasting.

"You will be killed by a poison that the West cannot detect nor treat!" The voice on the phone in London rasped out the threat in Bulgarian. Then the midnight caller hung up. Replacing his own receiver, Georgi Ivanov Markov stared in melancholy out the window of his flat. A light fog diffused the street lamps. It was mid-August, but the English nights were already chill. For nearly ten years, Markov had been living in London, and yet the Bulgarian secret police could reach out and strike him at will. Markov had made some powerful enemies. This was not the first death threat that he had received, but this time there had been an executioner's finality in the voice on the phone that troubled Markov deeply.

He had been a successful playwright in Sofia, a member of the small but energetic cultural elite that thrived in Bulgaria despite the heavy hand of the Communist regime. As a comrade of artists, actresses, and performers in the state theaters, he came into close contact with the leaders of the Communist party and government hierarchy who mixed with the performers, partied with them, and conducted furtive affairs. Markov observed with a playwright's eye, and took note of the secret liaisons, the sexual peccadilloes, the hushed-up scandals that swirled in the wake of the political elite.

In 1969, at the age of thirty-nine, Markov had defected. He had sought refuge in London as a political exile, and had soon found a job with the BBC, broadcasting news and commentary on cultural affairs in Eastern Europe and reviews of theater in London that would interest listeners behind the Iron Curtain. When he was not busy at the BBC, Markov held down another job—writing and broadcasting political commentary for Radio Free Europe.

Corruption was his favorite target. Regularly, he spoke to his listeners in Bulgaria and elsewhere in the Eastern Bloc about the private, personal deals of the bureaucrats and party leaders—deals that made them wealthy, surrounded them with luxuries beyond the reach of their countrymen, or demonstrated their skills at swindling and fraud. He recounted his personal memories of senior party leaders, including descriptions of their intimate behavior, and giving the names of their mistresses.

Friends, including other Bulgarians at BBC and Radio Free Europe, warned him that he was going too far. Through the pipeline of the emigré community in Western Europe came word that he had been marked for punishment by the secret police. There had been threatening phone calls before, but in August 1978 there was a new voice, and a new threat.

Markov's response, as always, was to point out to the caller, that his assassination would only make him a martyr. It would confirm the truth of his broadcasts forever. Blame for his murder would fall directly upon the Bulgarian leadership that he had so often attacked. It would demonstrate that they could not live with their own corruption.

"Not this time," said the midnight caller. "This time you will not become a martyr. You will simply die of natural causes. You will be killed by a poison that the West cannot detect nor treat." Once again he had repeated that statement with morbid certainty.

After the phone call, Markov slept poorly. The next day he told his closest friends about the new threat. Then, as the days passed, he became preoccupied with other matters.

On Thursday, September 7 at 1:30 P.M., he had a quiet lunch and walked back toward the BBC building in central London where he worked. At the south end of Waterloo Bridge he paused to look at the River Thames, while the swirl of pedestrians eddied around him. He felt a sudden, sharp pain in the back of his right thigh. It was the point of an umbrella. A powerfully built man of medium height had poked him with his brolly as he passed.

"Sorry," the man muttered. He got into a taxi that had pulled up to the curb, and vanished. Rubbing his thigh and staring after the taxi, Markov reflected that the man had spoken the one English word with a thick accent.

Markov went on his way to work, but as early evening settled over London he began to feel ill. There was still a sharp pain in his right thigh. He asked one of his friends, a Bulgarian exile named Teo Birkoff, to go to the men's rest room with him and have a look at his leg. In the back of the thigh there was "an angry red spot," Birkoff discovered, "like a pimple."

Markov told him about the encounter with the man and his umbrella.

That night, Markov was seriously ill. He had a high fever and what Birkoff called "a shocking cough." He had difficulty talking.

Birkoff took him to Saint James Hospital in Balham where Markov was admitted at 11:13 P.M.—nine hours and forty-five minutes after the umbrella incident—and was treated for "sepsis" (on the assumption that he had septicemia, a form of blood poisoning caused by bacteria).

By Saturday, September 9, Markov was in shock. At 9:45 A.M. on Monday, September 11, his heart stopped. Scotland Yard—alerted to the assassination threat by Markov's colleagues—announced that an autopsy would be performed the next day.

At Wandsworth Public Mortuary on Tuesday morning, Dr. Rufus Crompton removed large blocks of tissue for comparison from both of Markov's thighs, including the area from the right thigh that had a two-millimeter puncture wound from the umbrella. As Dr. Dennis Swanson and Dr. David Gall were examining the tissue on a porcelain autopsy table, they noticed that there was a tiny metal "pinhead" in the puncture spot, which they assumed had been placed there to mark the location of the wound. When they attempted to extract the "pin," a tiny pellet fell onto the table and nearly rolled down the drain. They examined the pellet closely, and then called the British Anti-Terrorist Squad, which was stepping in to handle the investigation because of the possibility of Bulgarian complicity. A BATS team came to the mortuary, retrieved the pieces of Markov's thigh and the tiny pellet, and took them to the Chemical Defense Establishment at Porton Down.

At Porton, a team of the world's foremost specialists in forensic medicine, including England's Dr. Robert Keeley and America's Dr. Christopher Green of the Central Intelligence Agency, studied the tissue and the pellet.

It was a 1.52-millimeter spherical jeweler's watch bearing, of a type commonly manufactured for precision watchmaking from platinum and titanium alloys. Two holes had been drilled through the tiny bearing, possibly using a high-technology laser and spark-erosion process, at right angles to each other, producing an X-shaped hollow in the pellet. The holes were empty.

The forensic specialists reviewed the original roentgenograms of the corpse and discovered where the tiny pellet had lain embedded in Markov's thigh. The doctors who had first examined the X ray had not seen the pellet, and had concluded that the picture was "normal." Whatever had been in the pellet was not there anymore. And there were no apparent traces in the pellet or in Markov's thigh. Nobody knew what to look for.

In Paris on August 26, 1978, less than two weeks before Markov was poked by the umbrella, the Bulgarian exile Vladimir Kostov was emerging from the Metro station beneath the Arc de Triomphe when he felt a sting in his back and heard a report that sounded like the firing of a compressed air gun.

Kostov had been the chief of the Paris bureau for the Bulgarian State Radio and Television network until the previous June, when he had defected and was given asylum by the French government. Approximately five hours after the incident at the Metro station, Kostov entered the emergency room of a Paris hospital, suffering from a raging fever. His wound was treated, and he was released.

Fourteen days later, on September 26, acting on a hunch, the team of forensic scientists and members of the British Anti-Terrorist Squad from Porton arrived in Paris and obtained a roentgenogram of Vladimir Kostov's back. There, at the puncture site where Kostov had been "stung" at the Metro station, was a pellet identical to the one that had just been taken from Markov's thigh. But there was a difference in its content.

Kostov had been wearing a bulky sweater when the incident occurred. The pellet had been slowed by the sweater and did not penetrate his skin as deeply as it would Markov's. A coating of wax, intended to melt at body temperature of $98.6°$ F had only partly melted, and had exposed the opening of only one of the X-shaped tunnels within the pellet. Only a portion of the 450 micrograms of deadly poison inside the pellet had leaked out into Kostov's body. And at age thirty, Kostov was a healthy man. He had become desperately ill, but he had not died.

Retrieving Kostov's pellet and extracting its remaining contents, the BATS team and scientists put the substance through laboratory tests to determine, if they could, what it was. When the poison was injected into lab animals, the signs and symptoms demonstrated were exactly those of ricin.

Markov's assassin had been busy. The powerfully built Bulgarian carrying a tightly rolled umbrella had first come to Paris to kill Kostov. Another emigré, named Dinio Dinev, a "friend" of Kostov, had fingered him for the assassination. The killer had followed Kostov till they exited from the Metro station. Then he had raised the umbrella and pressed its trigger, and the compressed air cartridge inside the handle had fired the tiny pellet into Kostov's back. Quickly leaving Paris for London, the assassin had then telephoned Georgi Markov to add a touch of terror, followed his victim to lunch, then to Waterloo Bridge, and shot him in the leg.

Two weeks later another Bulgarian was murdered in London. But this time the assassin apparently changed his weapon. There had been too much publicity about Markov's thigh wound and the ricin poison pellet.

The victim was Vladimir Simeonov. Like Markov, Simeonov worked for the overseas radio service of the BBC. He was an assistant program controller in the Bulgarian section, a colleague of Markov and an acquaintance of Kostov in Paris. In the weeks following the attack on Kostov and Markov's murder, Simeonov worried that he might be next. Just why he should be was unclear. He seemed to be no threat.

Simeonov was not his real name. He was actually Vladimir Dimitrov Bobchev, born in Assenovgrad, Bulgaria, on April 21, 1948. He was a solidly built lad of thirty, always in good health despite a faint heart murmur in his youth that kept him out of the Bulgarian army. After graduating from Sofia University in 1970 with a degree in psychology and fluency in Russian and French, he was allowed to travel with a group of young Bulgarian tourists to England. Five of them promptly defected, including Vladimir— and he immediately adopted his father's middle name and went into hiding at the home of a Bulgarian employed by the BBC. Eventually, he was able to get a job in the BBC canteen himself, and the following year, 1973, he was promoted from busboy to program assistant. By studying assiduously every evening, he had become fluent in English.

Nobody seemed especially fond of Simeonov—in fact, Markov gave every appearance of actively disliking the young man—and it was rumored that he might be "a Bulgarian plant" placed in the BBC to keep an eye on the political activists like Markov. Simeonov was making a decent salary by British white-collar standards, enough to put the money down on a little two-bedroom "maisonette" at 84 Western Road, in Plaistow, one of the London suburbs.

He spent money only on traveling each year, with holidays to India, Hong Kong, Kenya, Brazil, Italy, and Spain—inexpensive package tours. The rest of the time he kept to himself, addictively watching television at home. Aside from the ground-floor kitchen, he furnished his house with only a bed and a TV in one of the two upstairs bedrooms, arranged so that he could lie in bed for hours watching the telly across the room.

He made no political broadcasts, but served as a Bulgarian-language announcer reading news, commentaries, and features. He also compiled a harmless weekly childrens' program with items of interest to Bulgarian youth. As a relative novice, he got the odd hours to work, particularly the shift late Saturday night to Sunday morning, when he broadcast the news at five-thirty and then went home.

He did so on Sunday morning, October 1, 1978, three weeks after Markov's assassination and five weeks after the Kostov attempt. On Monday at 3:30 P.M.—an hour after he should have shown up for work—his BBC supervisor became anxious and eventually dispatched a secretary, Gabriella Connor, to see if Simeonov was at home.

"I got out of the taxi and opened the front gate," she narrated later. "I could not find a bell so I rattled the letter box. As I did so I looked in through the letter box and saw a person lying at the far end of the hall. He was lying on his stomach, his head against the wall, his body lying across the hall, so all I was able to see was his head, and the top half of his body. . . . I recognized the person as Vladimir Simeonov."

It was the third incident involving a Bulgarian in a matter of weeks, and only five days since the ricin pellet had been found in Kostov's back, so the British Anti-Terrorist Squad immediately joined the investigation. Doctors took Simeonov's corpse apart piece by piece and found nothing suspicious, or almost nothing. There was a peculiar bruise on his neck. There were a number of very suspicious circumstances surrounding the events leading up to the death and the condition of the house. But after an exhaustive inquiry, the Queens Road Coroners Court ruled that death was apparently accidental, the result of a fall down the stairs. Simeonov, they said, had broken his nose in the fall and drowned in his own blood.

It was this last quirk that bothered me. The circumstances were coincidental enough without the question of blood arising again. Could it be that Simeonov had been sprayed with an aerosol of something that caused him to hemorrhage and bleed to death? Or was the blood just another coincidence? Had the assassin struck again, this time changing his weapon to something new "that the West could neither detect nor treat"? If it had not been for the chance discovery of the tiny pellet rolling down the autopsy table when Markov was being examined, his death would have been ruled accidental, due to unknown infection. Had it not been for the discovery of an identical pellet in Kostov, with testable traces of ricin intact within it, his illness would never have been connected with an attempted assassination. Maybe in the case of Simeonov the assassin had not used a ricin pellet, but something else.

The only way to begin was by examining the documents from the inquest. Her Majesty's Coroner is not obliged to give out copies of inquests. It took months of dogged correspondence before the coroner, Dr. Harold Price, kindly agreed to let me see the records. The following is reconstructed from those files, with only a few remarks added for emphasis where the details struck me as provocative.

Several BBC employees testified that Simeonov had looked fine, happy, and healthy when he left after his broadcast that Sunday morning. But he had been extremely nervous. After the Markov incident, a Bulgarian "merchant seaman" caling himself Nedelko had come to the BBC and threatened to kill Simeonov. It was not clear whether he was an agent sent to do the job or, perhaps, a friend of Markov's who thought Simeonov had set up the assassination the way Dinio Dinev had fingered Kostov in Paris.

According to George Ivanov of the BBC, Simeonov "seemed extremely upset" after the incident with the merchant sailor. "Vladimir told me he was frightened to be on his own. He told me he wanted to sell his house and live with somebody instead of living on his own. He was frightened for his life, he felt that the Communists would try and eliminate him. He often used to speak of this; he was very frightened after the Markov incident."

After his 5:30 morning broadcast that Sunday, Simeonov was taken home by taxi as usual, this time in a minicab driven by Roger Simmons:

"During the journey I was not feeling particularly talkative," Simmons told the investigators, "but Mr. Simeonov seemed to want to talk. He told me that he was a bachelor, lived on his own, and that he came from Bulgaria. He also told me that he loved to travel. During the conversation . . . he asked me if I had heard about the two Bulgarians who worked for Radio Free Europe. . . . He then continued to say that both men, Markov and the man in Paris, were friends of his. . . . I said to him that as he was a friend of the two men he had better be careful. He replied that he had no need to worry because he didn't think that he was important, and he wasn't connected with Radio Free Europe, so why should they worry about him. I got the idea he was trying to convince himself rather than me . . ."

It was just after 6:00 A.M. Sunday when Simmons dropped Simeonov off in front of his home. It was a small house, narrow and two-storied, with a living room separated by stairs from a back dining room, kitchen, and bath. Up the narrow stairs there was an empty bedroom in the front with orange carpeting, and an identical bedroom in the back with the same carpeting, where Simeonov had his bed and TV.

Apparently he spent the rest of Sunday hurriedly packing all his possessions, stacking his suitcases in the otherwise empty front room. The front door was double-locked with a Yale lock in the usual place and a bolt at the bottom held by a bent ten-penny nail. As a frightened man, Simeonov must have made doubly certain of the locks. That Sunday evening, after finishing packing, he put on pajama bottoms with a yellow striped pattern, and two sweaters to ward off the chill, and got into bed to go over his personal papers.

He may have arisen to go downstairs to the bath, or he may have heard something. He turned the bedclothes aside, left his papers in a heap on the floor, and went downstairs. It is impossible to tell whether he turned on the lights first, because the switch had an automatic cutoff like most European staircase installations. It was around 9:00 P.M.

Roughly twenty hours later, the emergency call from Gabriella Connor brought an ambulance from West Ham Ambulance Station. Graham Mark Harris was driving, so medic Douglas Thacker was the first to the door at 4:45 P.M.

"I looked through the letter box and saw the upper portion of a male lying at the foot of a flight of stairs," Thacker reported. He used the ambulance radio to call for police help, then decided to force his way into the house. "I had earlier, when looking through the letter box, pushed the door with my hand, but it wouldn't open. I then pushed my foot against the door, and it opened comparatively easily. It wasn't as difficult to open as many doors which I've had to force open in the past." He went to the body and found no pulse. The man had been dead quite some time, judging from the stiffness of the corpse. Thacker quickly went upstairs and was puzzled by the emptiness of the rooms. He then found the crowd of suitcases downstairs. As he went outside to await the constables, he noticed that the bolt at the bottom of the door was shot in the locked position. He also saw a metal hair curler lying by the door on the right side. Simeonov had straight black hair and evidently no girlfriends or boyfriends.

When Harris followed Thacker out, he noticed the bolt also, and saw that the tongue of the Yale lock was set in the lock position, but that there was no sign of damage to the doorjamb anywhere. 'Which surprised me as it had been kicked open," he told the investigators.

How could the two locks on a frightened man's door give in to a preliminary nudge from a medic's foot? Could they have been kicked open the night before and then jammed back shut? If so, the investigators found no signs of forcible entry anywhere. Could the Yale lock have been picked and the bolt forced? Although no signs of force were found around the Yale lock, the bolt-holding ten-penny nail had somehow been bent straight so that it no longer restrained the lower lock. When the door was firmly shut, the investigators were able to force it open with simple body pressure. Very odd for a man in fear of assassination.

One of the two constables who arrived was Joseph Geoffrey Martin. He, too, was puzzled by the scene, but what attracted his attention most was the position of the arms and legs. "I did not move or touch the body but noticed that he was well built, had straight black hair, and was about five feet ten inches in height. The top of his head was against the south wall of the hallway and his legs and feet were lying on the bottom stairs. I noticed that the arms were down along the sides of the body. I noticed that there was what appeared to be blood on the carpet immediately to the right side of the head. I noticed how straight the legs appeared."

Humans falling down stairs to their death have a way of flailing about with arms and legs in a desperate effort to break their fall.

How could it be that Simeonov was so nicely arranged with his arms at his sides and his legs straight out, his feet neatly placed on the bottom stairs? Could it be that somebody had botched the attempt to make it look like Simeonov had fallen to his death?

Dr. Rufus Crompton, one of the pathologists who had done the original autopsy on Markov and a consultant at the Department of Forensic Medicine at Saint George's Hospital Medical School, was able to find nothing that would explain Simeonov's death except the blood in his throat, which might have strangled him. Dr. Crompton sent the heart to Dr. M. J. Davies, the professor of cardiovascular pathology at Saint George's, and learned that there was a tiny congenital lesion on the wall between the left and right ventricles of the heart with a small opening between the two chambers, accounting for the faint heart murmur that had kept him out of the Bulgarian army as a youth.

The coroner, Dr. Price, therefore reconstructed the death as follows: Simeonov had got up to go to the downstairs bath, had a "syncope"—a momentary interruption of his circulation caused by the defect in his heart—fainted, and fell down the staircase to fracture his nose and choke to death.

It was quite reasonable. However, given the sinister context created by the Stashinsky assassinations and the ricin attacks on Markov and Kostov, I think that it would be equally reasonable to conjecture that Simeonov heard something (perhaps the Yale lock being picked) and went downstairs armed with a curling iron, was surprised by an assassin hurtling through the front door, was sprayed or poked with saxitoxin, dropped the curling iron, and died almost instantly. The assassin then carried the body to the stairs, where he had originally planned to catch Simeonov, and placed the body deliberately with the feet on the bottom steps. Unimaginatively, the assassin failed to position the arms and legs in a realistic incongruity. He picked Simeonov's head up by the hair and smashed his nose into the carpet to provide a cause of death. If Simeonov was still in the process of dying from some nameless poison, it would be just enough to choke off the last rattle. The assassin, in this scenario, would then have pulled the front door shut firmly, leaving the door a bit sprung but undamaged—just enough to keep it from blowing open on a breeze, but not enough to bar the entrance of a man leaning on or kicking the door.

In the end, perhaps it does not matter whether Simeonov was assassinated or died a natural death. The point is that invisible assassination was carried out with almost total success on Markov— exposed only by a freak accident. In Paris, Kostov had already been released from the hospital when the investigators arrived from London to satisfy their curiosity and began going over Kostov's medical file, looking for pellets in his X rays. He was at that time still carrying the half-spent pellet around in the skin of his back. If somebody had not gone looking for it, the pellet never would have been found. Kostov might in time have gone to a massage parlor, had a back rub, and died mysteriously.

Simeonov could have been killed with scores of poisons, including Stashinsky's cyanide, saxitoxin, or something new, and it would have metabolized during the twenty hours the body lay undiscovered. Whatever was used, it was certainly "a poison that the West cannot detect nor treat."

If it was impossible to detect, how many other assassinations had gone undetected?

It is purely a conjecture, but I suspect that Simeonov really was a low-grade Bulgarian plant who did finger Markov for the umbrella assassin—and then was killed to keep the Bulgarian connection from unraveling further.

As I reconstructed the scene, Simeonov answered his door, and found an assassin like Stashinsky waiting, was sprayed in the face, and had his body arranged on the landing. The assassin then pulled the door shut and walked away, leaving the body to be discovered later through the mail slot.

If this is what happened to Simeonov, and it seems to me the only reasonable explanation, then the superpoison that killed him can only be guessed at. It could have been the same strange poison being used in Laos and Afghanistan. Simeonov after all had strangled in his own blood.

All potent chemicals can cause bleeding to some extent in heavy doses, and under certain conditions. But they are not particularly noted for that effect, and would not produce it if they were dispersed in aerosol vapor or spread in powder form by a bomb over a village. For that matter, they would not produce such an effect so suddenly if sprayed in a mist up the victim's nose. None of the familiar first- and second-generation synthetic chemical warfare agents suspected at different times of being used in Yemen, Laos, or Afghanistan—whether chlorine, phosgene, adamsite, mustard, or even nerve gas—produces that rather sudden, dramatic effect.

By mid-spring 1981, groups of scientists and researchers in various parts of the world were expending considerable effort searching for an explanation. Their investigations of the natural, biological toxins yielded surprising results.

9.
A Rampage of Pestilence

The hunt for the mysterious new Soviet blood agent—which I had already dubbed "Specter" in my own mind to keep it simple—began, as many hunts do, with a wild goose chase. According to a number of leading biochemists and clinical pharmacologists I had contacted, there were only a few substances that could cause the sort of sudden hemorrhage observed in Afghanistan, Laos, and Yemen. By far the most powerful of these was an awesome marine superpoison with a legendary, violent history. I knew from combing through the monographs published by scientists at Edgewood Arsenal, which are available unclassified through government data banks, that palytoxin had been under intense study for the past several years. If scientists at Edgewood were spellbound by palytoxin, it was a good sign that Soviet scientists were also. It seemed a bit farfetched to me that the Soviet Union could be milking superpoisons from coral reefs. But if palytoxin could be synthesized in the lab, that would be another matter. And there, among the "sabotage poisons" listed in the East German military manual on chemical warfare agents, was palytoxin.

On all my previous visits to Hawaii, I had found the alohas more than a little off-putting, so I had always made it a point to keep going till I reached Tokyo or Hong Kong. Give me paradise without Musak and a slap on the back, any day. This time, I sidestepped Honolulu by catching a feeder airline straight to Maui.

After a short hike down a black lava flow near the town of Hana, I found a tidal pool barely two meters long by less than a meter wide with a reddish moss growing beneath the surface. It is not really a moss or alga, but a coelenterate—a soft, invertebrate coral animal related to the sea anemone.

The Hawaiians call it *limu-make-o-Hana,* the deadly seaweed of Hana. This beautiful marine creature slowly sulking in the soft currents of the pool produces one of the deadliest supertoxins on earth—a whole order of magnitude more potent than the shellfish toxin, saxitoxin, or the frog poison, betrachotoxin. It is far, far deadlier than the ricin that killed Georgi Markov. Compared to it, cobra venom is a lazy, slovenly killer.

Polynesian legend has made much of the deadly *limu.* This pool is cloaked in ancient taboos. According to that legend, the people of Maui long ago discovered that a suspicious man in their midst was really only half man, the other half shark. So they murdered him and threw his body into this pool. Thereafter the *limu* in this pool alone became toxic. The taboo proclaimed that anyone who came to this pool to seek the *limu* would suffer misfortune. Despite the taboo, Hawaiians in the old days came here to smear their spear points with the secretion of the *limu,* to make the spears poisonous.

On December 31, 1961, Dr. Philip Helfrich of the Marine Laboratory at the University of Hawaii and Dr. Paul J. Scheuer of the Chemistry Department had trekked to the site with several associates to take the first known samples of the organism. They identified it as one of the genus *Palythoa,* and when they had isolated and purified its clear, colorless toxin, they named it palytoxin. It was so potent and fast acting that if it was given intravenously to any creature in the lab—dog, monkey, mouse, guinea pig, or rat—it killed in a few seconds. The symptons palytoxin produced began with drowsiness, weakness of the limbs, constriction of arteries throughout the body, sudden vomiting and defecation of blood, and general hemorrhage throughout the body, followed immediately by shock, heart failure, and death. The main effect appeared to be the constriction of the arteries, which caused the blood within the circulatory system to gush out wherever it could. Some creatures reacted more violently than others. Palytoxin was ten times more potent, for example, on a dog than on a monkey. It was not clear exactly how a human would react. There had been legends of divers who brushed against coral reefs and died in agony moments later. This may well have been palytoxin at work, because in spite of the belief that the deadly *limu* existed only in the pool near Hana, it is abundant in all warm coastal waters. However, the diver would have to cut himself first on the sharp coral, because palytoxin seemed to be lethal only when it entered the bloodstream. One student, who accidentally touched a colony of the *limu* to an open cut, became severely ill and had to be hospitalized for two days.

The investigators from the University of Hawaii were not engaged in a study of palytoxin for any reason other than scientific curiosity. But when they had isolated the poison, they shipped a sample of it to Edgewood Arsenal, where it was studied with fascination by Dr. James A. Vick and others and was added to the catalogue of the world's most violent poisons. When the search began for the cause of the phenomenal bleeding in Laos, the first poison to be seriously considered was palytoxin.

It was a logical candidate, at first glance. Here was a poison so potent that the tiniest droplet would cause immediate violent hemorrhage. And a scan of the data base turned up the curious information that the list of East German "sabotage poisons" included palytoxin. Presumably Soviet Bloc assassins had stocks available.

But unless Soviet scientists had achieved a miraculous breakthrough, there was one excellent reason why palytoxin could not be the key to the yellow rain. Palytoxin might work intravenously or through an open cut, but when the toxin was applied directly to the unbroken skin of lab animals it was totally ineffective. The molecules of the toxin were so large that they could not pass through the skin surface unless it was cut or perforated.

Surprisingly, this terrible superpoison also was harmless when given to lab animals orally. It was broken down by the stomach fluids.

To fit the descriptions of death in Laos, the poison had to be effective as a fine vapor or dust cloud, entering through the skin or the lungs of the victims. To my surprise, palytoxin would not be effective through the breathing passages because it would be neutralized by the mucous membranes. What had seemed to be the most obvious candidate of all was a total flop.

The Soviets, furthermore, would have had to harvest acres of coral reefs, or build and maintain vast hydroponic tanks, to produce more than a tiny amount of palytoxin. What investigators at Edgewood, Fort Detrick, and elsewhere were now seeking was not an individual killer of the type used on Markov or on Rebet and Bandera. The search was for a mass poison, effective in yellow brown clouds on whole villages.

For such a scale, palytoxin would have to be synthesized to produce a chemical analogue in great quantities. This was unlikely, even given the spectacular advances of chemistry and microbiology in recent years, because palytoxin's molecule turned out to be so big and complex.

Cobra venom had been successfully synthesized, and progressively more complex molecules were being reconstructed in the laboratory, but it might be years before an analogue of something as complicated as palytoxin could be created. Dazzling and conspicuous a killer as it was, the deceptive red "moss" from the little pool near Hana was set aside. The investigation moved elsewhere.

At the opposite end of the list of candidates causing radical bleeding was the ordinary rat poison, warfarin. It was ruled out because it worked only when dose after dose was absorbed over many days.

The symptoms reported from Laos, and more or less identically from Afghanistan, included constriction in the chest; burning in the eyes, lungs, and throat; sudden nausea; cramps; dizziness; internal hemorrhage; the violent purging of blood from all body openings; all accompanied by twitching, jerking, and convulsions and resulting in death in minutes. Some of these symptons could be caused by different agents, leading to the original conclusion of Dr. Charles Lewis and the army medical team that the yellow rain must be a compound of a burning agent, a nerve agent, and a bleeding agent. The inexplicable quality was the bleeding. Unlike palytoxin, which caused bleeding by constricting the arteries, the investigators assumed that they were looking for an agent that interfered with the coagulating factors of human blood.

There were two ways that this could occur. The poison could block coagulation so that the blood could not clot, and the victim would bleed to death like a hemophiliac. Or the poison could cause the blood clotting factors to act all at once, using them up; then there would be none left to halt the flow of blood, and the victim could bleed to death just as rapidly.

It was assumed that mustard or another burning agent was included in the Specter compound to speed the bleeding. In order for a coagulant or anticoagulant to work rapidly, the body tissue would have to be perforated to let the blood pass through quickly. A first-generation agent like mustard would burn countless tiny holes in the breathing passages, esophagus, and intestines, as well as the skin. The hunt for the coagulant or anticoagulant turned from palytoxin to the many snake venoms. Venoms can produce both effects. A small dose of a venom may cause coagulation, while a heavy dose may cause anticoagulation. Ultimately, snake venom kills by producing respiratory failure. Of the four families of venoms, the average dose per kilo of body weight needed to kill are 3.11 milligrams for crotalidae such as the rattlesnake, 1.90 mg for the viperidae like the puff adder, 1.09 mg for the elapidae including cobras, coral snakes, mambas, and kraits, and 0.07 mg for the hydrophidae or sea snakes. The problem with snake venom is that it makes a potent one-on-one killing agent for assassins, but you'd have to milk a million vipers to collect enough to spray on a village. The thought is intimidating.

Since cobra toxin has been synthesized, it is conceivable that large quantities of any venom could be manufactured, but even then cobra toxin—or a synthetic analogue of a potent sea snake venom—would not act fast enough through the skin or through inhalation.

After stirring up considerable initial excitement in the intelligence community, both palytoxin and the snake venoms proved to be letdowns. There were too many qualities that the potential Specter agent had to meet before it could be considered easy to produce in large quantities, easily dispensed over a target by aerosol or powder, easily absorbed by the skin and the lungs—and specifically able to cause massive bleeding in minutes.

It was then that the search hit what might be pay dirt, in a nightmarish poison from the Dark Ages.

Rampages of pestilence and black death beset the miserable souls of the Middle Ages so often that we have only the most confusing record of Saint Vitus's dance, epilepsy, Saint Anthony's fire, blindness, dementia, plague, and poisoning from which to deduce the true causes of their mortal suffering—yet the greatest cause, aside from contagious diseases spread by vermin, surprisingly, was bread. In the rye, the wheat and the barley, the rice, the oats, the malt and the hops, there grew such a curse of deadly fungus that it is a wonder anyone survived at all. More amazing, to us in an age when bread and other grain foods come prepackaged in sterile loaves, is the fact that these horrible epidemics raged from Hellenic Greece in 430 B.C. to as recently as the 1940s when part of the population of a Soviet province was wiped out by the lethal toxins in poorly wintered grain.

Together, these fungal poisons have accounted for hundreds of thousands of human lives and the devastation of livestock on an order comparable to the ravages of anthrax, typhus, smallpox, and all but the monumental bubonic plague itself, which had the singular and incomparable result of wiping out one-third of the human race between India and Iceland in the years 1348 to 1350. Bread poisons over two millennia may have killed almost as many.

The most familiar of these ghastly fungal poisons was ergot, which is now credited with many of those grisly deaths. But ergot is only one of the fantastic fungal killers, and by no means the most horrible. It is first mentioned in an Assyrian tablet dating from 600 B.C. as a noxious pustule found on ears of grain. A sacred text of the Parsis of Persia from 400 B.C. speaks of a deadly grass that caused abortions. Ergot is the most likely explanation of the plague that beset Athens during the Peloponnesian Wars, struck Duisberg, Germany, in 857 A.D., and France in 943 A.D.

From the tenth century on, conditions in medieval Europe were so grim, with famine ever present, that ergot and other fungal bread poisonings became epidemic. After the collapse of classical enlightenment, agriculture was no longer conducted with care and wisdom. The planting and harvesting of grain was done truculently, in dismal ignorance. Once grains were harvested, landlords hoarded it to maintain stocks in the face of famine, or to squeeze higher prices from the hungry. Because of Europe's damp winters, a broad spectrum of fungal growths developed on the stored grains. Although many different bread molds have now been identified, each with its own characteristic toxin, the accounts of the Dark Ages focus most frequently on the dramatic effects of ergot poisoning. As the epidemics spread, these effects were described by horrified chroniclers. H. E. Jacob has reconstructed the Latin and other period accounts in his book, *Six Thousand Years of Bread*:

> . . . in the early fall of that year of travail A.D. 943 more dreadful things began to happen. Shrieking, wailing, and writhing, men collapsed in the street. Many stood up from their tables and rolled like wheels through the room; others toppled

over and foamed in epileptic convulsions; still others vomited and showed signs of sudden insanity. Many of them screamed 'Fire! I'm burning!' . . . It was an *'invisibili ignis, carnem ab ossibus separens et consumens* [an invisible fire that separated the flesh from the bones and consumed it],' the chronicler wrote. *'Cum intolerabili cruciati,'* with intolerable, excruciating pain men, women and children perished. . . . First their toes turned black, then their fingers burst open, their arms and legs convulsed and broke off. . . . *A horrendissimus ululatus,* a horrible roar of pain, could be heard for miles, and the indescribable stench hung for weeks in the streets. . . . Infectious plagues were known. But this was not one of them. The undertakers who carried the thousands of rotting and twisted bodies to a pit, where they were all thrown together, remained healthy. And, on the other hand, in villages where there had been no deaths, the entire population died in a single day. At the same time, the bread of the people of Limoges became transformed upon their tables. When it was cut, it proved to be wet, and the inside poured out as a black, sticky substance.

They called the different symptoms holy fire, occult fire, Saint Anthony's fire, or Saint Vitus's dance. The symptoms were a sensation of cold hands and feet (caused by contraction of the veins and arteries in the extremities) followed by terrible burning because of the cutting off of circulation. Then came gangrene. The limbs quickly turned black from necrosis, and finally arms, legs, ears, and genitals fell off. In many cases this was accompanied by blindness, convulsions, abortion, hallucinations, and purging of blood—with death following quickly.

Desperate victims sought succor from the church by visiting the shrines of Saint Anthony or Saint Vitus, hence their association with bodily fire and epileptic convulsions. Neither saint produced those effects, suffered from them, or cured them. But the trip to the shrines took the pilgrims away from the source of tainted grain, and they survived by changing their diet in the new region they were passing through. This was especially remarkable with the shrine of Saint Anthony, because it was in mountains of the Dauphiné, where it was dry, clear, and cold, and no mold grew on the bread grains. (The relics and remains of the saint had been transferred there from Saint Anthony's burial place in Egypt.)

The ergot itself was a black or dark purple mass, a long, hard, club-shaped structure that formed as a strain of the mold *Claviceps purpurea*, which grew in the female sex organs of grasses, including the edible food grains. The mold pods contained alkaloids that are derivatives of lysergic acid. They block nerve impulses, cause constriction of the veins and arteries in all extremities, stimulate and depress different parts of the brain, and cause progressive paralysis and uterine contractions.

In enlightened classical Greece or Rome no farmer would have threshed such polluted grain. No miller would have ground it. But in the Dark Ages, famine aggravated ignorance and caused peasants to bake the sickening grain and eat it.

It is no wonder that the people of the Dark Ages believed so firmly in the devil, for he cursed even their daily bread.

Ergot was only one of the fungal poisons—or mycotoxins. There were others that contributed to these horrible medieval afflictions. Others that had no name, but were specifically responsible for the purging of blood. And it was here in a bizarre hemorrhaging disease that plagued Mother Russia that the investigators at last found the thread of an explanation for Laos and Afghanistan.

The earliest recorded outbreak that can be associated exclusively with this noxious killer occurred in 1891 in the Ussuri district of eastern Siberia, during the reign of Czar Nicholas II. It was first called the "staggering" sickness, because humans who consumed the contaminated grain were sticken with vertigo, headache, chills, nausea, and vomiting. There may have been horrible outbreaks every year before that, and every year thereafter, which went undistinguished from the rest of the human suffering through which Russia was passing at the time. Most cases were wrongly believed to be epidemics of cholera or diphtheria. Because of the total rupture of Russian society on all levels during the Revolution and the subsequent civil war, there is no way to separate one cause of misery and death from another—millions were dying. In 1934, however, the new Soviet government had brought sufficient domestic control that such distinctions were once again possible. In that year, the bleeding or staggering disease was recognized once again, this time by an observer in western Siberia. Once it was recognized, it became possible to distinguish a pattern of recurrences through the rest of the 1930s, as it hit Ryazan, Molotov, Sverdlovsk, Omsk, and Novosibirsk.

When World War II began, Soviet agriculture was again disrupted, bringing on severe hardship and famine throughout much of the nation. The disease became epidemic in a number of districts and republics. It spread through the Urals, Moldavia, the Ukraine, central Asia, and Siberia. In many of those regions, 60 percent of the population was stricken. It hit hardest, because of certain favorable environmental conditions, in the Orenburg district—an area the size of Czechoslovakia—where 10 percent of the population of roughly 300,000 died hideously.

It was, above all, a bleeding disease. Minutes after the poisoned grain was eaten, the victim began to burn in the mouth, throat, esophagus, and stomach, as the poison quickly went to work on the mucous membranes, causing surface hemorrhages. Then came a hemorrhagic rash on the skin of the chest, spreading within the hour to the abdomen, legs, arms, and face. The rapid onslaught of internal bleeding was accompanied by violent headaches, dizziness, vertigo, weakness and fatigue, fever, sweating, angina, neurological tremors, spasms, and then convulsions. The blood pressure fell, bleeding became heavy in the intestines and all the vital organs and glands—particularly in the adrenal and thyroid glands, gonads, uterus, and pleura. Suddenly, the lungs gushed blood, filling quickly with it. The heart began to fail as the bleeding spread to the liver, the kidneys, the central and autonomic nervous systems, the ganglia, and finally the brain. There was severe destruction of the bone marrow, and the hemoglobin count dropped to 8 percent of normal. In agony, the terminal victim spewed blood from every body opening. In the few cases where people survived, there was blood seeping from the eyes and ears—and all other orifices—all symptoms and signs apparent in Laos, Yemen, and Afghanistan. Aside from the bleeding, there were hematological spots or small blisters on the skin—angry red welts accompanied by a general pink inflammation that soon became mottled and turned black as necrosis set in—again all symptoms described in Laos, Afghanistan, and Yemen where the difference from mustard blisters was striking. The following is an extract from a previously classified interagency report prepared by scientists at Fort Detrick:

These symptoms call to mind the symptoms reported by the Mong [sic] tribesmen after the attacks with the "yellow rain" in Laos. The following was taken from an interview with a Lao refugee in Thailand who witnessed a chemical attack that occurred in May of 1977. After exposure to the agent, he immediately felt dizzy with the desire to vomit. He experienced frontal headache, vertigo, painful burning of eyes and throat. He had difficulty breathing and was extremely nauseated; vomiting blood on several occasions. He suffered from bloody diarrhea and his skin itched all over, developing small blisters and numerous hemorrhages under the skin. The symptoms described are very similar to those described for ATA [Alimentary Toxic Aleukia] and other classical tricothecene intoxications.

The next passage of the Fort Detrick report was deleted for security reasons. The report fails to note that the symptoms of the disease in Russia also include muscular and neurological spasms, causing victims to twitch, jerk, and dance as if they had been stricken by nerve gas. This, too, was constantly reported in Laos. The witnesses and survivors interviewed for this book along the border of Afghanistan also specified these symptoms. The eyewitness accounts from Yemen also include them. In each case they followed aerial bombardment with chemical agents.

Soviet scientists began studying the disease intensively in the late 1930s—almost thirty years before fungal poisons attracted attention in America, England, and Japan.

It had been customary for centuries in Russia to harvest some cereal grains in the autumn, but to leave others in the fields through the winter for harvest after the first thaws in the spring. In some cases, this was the result of extremely primitive farming methods and the early onset of the brutal Russian winter—which forced the peasants out of the fields and into shelter before they could gather all the crops. In other areas, as in Orenberg, the rich soil of the southern Caucasus produced such a bountiful crop of grain that it was impossible to harvest it all before winter even with the best effort and methods available at the time. The ground froze and blizzards piled deep drifts, burying the grain beneath a crust. During the winter there were repeated freezings and thawings in the southern Caucasus that did not occur farther to the north. Because of this, not only did one fungal growth begin to develop in the cereals but several poisonous fungal species, with different toxic properties, developed in combination on the same grain. Even within one mold, there would be several toxins produced and secreted in the grain. These slightly different poisons combined to produce a synergistic effect—in which the results of the combination were greater than the deadly effects of any single toxin.

In the spring thaws, this wretched grain was taken in by hungry peasants determined not to waste a single stalk. In areas beset by famine, even the trampled grains would be collected by the poorest wretches and eaten.

There was no squeamishness when it came to cooking the foul grain, either. Baked breads and cakes were immediately covered with thick furry growths of mold, but were eaten anyway. The symptoms took a few minutes to appear, so nobody suspected the bread. Since the people did not know what was causing everyone to die, they continued to eat the grain. Given the system of communal farms enforced by the Soviets on the peasantry, and the determination of the government to extract as much grain as possible from each commune for distribution to other parts of the Soviet Union, the poisons were widely and unwittingly spread.

Once Soviet scientists began to understand the nature of the poisons, they christened the disease alimentary toxic aleukia, or ATA. The two primary fungal growths identified with it at first were *Fusarium poae* and *Fusarium sporotrichioides*. These are only two of the fusaria. The deadly toxins they produce are now identified as T_2 toxins, or trichothecenes. These are a variety of chemically related, biologically active fungal metabolites, produced primarily by various species of *Fusarium*. Because of the special circumstances of Russian agriculture and environment, most human deaths caused by T_2 have been in the Soviet Union. Deaths that have occurred elsewhere have not been traced to T_2 toxins as virulent as those in the Soviet Union—leading some scientists to conclude that since the toxins have thrived in Russia, they may have become especially potent there.

Outbreaks of ATA, the bleeding disease, continued through 1947. Similar afflictions hit horses and cattle in Russia and Eastern Europe in 1958 and 1959, through infected feedgrains. There have been instances of T_2 poisonings all over the world—from peanuts and other contaminated sources—but on a comparatively minor scale. Western interests were aroused by the outbreak of a similar disease that killed no less than 100,000 turkeys in England in 1960, after they ate peanut meal contaminated with the mycotoxin called aflatoxin. Scientists then discovered that aflatoxin was a potent carcinogen and was present in many foodstuffs, leading to the generation of major scientific research worldwide.

T_2 toxin was studied intensively in the Soviet Union, particularly at the Institute of Microbiology and Virology at Kiev in the Ukraine. It was found that millet produced the most potent toxins, with large doses of the crude extract causing an agonizing death in less than one day. It was soon possible for Soviet scientists to reproduce the toxin in large quantities using biosynthesis. Interestingly, of fifty articles on the trichothecenes in Soviet open source literature, twenty-two deal with defining optimum conditions for biosynthesis of the compounds. This means, quite simply, that as long as two decades ago—well before the Yemen civil war—the Soviet Union was able to produce as much T_2 toxin as it wished, and was obviously fascinated with the desire to find better ways to produce still more. Western scientists are unable to come up with any benign reason why Moscow would want to produce such vast quantities of a poison that has no apparent use whatever except to cause people to drown in their own blood. As an agricultural problem, *Fusarium* is now well understood, easily avoided by exercising ordinary public health precautions and agricultural inspection methods.

Some T_2 toxins have been synthesized chemically, but there is no reason to manufacture a synthetic version when the natural forms can be produced so readily with biosynthesis.

The T_2 toxins are very stable, especially in solid form, and may be stored for years at room temperature without loss of potency, even at temperatures of 100° F. The toxins range in molecular weight from 154 to 697, but most fall between 300 and 600, making them easily absorbed through the skin or internal membranes. A dose as small as 0.1 mg/kg is fatal—so it is more potent than cobra venom. But T_2 can be modified easily in the laboratory to increase its ability to penetrate the skin or to be absorbed through the tissues of the nose and throat. This would help accelerate the impact, so the poison would go to work in minutes rather than hours.

Using biochemical engineering methods developed over the last several decades, it is also possible to enhance the potency of the toxins radically by playing around with the molecules and then mass-producing the modified form with biosynthesis. This could easily move the T_2 toxins into the category of supertoxins. It would also follow that anyone determined to produce large quantities of such a poison and aware of its various forms and actions would also fully understand the perversity with which these toxins interact synergistically. The Soviets would know how to combine several of them to gain maximum killing effect, maximum speed of action, or symptoms made to order. The killing agent could be made lethally effective in five to ten minutes with heavy aerial dosages, which is in keeping with reports from Laos and Afghanistan.

A T_2 toxin would be suitable for delivery as an aerosol because it is stable in solution, or as a powder of its solid form. For ease of dispersal, it could be bound to other substances that would serve as "carriers," or could be microencapsulated, for release at the target. Because of its remarkable stability, it would tend to be persistent at the site of attack. However, if nobody knew what to look for, one could hardly be expected to look for T_2 toxin residues, particularly in a world familiar only with the first- and second-generation killing agents such as mustard or nerve gas. In an effort to rid the target of T_2 residue, it would be a simple matter to bond the toxins with a surfactant base, to take advantage of the heavy rains in Laos, for example, and let the bulk of toxin residue be washed away. Laboratory analysis of leaves brought from target sites in Laos showed the presence of a surfactant—lauryl sulfonate. There is no reason for the presence of such an ingredient of household detergent on the leaves of the most primitive and remote sections of north-central Laos, unless the surfactant was sprayed on the leaves for some purpose.

The symptoms demonstrated in Laos, Afghanistan, and Yemen have all been interpreted as caused by various known first- and second-generation agents in one combination or another, including phosgene, chlorine, tear gas, mustard, phosgene oxime, modified adamsite, lewisite, and the nerve agents soman and VR-55. The original conclusion reached by Dr. Charles Lewis after the visit of the U.S. Army medical team to Ban Vinai refugee camp on the Thai-Lao border was that three agents appeared to be involved in the compound: a vesicant or burning agent such as mustard to produce the blisters and other symptoms of burning in the nose and throat; a nerve agent to produce the muscular and neurological symptoms of trembling, twitching, and convulsions, and an unknown agent—the unknown Specter—to produce the incredible bleeding.

It is clear from a study of T_2 toxins that they can produce all these symptoms including radical bleeding, burning, and convulsions. However, there are two reasons for concluding that it was not with

T_2 toxins alone that the Soviets have been experimenting in Yemen, Laos, and Afghanistan.

The first is the obvious experimental nature of the attacks, typified by frequent minor variations in the signs and symptoms, in the overlying perceptions of the agents by survivors (a smell of garlic, a smell of fresh fruit, no smell at all), and the endless variations in the forms of attack and types of munitions employed (sprays, air-bursting bags, rockets, cluster bombs, canisters), and even the infusion of bright colors, which could have begun as a means of identifying the dispersal of different agents for color photographic overflights, or could simply have been a device to confuse any witnesses who survived. There is also the incident in which a Hmong victim was carried out to a field station and was dosed with assorted medications, presumably antidotes, by Vietnamese doctors.

The other reason is the variation in signs and symptoms. Some of these could be explained by adjustments in the ratio of one T_2 toxin to another as the experiments continued over a number of years. However, in Yemen in particular but to some extent in Afghanistan and Laos as well, there were fatal incidents involving what seemed to be heavy overlays of mustard gas or phosgene, and others that suggested the presence of nerve agents. Therefore, it appears that a variety of agents were being tested in a program of which the T_2 toxins were only a part. Indeed, there are many instances where no bleeding whatever was reported. What we have been witnessing has been the wholesale field-testing of an impressive variety of Soviet war agents and poisons on human beings, from the Middle East to the Far East, over a period of roughly fifteen years.

We have also witnessed the widespread use of a "nonlethal" agent now called "Blue-X" that knocks victims out for six to eight hours without any evidence of injury. Among the mycotoxins now under study in the United States there is a group called "neurotoxins" that have precisely that effect. It seems the Soviet scientists, while working on T_2 toxins, came up with the related neurotoxins, and these have proved remarkably useful, especially in Afghanistan.

Even in the bleeding cases, there is a peculiar aspect implying the presence of a secondary agent. This was the occasional report of defoliation accompanying the bleeding-agent attack. This draws attention to a second line of investigation that has been going on simultaneously to the scrutiny of T_2 as a possible new Soviet super-poison.

The second line of study has been the long-term Soviet development of modified organic arsenic compounds.

Arsenic principally attacks the heart and gastrointestinal tract, damages the liver and kidneys, and inhibits some enzymes. Symptoms of arsenic poisoning include garlic odor of the breath, burning in the stomach, bloody diarrhea, nausea, cramps and vomiting, headache, vertigo, convulsions, paralysis, and shock. It is commonly used as a pesticide, weed killer, and defoliant.

One of the chemical warfare agents developed in World War I was an organoarsine named adamsite, or diphenylaminechlorarsine. Professor D. E. Lauppi, director of the Institute of Forensic Medicine of the University of Bern, Switzerland, concluded on the basis of Red Cross medical reports from the attack on Gahar in Yemen, on May 15, 1967, that adamsite or another organoarsine, lewisite, might have been the killing agent. It is known that the Soviets have been experimenting in recent years with modifications of adamsite and other organoarsines that would make them a great deal more potent.

Dr. Matthew Meselson of Harvard drew up charts of the various signs and symptoms reported in the three countries, and concluded that adamsite—or a compound similar to it—would fit many of them. He also remarked that the Soviet literature showed considerable interest in synthesizing modified derivatives of arsenic.

Meselson pointed out that adamsite, when it is hydrolyzed by contact with water, becomes diphenylarseneous oxide, which is a very poisonous form of arsenic. Anyone who swallowed it would be killed. Adamsite was stocked by the U.S. Army in Vietnam, in hand grenades as a riot-control agent, marked "not to be used where deaths are not acceptable."

What the Soviets are using may well be a compound of any number of agents, including T_2 toxins and modified adamsite, experimenting at one time or another with different fatal combinations. It may be that modified adamsite is, as Dr. Meselson believes, one of the major components, explaining the defoliation and the reported burning of holes in leaves.

But the leaves that have been brought out from attack sites have not been found to have any arsenic residues. Nor have more recent samples of yellow powder left by the mysterious yellow rain, analyzed in spring and summer 1981. There is only the surfactant, or carrier.

If T_2 toxins are actually being used, their use would illustrate a disturbing ambiguity in existing treaties. The toxins are produced by living organisms, and therefore constitute biological warfare agents as opposed to synthetic chemical warfare agents. However, the Soviet Union considers toxins to be chemical, rather than biological, because they are secretions or products of living organisms but are not themselves living organisms.

The capability of the Soviet Union to modify and mass-produce T_2 and other toxins a thousand times more powerful than the most potent nerve agent makes it clear that we have arrived at the dawn of a third generation of war poisons, in which the most dangerous factor is our own ignorance. Fifteen years after Yemen, we have no positive determination of killing agents used there. Five years after the start of the wholesale slaughter of Hmong hill tribes in Laos, there is still quibbling over whether the Hmong accounts can be believed. Two years after the invasion of Afghanistan, there is controversy within the American government about what it should say or not say about well-established gas attacks there. Within the responsible agencies there are factions opposed to discussion of the superpoisons because it might jeopardize disarmament negotiations, which have broken down in any case. In the U.S. Congress, with its massive ignorance of the state of the art of war poisons, the appropriation of billions of dollars for production of a binary storage and delivery system for the old-fashioned nerve agents is being pondered in a debate that has its reasoning rooted in the Ice Age. Before the United States commits itself to yet another expensive detour, it would do well to find out exactly what the Soviet Union is using in the field. Serious research into T_2 toxins and other new chemical and biological agents is proceeding slowly, with only modest support and funding. Efforts in the field by diplomatic and military intelligence people to obtain samples of the yellow rain have been hampered endlessly by political obstacles and reluctance in Washington to go all out in resolving the mystery. The Carter administration sought actively to block every effort to investigate the Laotian and Afghan reports, apparently in the misguided conviction that the discovery of Soviet misconduct would interfere with ongoing treaty negotiations. The Reagan administration took a much more aggressive stand on chemical warfare and encouraged field investigation so that some samples did begin to come from Laos. But the greatest amount of energy has been devoted not to figuring out where we stand before we plunge ahead but to plunging ahead into binaries without knowing where we stand. Congress and the Pentagon seem to believe that the answer lies in purchasing more hardware. Purchasing expensive hardware gives the illusion that something meaningful is being done. The Pentagon remains obsessed with waging a World War II-style tank war in Europe with old-fashioned chemical agents. In the new era of biological toxins, this demonstrates the genius of George Custer and the dynamics of the Indian Wars. Washington might just as well be on the Little Big Horn as on the Potomac.

10.
Myth and Reality

The Swedish Foreign Ministry is in a fine old gray stone building beside the Norrström, a fast-moving canal in the heart of Stockholm that links the Riddarfjarden and Lake Malaren with the Baltic Sea. Across the Norrström on an island sits the royal palace and the Old Town—a tidy medieval city that has survived centuries of European conflict without damage of any kind. Nowhere in the world has survival been practiced so effectively. Sweden enjoys a resplendent past free of the pockmarks of bullets while indulging in the social experiments of the future. It would like to have things remain that way. So Swedes like to cover both sides of a bet. They do not engage in war, but they regularly send troops on peacekeeping missions for the United Nations—they did much of the fighting in the Congo. They do not participate in the arms race, but they manufacture fine Bofors guns and excellent jet fighters like the Viggen. They see themselves as being above the sort of pugnacious rivalry that often brings down both sides in European wars. And while demonstrating their restraint, Swedes reward brilliance with the presentation of Nobel Prizes, one of which went to Fritz Haber, the father of chemical warfare.

Part of Sweden's success in avoiding entanglement with other nations lies in its diplomatic skill, a process of endless discussion, evasion, and negotiation roughly equivalent to fencing with foils while wearing full padding and a wire mesh mask.

I had come to Sweden late in 1980 to visit SIPRI—the Stockholm International Peace Research Institute—before proceeding to the headquarters of NATO and SHAFE [Supreme Headquarters Allied Forces Europe] in Belgium. I was looking for historical data, but I was given instead a practical lesson in the wit and wisdom of chemical survival.

SIPRI is a government-funded organization of scientists and investigators who have devoted many years to the close examination of war and its damage, including the definitive historical study of chemical and biological warfare. I wanted to spend some time at SIPRI making certain that I had all the material I could possibly absorb on chemical weapons, but I had also made appointments with officials at the Foreign Ministry and the Swedish Civil Defense Agency to see what they knew of developments in Afghanistan and Indochina, and what precautions Sweden was taking, if any.

So, early the next morning, I was ushered into a small office off a courtyard in the Foreign Ministry for a talk with one of its diplomats. In the course of our conversation, he assured me that Sweden was not aware of any chemicals being used by anyone, anywhere—since the American spraying of Agent Orange in Vietnam, of course. So far as Sweden had been able to determine, the reports from Indochina and Afghanistan were merely unfounded contrivances. Sweden certainly did not feel that there was anything worth becoming excited about in the field of chemical or biological warfare.

He was an engaging fellow and we had a thoroughly enjoyable conversation leading nowhere.

In Sweden, the politics of disarmament are a fundamental part of survival theory. The Foreign Ministry pushes constantly for new talks and new treaties while adamantly denying that any of the parties involved could possibly be using lethal chemicals or even thinking about using them. If anyone was guilty of using them, it was the United States in Vietnam. But that, of course, was long ago. The world was now on the verge of entirely new agreements banning any and all use of bugs and gas, and Sweden was in the forefront of pushing for these accords.

After leaving the Foreign Ministry, I strolled a few blocks to the Sturegaten near the national library and rode up in a tiny elevator to the third floor of a small brownstone. A press conference was about to begin. There, in the course of the next two hours, contrary to everything I had just been told at the Foreign Ministry, the director general of Sweden's Civil Defense Agency announced a new multimillion-dollar crash program to upgrade Swedish defenses against chemical warfare. Included would be new gas masks for every man, woman, and child in the nation. There was no alarm. It was very matter-of-fact. Chemical warfare is imminent and when it comes is likely to be so widespread that it includes neutral Sweden. Therefore more underground shelters need to be built in addition to already elaborate complexes dug out of solid rock. New masks with new filtration systems need to be distributed, along with the latest designs in chemical costumes, for everyone including children in the crib. That night Swedish television carried the announcement and conducted elaborate discussions of the new masks and shelter systems.

Diplomatically, Sweden did not know that chemical warfare existed. Realistically, it was preparing for chemical and biological warfare at a rate surpassing any other country on earth.

With heavy infusions of funds from the government, Swedish scientists had developed chemical ensembles that were secure against all known chemical agents, specifically against what the Swedes call Agent F, which is their designation for thickened soman or VR-55, the Soviet persistent nerve agent.

The lesson was clear: Strive to obtain chemical disarmament, but just in case that fails, be prepared for the worst. Deny that anything sinister is going on, but meanwhile get ready for it to happen to you.

Juggling fantasy and reality is fine so long as it is deftly done, and the Swedes do it deftly. That is not so in NATO. Sweden, to be sure, is not a member of NATO. But the nations that are allied in this most extraordinary of all country clubs like to believe that NATO handles myth and reality as smartly as Sweden. It soon becomes apparent that they do not. At NATO, fantasy rules supreme.

Compared to Stockholm's dignified, centuries-old Foreign Ministry building, the headquarters of SHAFE look like a group of budget motels clustered together on the bruised hills outside Mons, Belgium. Across the street from the entrance to SHAFE is the European version of a Howard Johnson's. Like SHAFE, it is prefab. The entire complex, SHAFE and restaurant, could be beside a highway in Silicon Valley in California. All that is European is the food. The rest is polyester and Styrofoam.

Deep inside the polyester halls of SHAFE, inside a Styrofoam conference hall, a clean-cut American major with a very sincere grin told me that I could relax because America had taken the whole CBW and NBC game in hand. Up at Ramstein Air Force Base, the USAF was now equipped with a full set of ensembles for all pilots and operational crews. Phase two of the program would provide a second ensemble for every crew member so that they could return to base for decontamination, put on a fresh ensemble, and get back into combat quickly.

The major gave me the full rundown with all the backups. He also gave me the scenarios and game plans. He assured me that so far as U.S. Army was concerned in Europe, everybody was on his toes and ready to get that mask on in less than ten seconds, which was the time lapse it was estimated that a soldier would have after his alarm system told him chemical agents were being used. America was on the ball in NATO. Soon it would have the rest of NATO in line.

After the major left, two Dutch officers took me aside and advised me not to believe a word I had been told. NATO was in a hell of a mess. Nobody knew how to put on a mask, half the troops did not have them, and there was no way any European country could afford to buy them.

"It is a political issue," one Dutch officer said, confidentially. "The public would never stand for it if the political party in power tried to equip the military with masks. Everybody knows that poison gas kills civilians as fast as it kills soldiers. Putting masks on the armed forces does nothing to save civilian lives. So any government that tries to equip the armed forces for chemical warfare is going to lose power quickly."

"That major," the other Dutchman said, "the American who was just talking to you—he may know how to put on a mask and costume, but he is probably the only American soldier in Europe who does. And he just came over recently to try to straighten the mess out. He has his work cut out for him, believe me."

The two Dutch officers assured me that Americans are vastly misled by their own propaganda. After they left, I went across the road to ponder what I had been told, over a glass of 1937 Latriciere Chambertin. Not bad for a polyester roadhouse. Now I knew why SHAFE reminded me of a movie set on a Hollywood back lot. Because that is exactly what it was. Here everybody played bit parts in a high-budget fantasy. America was producing *Star Wars* on· location in Europe. In the midst of it I could have sworn that I had stumbled onto the set of a low-budget western where the cavalry officer assures the settlers that they have nothing to fear from the Apaches.

There is definitely something of the Old West, and of the logic and inspiration of George Custer, in American thinking about NATO. And in time this fantasy has penetrated the minds of British officers as well, a sort of wishful thinking, of whistling in the dark, and of reliving the good old days of armored cavalry in World War II when masses of tanks rumbled back and forth across Europe. They imagine that World War III will happen that way, and they see themselves riding around in tanks and armored cars dealing with it.

Nowhere is this better demonstrated than in the fictionalized narrative of NATO game plans published in 1979 under the title *The Third World War*. The book became a best-seller partly because it was written by a team of NATO officers headed by Britain's General Sir John Hackett and was based upon "actual NATO and Soviet battle strategies." There were in fact long passages that I recognized as being lifted from current NATO defense studies. The portions of the battle dealing with Soviet chemical attacks were clearly based on the analyses of John Erickson at Edinburgh University. The following extracts give an idea of how NATO generals think poisons would be brought into play, and what NATO would do about it:

> Chemical agents were used in the attack from the start, but only on some sectors of the front. They were not used against the two US corps, perhaps because USAREUR possessed integral and effective chemical offensive weapons of its own. US policy had consistently been that US troops would retaliate in kind if attacked with chemical agents but would not use them otherwise. The Soviet commanders seemed to have taken this threat seriously and did not use chemicals against any formation in CENTAG.

British army forces defending northwestern Germany, however, did not fare so well:

> In the NORTHAG sector none of the national corps possessed a chemical offensive capability. This position had persisted in the 1980s despite the growing strength of the argument that possession of a retaliatory capability would be a relatively

unsophisticated and economic means of discouraging recourse by the Soviet Union to chemical weapons. . . . There was now widespread use by the enemy of chemicals to support attacks against NORTHAG, principally launched in BM-21 rockets. These equipments operated in battalion groups of eighteen which, when fired in unison, were able to land 720 rockets on a square kilometre within fifteen seconds. The warm weather was ideal for the use of non-persistent agents such as HCN. This has a hazard duration of only a few minutes at 10°C in moderate wind conditions with rain, or at 15°C in sunny conditions with a light breeze. Soldiers not wearing respirators within the target area died within a few minutes of inhaling the vapour. The agent evaporated so quickly that Soviet assault troops would be able to move through the target area with only minor precautions. Despite peacetime training, Allied casualties in forward areas as the offensive opened were considerable. At the same time, major airfields were attacked with chemical agents (usually mustard, or G- or V-type nerve gases) delivered by missiles, each one of which could put down sufficient of a persistent agent to cause severe disruption over the whole airfield complex. Ground crews were forced to wear full protective equipment to carry out maintenance and aircraft refuelling and re-arming. This severely handicapped their performance and increased aircraft turn-around times significantly.

This is an essentially straightforward dramatization of prevailing theory about how the Soviets might employ chemicals in a typical game plan. The only major flaws are that General Hackett, being both British and a gentleman, allows British forces to come under criticism for lack of preparedness while flattering America's notion that its forces in NATO are better prepared. And Hackett ignores the serious danger posed by aircraft moving in and out of bases contaminated with persistent V agents; the result would be widespread dispersal of nerve gas across the landscape.

Sir John does foresee civilian chemical casualties of some severity, however:

Major logistic installations and communications points, where large numbers of the civilians operating them had no protective equipment, received similar treatment. Physical removal of persistent agents was virtually impossible while further missile attacks maintained a high level of lethal contamination. Such attacks upon airfields and logistic installations caused more prolonged disruption than sustained high-explosive bombardment. . . . Medical services soon overloaded with battle casualties were severely taxed to cope with casualties caused by chemicals as well. . . . The main result of chemical attack was less the infliction of casualties, which were never intolerably high after the initial attacks, than the severe constraint on physical activity occasioned by defensive precautions, particularly the wearing of respirators and cumbrous protective clothing. The performance of combat infantry was degraded under full precautions by as much as 60 percent. Mobility was reduced in avoiding contaminated areas. The requirement for chemical reconnaissance took time and units were frequently forced for lack of it to fight in a contaminated environment.

What is left out of General Hackett's narrative are downwind deaths, particularly among civilians. A grim picture of what would happen to the civilian population emerges from a study prepared by Dr. Messelson of Harvard and Dr. Julian Perry Robinson of the University of Sussex:

Since civilians are unlikely to be provided with protective equipment and trained in its use to the same extent as combat units, noncombatants stand to suffer more severely from the effects of chemical attack. Existing chemical weapons are not designed for strategic purposes, and military doctrine does not envision intentional chemical attacks on civilians. Clouds of nerve-gas vapor could drift long distances downwind of a battlefield before becoming harmless, however, and terrain contaminated by nerve gases may remain hazardous long after fighting in the region has ended. Battlefield chemical weapons thus carry with them an immense potential for causing civilian casualties. It can be estimated that on-target sarin contamination intended to cause 20 percent casualties among soldiers carrying respirators but not at first wearing them could, under weather conditions frequent in central Germany, kill unprotected people 20 kilometers or more downwind and seriously incapacitate people out to about twice that distance. Civilian casualties on the order of millions could result from battlefield chemical warfare in Europe.

Drs. Messelson and Perry Robinson based their calculations, of course, on known killing agents including mustard, hydrogen cyanide, and nerve gas. If the lethal agents included unexpected or unknown poisons such as T_2 toxins, the casualties would be sharply increased. Among the additional deaths would be civilians who took precautions against familiar agents but discovered too late that their filtration units in shelters or gas masks were unable to block the unexpected poisons. The Soviet Union was looking for a route to bypass gas mask filters as early as the 1920s, when its chemists sought a means to introduce an agent that would be converted into toxic carbon monoxide by the victim's own mask filter. Another way of attaining the same end has been to hit the victim with an agent that produces severe nausea so quickly that even if he dons a mask, he will have to remove it to vomit—at which point he would be exposed to nerve gas or another lethal agent.

The calculations also are based on the nerve agent sarin, which is a nonpersistent vapor at the time of delivery—roughly equivalent in potency to the Soviet agent soman. This would dissipate rapidly. If thickened soman (VR-55) or any other oily V agent were mixed into the calculations, casualties would be sharply increased because of the agent's persistence. Rather than dissipating, the V agents would remain for weeks or months, gradually being spread by vehicle movement, human movement, or normal weather. Contaminated areas of hundreds of square miles would be impassable except in special vehicles. It would be impossible to prevent a panicked population from entering contaminated zones and dying immediately.

Sir John Hackett's dramatization concludes its brief passages on chemical attacks with a note of reassurance that American forces would retaliate against the Soviet use of poisons:

> In theory a nuclear response had always been considered a possibility, at least by the British, but at this stage [three days after the Soviet invasion] SACEUR was in no doubt that such a response would be an irrational risk. He was, however, prepared to see chemicals used in retaliation; indeed, authority for their use had already been delegated to local U.S. commanders. . . . A squadron of US Air Force F-4 *Phantoms* equipped with spray tanks . . . attacked second echelon and reserve Soviet divisions with extensive and heavy concentrations of persistent lethal agents. These attacks forced Soviet units into unplanned

moves. The personnel protective equipment used by Soviet soldiers was not suitable for prolonged wear and under continued attack by persistent gases grew almost intolerably irksome. . . . Their less flexible command and control procedures were more easily impeded. On balance, Soviet commanders considered a chemical exchange to be to their disadvantage.

Here Sir John's narrative indulges in sheer fantasy, the wishful thinking about poison gas typical of military minds in World War I. Any Soviet force engaged in dousing its enemy with G and V agents (or worse) will be constantly alert to chemical counterattack, and will be prepared to don full regalia instantly—if they have not already put them on as a precaution. Thus the likelihood of catching many Soviet troops off guard is remote. They would also have advance warning from spies, or from the well-trained vanguard of General Pikolov's Chemical Corps, whose sole function is to locate enemy chemical depots and assist in their capture or destruction. Once in their chemical ensembles, Soviet soldiers would certainly demonstrate less efficiency and mobility, but far from the degree suggested. After years of hardship training in these suits, up to twelve hours at a time while conducting maneuvers and performing all duties—something no Western trooper has been obliged to endure, outside of a few showpiece units—the Soviet soldier could be expected to perform better in his uncomfortable suit and mask than his NATO counterpart in the latest and most comfortable ensemble of Western manufacture. For that matter, by the third day of such an invasion, it is unlikely that many NATO soldiers would still have their masks and costumes at hand to put on.

The fascination with discomfort in chemical war tells less about the Soviet soldier than about the self-indulgence of Western troops. Whoever suggested that war should be comfortable? Gas masks and protective garments and gloves are a terrible nuisance. They are uncomfortable under the best circumstances, clumsy to put on, suffocating and claustrophobic to wear for more than a minute.

Front-line American troops in NATO, those within sight of Soviet units, are equipped with masks and breathing filters containing activated charcoal to absorb vapor and paper filters to block particles. The charcoal is impregnated with copper compounds to be more effective against small molecule agents such as hydrogen cyanide. According to descriptive material published by the Pentagon, these masks could be donned in less than ten seconds and worn even while asleep. Yet soldiers attempting to demonstrate the masks before television news cameras were unable to put them on in the prescribed time, got them on askew in any case, and then could not figure out how to work the valve connection that would make it possible to drink through a pipe from their canteens. Would they get them on faster or better under attack?

A new American mask that is lighter, with fittings for voicemitters, and large lenses designed to accommodate sighting a rifle or using guided missile sights, is in final stages of development. This new mask is also handsomer and more stylish, which presumably guarantees that it would find wider acceptance among more fashion-conscious GIs.

All GIs in NATO are supposedly equipped with the British Mark 3 disposable two-piece overgarment to be worn with overboots and Butyl rubber gloves. It weighs only four pounds and sheds rain while allowing the evaporation of perspiration. Any nerve vapor that penetrates the surface is absorbed by activated carbon bonded between the outer and inner layers. It is said to be comfortable for prolonged wearing except when temperatures rise above 75° or 80° F—which is not typical of northern Europe. On such an unusually warm day, the soldier would not be able to engage in heavy exertion for more than an hour before getting out of the suit for a break. A similar suit is provided for combat pilots, whose cockpits are not protected against chemicals. Pilots engaged in the severe duress of an hour's combat would have to land, find their way to an uncontaminated chamber, remove their ensembles, and rest before resuming combat.

Soldiers are trained (when they are trained at all) to put these suits on at a signal from their officers, the sounding of an alarm, or first sensing such telltale signs as a runny nose, dimming vision, or tightening in the chest. However, nerve agents are so potent that a killing dose can be absorbed before it is detected by the senses. So unless troops are given advance notice—time to fumble with their masks for a minute or more—they are likely to receive a lethal dose or enough to make them ill and useless for battle.

Protective gear is regarded with so much irritation that it is likely to be worn only when the threat is overwhelming. One high-ranking U.S. Army officer told me privately that American soldiers are so unprepared for chemical attack that "if they saw the Russians advancing toward them behind a yellow brown cloud, they'd say 'Oh, yeah, the Russians always lay down smoke to hide their armor from our antitank missiles,' and by the time they realized it was not smoke, they'd be dead."

This problem is simplified when soldiers can fight in tanks or armored personnel carriers that are secure against chemicals in the same fashion as current Soviet armor. The latest NATO tanks have such seals—with positive-pressure filtered air supplies. The crews do not have to wear gas masks. Presumably, the European members of NATO will follow the Soviet pattern and extend this group protection to other vehicles, including APCs [Armored Personnel Carriers]. The Soviet experience in Afghanistan has shifted emphasis from heavy armor to highly maneuverable lightweight vehicles— the BMPs and BRDMs—so group chemical security systems are gradually becoming a basic design feature of all Soviet combat vehicles. Presumably, this will be emulated by the NATO allies as new equipment rolls out onto the line. It tells us a great deal about the shape of future wars to know that the most advanced equipment is built to be secure against a wide range of poisons.

NATO also stocks basic antidote kits against the known agents, and has simple decontamination equipment—nothing on the order of the Soviet TMS-65 turbojet decon vehicle. No matter how advanced some equipment is, and how crude the rest, the key to survival and performance in combat lies not in the equipment but in the training. A soldier forced to learn how to make the best long-term use of a clumsy suit and mask has a better chance of survival than a soldier equipped with the most elegant equipment money can buy but unable, unwilling, or untrained to use it.

After what I had already learned about the mismanagement of chemical weapons, I was hardly surprised to find that there is no definitive U.S. or NATO doctrine on chemical warfare. What is put in writing remains ambiguous. Nobody seems to have a clear idea or a central purpose. At first I thought that this was entirely a reflection of the public attitude in America, which—when it exists at all— shows a mixture of fear and apathy. Until the Nixon ban in 1969, there had been strenuous opposition growing. After the ban, apathy took over. Americans would have to bear the stigma of military poisons until the many wounds of Vietnam were healed. Meanwhile, the Soviet Union did not appear to be up to anything sinister with chemicals—Yemen had passed virtually unnoticed.

There were times when it struck me that this was, rather fiendishly, the real result of the Nixon ban: that the public was falsely lulled into a state of inertia and bogus security regarding the forward thrust of biological and chemical warfare. It was as if people said, "We have been assured that the beast does not exist after all, so there is no reason to be alarmed." Newsmen generally lost interest in it as a story, and when an occasional story was written the reception was distinctly to regard it as freakish. The Pentagon, for its own reasons, encouraged this. From its point of view, the less written about bugs and gas the better.

It was only with the Arab-Israeli War of 1973 that there was a flurry of military attention to the remarkable chemical warfare capabilities built into Soviet tanks and other equipment captured from the Arabs. Once the Department of Defense had digested this disturbing information and compared the Russian equipment with what American troops drove around, a crash program was launched with $1.5 billion to upgrade U.S. chemical defense gear and operational ability. The Pentagon had been surprised, if not startled, possibly because it had been so self-absorbed that it failed to digest intelligence data received earlier.

But this did nothing to bring about a clear-cut restatement of U.S. and NATO chemical doctrine. As put in the current field manuals:

> The objective of U.S. policy is to deter the use of chemical weapons by other nations. If this deterrence fails, and the use of chemical weapons is authorized by national command authorities, the primary objective is to achieve early termination of chemical warfare operations at the lowest level of intensity.

It sounded reasonable, but it was neither fish nor fowl. America would deter by maintaining "a limited offensive capability" and by the threat of "retaliation in kind." This is obviously the kind of policy statement written not by the generals but by the public affairs officers who are primarily responsible for keeping issues clouded in gobbledygook.

In Europe this murkiness produced mixed feelings. Some Europeans longed for SALT II. They hoped that it would bring an agreement to ban all chemical and biological weapons once and for all. European realists were equally unrealistic. They dwelt in the fantasy that in the event of war, America and the Soviet Union could somehow be induced to fight it out between themselves—leaving Europe unscathed. Still others believed that any war would risk crossing the nuclear threshold, therefore neither Russia nor the United States would fight. Meanwhile, Europeans uneasily watched the Swedes and Swiss dig in.

In the midst of such confusion, in the absence of a clear-cut policy, it was agreed only that NATO should have its own "limited offensive capability" to carry out a chemical counterattack—just enough to discourage Moscow from introducing chemicals. This was labeled a "credible retaliatory threat," meaning that any use of chemicals by Moscow would risk immediate chemical reprisal, canceling any advantage.

It sounded believable as rhetoric, but it did not stand up to scrutiny. Each member of NATO had its own idea of what constituted a credible reprisal. Some were based purely on defensive preparations, others relied entirely upon borrowing from the American chemical arsenal if the need arose. France, meanwhile, jealously retained its own offensive chemical option and its own chemical and biological weapons production facilities.

England's role waxed and waned depending on its budgets.

The backbone of NATO traditionally has been the alliance of Britain and America. Britain's historic role in chemical warfare was sharply curtailed after World War II for economic reasons as it retrenched from empire and struggled to find a new national identity. In the meantime, while depending on Washington for chemical weapons, England disposed of its stocks of World War II agents and closed down her nerve gas production plant at Nancekuke, in Cornwall. That automated pilot plant had produced some twenty tons of sarin from 1953 to 1955. The burden of chemical warfare research, along with that for biological warfare, was carried by the Chemical Defense Establishment at Porton Down in Wiltshire, founded in 1916. Some 70 scientists and 750 technicians and staff at Porton conducted research and development, and intelligence analysis in collaboration with Australia, Canada, and the United States. NATO's chemical weapons remained British in design, the United States took over development and manufacture, and field testing and evaluation were carried on jointly at testing grounds in Canada and the western United States.

Britain retains bulk storage of one hundred kilograms of sarin and VX. Its national police forces are equipped with CS weapons, and the British army has both CS capability and a modified BZ-type psychochemical incapacitant (lethal in heavy concentrations) that has been used repeatedly, if surreptitiously, in Northern Ireland.

British policy was voiced by Defense Secretary Denis Healey in the House of Commons in 1970:

NATO as a whole has chemical weapons available to it because the United States maintains an offensive chemical capability. However, I believe that both the former and the present government in Britain were right not to stockpile offensive chemical weapons in the United Kingdom. If the House really considers the situation, I believe that it will recognize that it is almost inconceivable that enemy forces would use chemical weapons against NATO forces except in circumstances of a mass invasion—in which event even more terrible weapons would surely come into play.

This was the nuclear threshold argument.

The French are the only European members of NATO to possess their own chemical strike force, their own large-scale production capacity for lethal agents, and their own substantial stockpiles of bulk chemicals and filled munitions. There has been some liaison between Paris and Washington on research, development, and testing, but the French have been as secretive and guarded about their chemical warfare capacity as they have been about their own nuclear strike force. Both nuclear weapons and chemical munitions are characterized as *armes speciales,* under the supervision of AS officers.

The main French chemical research facility is the Centre d'etudes du bouchet, outside Paris. Prior to World War II there was a production plant for lethal agents at Le Bouchet, and others at Vincennes and Aubervilliers. Tests were conducted at the Polygonne d'entressen proving ground at Bouches-du-Rhone, near Arles. While Algeria was still a French colony, there was a 5,000-square-kilometer testing ground called B2-Namous at Beni Ounif in the Sahara. A nerve agent production plant apparently remains in operation near Toulouse and is said to have produced several hundred tons of agents, and there is a Service des poudres factory at Pont-de-Claix, employing 1,700 workers, that specializes in the production or filling of *armements chemiques*. In all, it is thought that France stocks about one thousand tons of nerve gases, apparently sarin and VX. The French armed forces, given their continued exposure to the brutalities of combat from Dienbienphu to Algeria, may be presumed to be well trained in the use of chemicals, and prepared to use them offensively if necessary.

A similar stockpile of about one thousand tons of nerve agent—sarin and VX—is maintained in West Germany by the United States, under exclusive U.S. control. This includes 155-millimeter sarin rockets.

West Germany renounced chemical weapons after World War II. Bonn's position is embodied in the following 1970 white paper: "The Federal Republic neither possesses nor does she store any . . . chemical weapons; she does not seek possession of, or control over, weapons of that kind, she has made no preparation for using them, does not train military personnel for that purpose, and will abstain from doing so in the future."

The presence of the American nerve agents in Germany has produced some bitterness and criticism, as illustrated by the comments of Willy Brandt when he was foreign minister in 1969: "Should the American government, in the further process of the inner American treatment of this question, come to the conclusion that withdrawal of American supplies of chemical weapons from the Federal Republic of Germany was desirable, I would have nothing against it. Such an American decision would certainly not endanger our security. I don't need to make myself plainer."

The old pre-World War II German chemical warfare research and development center at Heeresversuchstelle on Lüneberg Heath, with a pilot plant at Munsterlager and 120-square-kilometer testing grounds at Raubkammer, has been turned into the Nuclear-Biological-Chemical Defense Research and Development Institute of the Federal Armed Forces. It is apparently concerned strictly with defensive, protection measures. Thanks to its advanced research into chemical defense, West Germany has fully equipped its navy with on-board environmental systems that make German ships at sea more or less impermeable to chemical or biological agents. This is built into the shipboard air-conditioning system, and represents one of the few truly effective CW defense programs outside of Sweden.

Stocks of lethal agents left from World War II that were not confiscated by the Soviet Union, Britain, France, or the United States amount to only a few tons stored at Lüneberg Heath awaiting completion of a special furnace for their destruction. A few additional quantities have been unearthed from unmarked burial sites from time to time, and some bulk chemicals were discovered in September 1979 at a derelict factory in Hamburg. These have been moved to Lüneberg Heath to await destruction.

In Italy, which is still subject to the 1947 peace treaty restrictions on chemical weapons, there are no significant stocks of agents known, and there seems to be no disposition to develop them again.

Among the other members of NATO, Belgium possesses a small stock of artillery shells filled with sarin and possibly some stocks of similarly loaded rockets. Holland appears to have even less, if any at all, and Canada has reduced its chemical warfare research and development at Suffield in Ontario to a low-level operation concerned primarily with developing defensive paraphernalia. The 4,000-square-kilometer proving ground tests systems developed jointly with Britain.

The remaining NATO members—Denmark, Norway, Iceland, Luxembourg, Greece, and Turkey—maintain small research and development projects intended to keep them, to varying degrees of refinement, up to date on chemical defense technology. All depend, to a considerable extent, on the United States for guidance. Of these last, only Norway—sharing a strategic arctic frontier with the Soviet Union—seems anxious to be prepared to retaliate with chemicals if attacked. They all submit their requirements to NATO headquarters on the expectation that the United States will provide whatever chemical munitions or defensive equipment they need.

Since the discoveries of the 1973 Arab-Israeli War, the United States has pushed its NATO partners to expand their retaliatory capabilities, but with the exception of Britain and France, already better equipped than the others, there has been stubborn resistance. According to Dutch senior officers, serious economic problems made it political folly to increase spending for chemical weapons. Even defensive equipment such as gas masks pose political problems if they are purchased for military forces rather than for the population as a whole. This is partly because of a basic European disenchantment with the armed forces as an institution with a knack for misrepresentation and an insatiable appetite for public funds.

There is a widespread perception among Europeans, particularly in northern Europe, that elaborate chemical defensive hardware and clothing for the armed forces does nothing to protect the civilian population.

The Dutch officers at NATO objected that American understanding of the predicament was totally unrealistic. The moment a Soviet chemical attack began, they argued, the entire European transportation network would come to an immediate halt. Dockyards and rail yards would be emptied of workers. Industry would cease to function as workers and managers alike frantically sought shelter.

In Edinburgh, Dr. Erickson remarked that it would be unnecessary for such an attack even to take place. Just the threat of impending use of lethal poisons would be sufficient, he said—for example—to shut down the port of Hamburg.

Only in the non-NATO countries of Sweden and Switzerland has this threat been faced squarely. In Switzerland, bank customers find glossy magazines in the lobbies explaining with color photography how to decontaminate personal clothing in family shelters; laws have been passed making it illegal to construct a new residence without including a shelter secure against chemical attack as well as nuclear fallout. Swiss towns incorporate group shelters on the communal level, and cities such as Luzern regard the improvement of mass shelters underground as part of municipal responsibility.

The smooth performance of chemical defense in both Sweden and Switzerland demonstrates that the confusion, paranoia, and hectoring typical of NATO are simply the result of dwelling in fantasy. If a country wants chemical protection, it is there to be had.

From all this it is clear that the portrayal of World War III by General Sir John Hackett is written from the point of view of old hands at cavalry maneuvers. It represents a dated concept of ground warfare being waged as it was forty years ago by Gen. Hans Guderian, the brilliant German tank corps commander, who made a deep impression on the Soviet Union, as he did on nearly everyone in the early stages of World War II.

To be sure, Soviet strategy is based similarly upon blitzkrieg—sudden thrust and rapid movement of heavy armor backed by light, fast armored personnel carriers and motorized rifles. No weapon is better suited to such surprise attack than lethal chemicals. In fact, chemicals are rarely effective without surprise. A Ukrainian nationalist surprised on the staircase, a Bulgarian broadcaster poked in a crowd, a secret agent in Cuba not equipped with the right antidotes —all are examples of superpoisons in the attack mode.

Where the attack is not one on one, but mass invasion by heavy armor, fast tactical aircraft, massed artillery, and missiles, the use of war poisons still relies on surprise. In a war that could escalate at any moment to strategic nuclear exchange, surprise and finality are so important that the notion of a week-long engagement of main battle tanks is ridiculous.

Vietnam proved, and Afghanistan reaffirmed, that a serious war is either won suddenly, brutally, and totally—or never won at all. The attacker who hesitates forfeits all. The war then becomes a process of erosion by partisans.

In nuclear war there is no turning back. In anything short of nuclear war, the quick, dirty, fatal blow is dealt by the sudden mass strike of every missile in the arsenal, loaded with enough lethal killing agents to wash the green cheeks of Europe clean of human life for a decade—without disturbing any of the buildings, factories, ports, railways, airports, technical complexes, or medical facilities.

We are usually encouraged to believe that such a Soviet attack on NATO is imminent at all times, and that when it comes it would take place across Germany. This is politically the most convenient scenario because it serves to alarm the most NATO allies. A Soviet attack through Germany would quickly tend to involve all the NATO members around its perimeter. So the endless replay of this scenario keeps the alliance nervous and eager to cooperate.

Some senior European officers believe that Germany, in fact, is the last place a Soviet attack would occur. It is the center of the NATO line, where most troops and weapons are concentrated. A Soviet attack on Norway, on the other hand, would not directly threaten most NATO partners, and in the most extreme circumstances it is possible that some members of NATO might be reluctant to commit everything to the defense of Norway when its conquest would not directly threaten their own survival. For this and other reasons, the Norway scenario is rarely played. It is my own conclusion that a Soviet attack on NATO is extremely unlikely under any circumstances—but if it were to occur, Norway would be the weak spot.

In such a Norwegian invasion, the opening move might be the simultaneous chemical bath of all military installations with T_2, VR-55, and mustard; similar isolation of all military and governmental command posts and headquarters; and the sealing of all harbors and fjords, major roads, rail yards, and airports. All functions would cease. The population would seek what shelter was available. Soviet forces striking quickly from the Kola Peninsula and across Finland would first clear the opposing Norwegian forces with short-term soman, or hydrogen cyanide, mixed with quick-dispersing, highly volatile super-toxins for which the defenders would be unprepared either with antidotes or with effective filtration. Those not killed by one poison would be killed by another. Once inside Norway, on land from the north, by sea in the west and south, and by airlift inland, Soviet troops would quell and disarm the surviving population with nonlethal Blue-X while cleaning out pockets of armed resistance.

Because of the confusion within NATO and the profound ambiguity of the United States' own national policy, it is not likely that any serious defense of Norway could be organized before the takeover was complete. It would then become a matter for endless negotiation between Washington and Moscow.

I was able to find no consensus in Europe on any scenario for NATO. But I was persuaded that many NATO officers believe no immediate threat exists unless NATO overreacts to the kind of crisis in the Communist camp raised by Poland. There was a general conviction that it serves the long-range political interests of Moscow and Washington to keep the Warsaw Pact countries and the NATO countries locked in alliance against each other, thereby maintaining an illusion of unity and coherent purpose.

Almost without exception, NATO officers with whom I spoke believed that the serious threat of Soviet attack was not against NATO but against China. They argued that the emphasis placed on NATO was hazardous because it drew political energies away from other areas. They worried that Washington's tendency to see China in terms of relations with Taiwan blinded American politicians to the possibility that Moscow was slowly but inexorably moving toward a position where it could stage a preemptive strike on Peking. In the meantime, Moscow uses NATO as a distraction.

It was along the Sino-Soviet border, they said, that the world's first massive chemical strike would take place.

11.

Dig Tunnels Deep

Early that day in March 1979, there had been storm warnings all over Hong Kong, and fleets of junks had raised sail and scurried around the western tip of the island into shelter. But the storm had fizzled or blown off, and the junks returned again as an armada of lanteen sails to their original moorings. By nightfall, a cold fog had settled over Kowloon and Victoria, so there was nothing visible through the plate glass windows of the press club. I was waiting impatiently at the bar, listening to an Australian journalist explain the virtues of sour mash whiskey as a digestive for nervous stomachs, when at last came my friend from the *Far Eastern Economic Review*. There was an expectant gleam in his eye and a tightly rolled journal in his fist. We found the quietest table by the plate glass, so that we could talk without interrupting the ulcerated Australian, and the editor unfurled his rolled-up journal. It was one of the latest *FBIS Reports*—the worldwide summary of radio transmissions intercepted by the U.S. government and translated by the Foreign Broadcast Information Service. He spread the pages open and tapped his index finger on one entry from the section on China.

"Read this," he urged. "You'll see what I mean. It confirms the flurry of American field intercepts that you heard about. The Vietnamese must be hitting the Chinese with some sort of poison gas, and the Chinese are really upset about it."

China had invaded Vietnam the month before—on February 17, 1979—to "punish" Hanoi for seizing Cambodia, for mistreating the overseas Chinese who were living in Vietnam, and for forcing more than 50,000 of them to flee overland to China during the previous two years. The Chinese invasion had gone well at first, with 30,000 soldiers of the People's Liberation Army penetrating about ten miles into Vietnam. Then, suddenly and without explanation, one main Chinese army force pulled back hastily as if it had been stung by killer bees. There were unconfirmed reports of up to an entire battalion of Chinese wiped out in one battle by Vietnamese chemicals. In Bangkok and Hong Kong, I had been told by American diplomats of a number of terse, cryptic Chinese army radio transmissions, from unit to unit, mentioning coming under chemical attack. These were short broadcasts on field radios, of the category the CIA calls "secrets spoke." The bits and pieces are assembled to see if they make sense as a whole. I had been unable to get anyone to confirm that the intercepts formed a revealing pattern. But the radio broadcast published in the *FBIS Report* of February 22, 1979, here in front of me, went a long way toward confirming the reports and putting them into context. It began with a headline:

KYODO CITES BEIJING SOURCES ON SRV USE OF POISON GAS CW201245 Tokyo KYODO in English 1239 GMT 20 Feb 79 OW [Text] Beijing, 20 Feb (KYODO)—Sources close to Chinese authorities have learned that 240,000 Chinese soldiers (?are deployed) in the war against Vietnam and 30,000 of them crossed the border into Vietnam while the Vietnamese countered with unspecified poison gas, killing at least a few of the Chinese.

The sources said the People's Liberation Army has ranged eight divisions composed mainly from the Kunming and Guangzhou units along the southern border. Each division consists of 30,000 soldiers. The divisions, under the overall command of the Liberation Army's general staff (?headquarters) are directed at the battlefronts by Xu Shiyou, commander of the Guangzhou units, and Yang Dezhi, commander of the Chinese Forces during the Korean war in the early 1950s.

Meanwhile, three units in Xinjiang, Lanzhou and Shenyang in the far west and north have been placed on full alert against possible intrusion by the Soviet Union, the sources said. They added that people living within 30 kilometers of the Chinese-Soviet border in northern Heilongjiang Province have been evacuated. Some areas in the western frontier of the Xinjiang-Uygur Autonomous Region have also been evacuated.

The sources suggested that the Vietnamese forces employed the poison gas even before China's massive assault on Vietnam last Saturday, saying that recent war dead included about 20 men from a people's commune outside Beijing who were killed by gas in Vietnam.

This FBIS report was taken from a broadcast by the Japanese news agency, Kyodo, transmitted from Tokyo but reported directly from Peking. The Japanese correspondent in Peking evidently had well-informed sources within the Chinese government or its Defense Ministry, judging from the data he obtained only three days after the invasion began, including the names of the Chinese field commanders; the access to specific information on evacuations of Chinese population who might be directly in the way if a Soviet invasion took place; and, finally, the unusual information about the twenty men from a commune outside Peking who were among those killed by Vietnamese chemicals. This is not the sort of information that is readily available to foreign correspondents in Peking, who are normally obliged to gather facts as if they were soothsayers casting fortunes from the color and shape of chicken intestines. The Kyodo report is also remarkably restrained. It does not elaborate on the rather shocking bit of information implicit that, for the first time since World War I, poison gas was being used in battle between two major national armies.

Previously, the Soviets had sprinkled chemicals over desolate towns in the wasteland of Yemen, the Vietnamese had sprayed Russian chemicals on defenseless hill-tribe villages in Laos, and the United States had poisoned the ecology of Indochina with Agent Orange and dioxin. But this time it was no incident of big-power bullying. This time it was a slugging match between two established world-class armies equipped on both sides with tanks, planes, and artillery. And the army being clobbered with poison had nuclear weapons in its arsenal. Here was one belligerent power giving another big power a slap in the face with Soviet chemicals—with potential consequences that boggle the mind.

Perhaps it is not surprising then, given the low-key tone of this report and the fact that it was broadcast in the midst of a welter of other major news stories, that it passed almost unnoticed. Nor was it ever followed up by anyone. The Chinese clamped down on news after that, because it reflected badly upon the performance of the Chinese army, which seemed to have been taken completely off guard.

In Hong Kong, we argued the possible ramifications of the gas story. The *Review* editor contended that Chinese intelligence was extremely good on Russia and Vietnam. So it followed that Peking should know all about the chemical capability of the Soviet Union, and know that the Vietnamese had been using Soviet chemicals to kill the Hmong. To anyone keeping closely informed of chemical warfare developments, superpoisons were no longer the exception but the rule. For example, one of the world's most astute leaders, Prime Minister Lee Kuan Yew of Singapore, told a visitor in January 1980—one month after the Soviet invasion of Afghanistan—that the Russian generals would not put up with resistance from the Moslem guerrillas, but would "use gas and bacteria." The Russians did not use bacteria, so far as anyone knows, but did employ gas and biotoxins. If the Singapore prime minister was able to read the signs, presumably so were the Chinese leaders in Peking. There was no reason for the Chinese to be surprised when the Vietnamese used chemicals. All levels of the People's Liberation Army had chemical warfare defense units attached. So if the chemicals used against them were familiar first- and second-generation agents such as mustard or nerve gas, it would be a relatively simple matter to bring up antidotes and distribute protective garments and masks.

There was no earthly reason, the *Review* editor claimed, for the PLA to be caught flat-footed, get hit badly, lose a whole battalion, then have to turn tail in a humiliating fashion and withdraw to the relative safety of the border. If twenty men from one single commune had been killed by gas, meaning an entire platoon, how many dead were there from all the other communes fighting inside Vietnam—five hundred, a thousand? I had been given educated guesses of 1,200 Chinese dead, and a senior commander was said to have been blinded. The report of an entire battalion, therefore, was not farfetched. But it was astounding. Especially since the Chinese apparently had been hit by chemicals by the Soviets ten years earlier on the Sino-Soviet border, and had a whole decade since then to work up proper defensive measures for their front-line troops.

The editor was speaking of the bitter border clashes between Russian and Chinese soldiers along the Ussuri River, north of Vladivostok in Siberia, in 1969. Few details of those clashes had ever become known to the outside world. But among the provocative reports was one telling how Chinese troops had been completely immobilized by some mysterious Soviet chemical agent that knocked them out for a few hours and then had no serious side effects when they regained their senses. Nobody in 1969 had any idea what sort of agent could do something so extraordinary (although it now seems strikingly similar to the Blue-X incapacitant used in Afghanistan). There were also unconfirmed reports that Chinese soldiers along the Ussuri River had been killed by another Russian chemical agent, as powerful and fast acting as the nerve agents. John Erickson in Edinburgh seemed to give those reports a good deal of credence.

It was only a matter of weeks after the 1969 border clashes with the Russians that China began building an elaborate defensive system of caves. Tunnels were dug under all the major cities of China, including Peking, Dairen, Mukden, and Huhehot—all of these in the strategic northeast and ranging from Inner Mongolia to Manchuria, the area under most serious threat. Similar, smaller tunnel systems were dug under small cities, towns, and villages, and even under isolated farming communities. The Chinese leadership at the time exhorted the people to "heighten our vigilance, strengthen education for defense against nuclear attack, mobilize the masses to dig tunnels deep, store grain everywhere, and make adequate preparation against such an attack."

The Chinese tunnels provide a remarkable example of a country trying to protect its civilian population against not only nuclear war but chemical and biological attack from the Soviet Union. Elsewhere, only in Sweden has the threat of chemical warfare inspired such extraordinary civil defense measures. But in scale if not in sophistication, the Chinese caves put the Swedes to shame.

Senior American military intelligence experts specializing in Soviet analysis told me that they believe it is the threat of China that has spurred Russia's drive in chemical warfare.

"China is the one place where conventional weapons—even nuclear weapons—will not suffice," one of them said. "In a war with China, the Soviets could throw everything they had available, including stones from Red Square, and there would still be hundreds of thousands of Chinese survivors who would not stop fighting until they had crossed the Urals and pushed the Russians into the Baltic. That is what scares hell out of the Russians. They have been invaded by Mongol hordes before, practically on the doorstep in European Russia, and they never stop fearing that it will happen again. It is not sufficient for the Soviets to bomb the big Chinese cities and the industrial areas in the east, and to hit the scattered military and scientific complexes in the western mountains and deserts. There are tremendous distances in between that are packed with Chinese. Many of them would survive the fallout. So the Soviets need lethal chemical agents on a massive scale to fill the space between the nukes and complete the job. Any war between Russia and China, is going to involve chemicals on a vast scale—probably biologicals as well—even if it stops short of nuclear weapons."

To the Russians, the threat of China may seem very real. It is so well established that Western strategists periodically raise the prospect as a device to take Soviet pressure off Europe. One recent example was when the Soviets seemed poised to invade Poland at the end of March 1981. Secretary of Defense Caspar Weinberger announced that if such a Soviet invasion took place, the United States would respond by offering to sell military hardware to China. Possibly this unusual public statement had something to do with the abrupt reduction in Soviet military pressure on Poland in the days immediately following.

To me the idea that China is a serious military threat to the Soviet Union is ridiculous. The Kremlin only uses the prospect to scare Russians with the Yellow Peril. The real value to the Politburo is that the imaginary threat of China justifies massing Soviet troops on the Chinese border, and could also justify a preemptive strike on Peking. The Chinese are more of an embarrassment to Russia than a military threat, particularly a political embarrassment within the world Communist movement. China has a gift for vitriolic propaganda—typified by such celebrated phrases as "running dog of the capitalist-imperialist warmongers, fascist bandits and insects"—and nobody else routinely speaks to Moscow that way. If Weinberger's warning worked, it did so not because arming China would increase its military threat to the Soviets, but because Peking would never let Moscow forget it.

Although the threat may be political rather than military, there is no issue more basic to Soviet strategy than its vulnerability to China. The Sino-Soviet fracture was probably the most significant single event in the Communist movement since the October Revolution. Following that historic split, China has posed a challenge to Moscow's authority that jeopardizes the security of the entire Soviet Asian domain east of the Urals. Since 1968, as a result, Moscow has steadily increased its armed forces in the Far East, with major garrisons stretching from the Afghan-Tibetan border, along the western deserts of China's Sinkiang Province, across Outer Mongolia to Manchuria and North Korea.

Hand in hand with this constant upgrading along the Sino-Soviet land border has come a diplomatic effort to isolate China by disrupting Sino-Japanese negotiations, provoking Vietnamese belligerence and expansion in Indochina, undermining Chinese initiatives in Burma, supporting anti-Chinese politicians in India, and most recently invading Afghanistan—which provides a corridor reaching nearly to the Indian Ocean.

If these moves seem Byzantine in the extreme, they are nonetheless typically Russian. John Erickson sees this encircling effort, accompanied by the expansion of Soviet naval forces in the Indian Ocean and the western Pacific, as a way of turning the long-standing strategic encirclement of the Soviet Union into a strategic encirclement of China.

As the Soviet military pressure has increased, China has shown genuine alarm, of which the cave system is just one of the more dramatic evidences. As a civil defense network to house millions of people, it is unique in history. A visit to the caves has become something of a must for travelers to China. Peoples' cadres seem to take great pleasure in showing them off.

Most famous of the cave networks is the one off Ta Sha Lane in Peking. It lies just outside the old city wall, near Tien An Men Square, in the old merchant quarter among two movie theaters and an opera house. There are thousands of narrow alleys in Peking, and of them all this is the busiest, with more than ten thousand shoppers and workers milling around at any one time. There are about forty-five stores in the lane. One of the larger department stores occupies an old theater. Foreign visitors are usually taken to a particular clothing store specializing in padded clothes. There the clerk obligingly slides a hand behind a wall calendar above a display case and presses a hidden button. A section of pink tiled floor moves away to reveal a subterranean passage. Visitors are led down a spiral staircase of thirty-five steps, a distance of twenty-six feet beneath the city, where a brightly lit tunnel begins. It is narrow at first, but quickly widens to enable four people to walk abreast. The walls are brick up to shoulder height. Overhead, there is a whitewashed arched ceiling of reinforced concrete. Chinese martial music plays softly from loudspeakers spaced throughout the tunnels. These speakers, in an emergency, would issue instructions on where to go through the tunnels. The labyrinth links up to others beneath Peking, forming a network many kilometers long. It is linked, also, to the new Peking subway system.

According to Chinese officials, every factory, school, apartment building, restaurant, government office, and shop has hidden access to the tunnels below. They state flatly that 80 percent of the population of the Chinese capital could be safely inside the tunnels within six minutes. There are roughly 8 million people in Peking, so more that 6½ million souls would fit into these tunnels at one time, if the official statement is accurate, as it may well be.

The tunnels are intended not to house those people indefinitely but to give them a safe means of passage to the countryside outside Peking. Presumably, in the event of a nuclear attack, those citizens not melted by a direct hit could escape radiation and blast by being inside the tunnels, at least those deep enough and far enough from each nuclear crater. This might allow a portion of Peking's population to survive and take up the fight.

In anything short of nuclear attack—say, a massive air assault with chemicals and biologicals—an even larger percentage might escape direct toxic effects and reach the clean air outside Peking because the shallow tunnels would not be caved in by blast. The tunnels would not be secure against gas penetration by saboteurs or enemy troops, but in the early stages of a Soviet attack on Peking the chemicals would probably be delivered in windborne clouds and in air-bursting and ground-bursting munitions. While a few saboteurs might be effective in releasing toxic agents into the cave networks, the ubiquitous cadres of the Ministry of Public Security, and the general vigilance of the Chinese, might be successful in reducing sabotage to a minimum.

It is difficult to imagine how the tunnels could accommodate so many millions without panic causing a disaster. During World War II, panicky Chinese crowds jamming Jing Bow air-raid tunnels trampled untold thousands. But the Chinese today are better disciplined.

Chinese officials say that special care has been taken to acquaint everybody in Peking with his or her particular entrance at home and at work, and with routines to be observed inside the tunnels to avoid panic and stampede.

Realistically, the Chinese admit that the tunnel system is not foolproof, and that it is not far enough below ground to provide real security from nuclear attack, but the object is only to assure survival of a portion of the population. China's greatest deterrent, they argue, is its long-established ability to fight on and on in a peasant guerrilla war of murderous attrition. So the prospect of tens of thousands of Chinese, perhaps up to a hundred million survivors, determined to exact vengeance and retaliate however possible must serve to remind Moscow that any attack on China must be absolutely thorough. Continual improvements are being made to the tunnel networks, and filtration units are being developed to remove chemical, biological, and radiological contamination from air supplies, apparently along the same lines employed by the West German navy in recent years to make its ships secure.

Similar tunnel complexes exist beneath the major cities of Shanghai, Tientsin, and Canton, but it is in the northeast—close to the Soviet border—that they have reached their greatest refinement. There, at depths of forty feet and more, the tunnels under Dairen in Manchuria, for example, include barbershops, small hospital clinics fully stocked with medicines, classrooms, cultural clubrooms, day-care centers, post offices, and bookstores. There are five systems in Dairen, all linked together, among them the City Zoo network, the March 8 network, the East Mountain network, and the Victory Bridge network, totaling more than eight miles within the city before they branch out into the countryside. More than 80,000 people from Dairen's population of 1,400,000 could be accommodated—or well over half the city. In the adjacent countryside, the tunnels are even bigger to accommodate the arrival of great throngs of city dwellers; some are big enough for trucks and buses to drive through, others contain small factories, with dormitories for workers, dining halls, schools—everything that would be needed to sustain life and continue production, albeit on a reduced scale.

Dairen is only 800 miles from the Soviet border—a short distance by Chinese standards— and just across the water from Pyongyang, North Korea. So Dairen feels more threatened than the rest of China. It was in March 1969 that bitter fighting with Soviet army units broke out north of Dairen on the island called Chen Pao in the Ussuri River, which forms the north-south border of Manchuria with Siberia.

"The social imperialists waged an aggressive attack against us on the island," said a Chinese official, "and they continue to threaten us. Chairman Mao urged us at the time to 'dig tunnels deep, store grain everywhere, and never seek hegemony.' That is why we worked day and night for 300,000 workdays to complete these tunnels. The tunnels safeguard China and socialist construction. We believe that the Russians are prepared to launch a surprise attack as soon as they see us weaken our resolve."

Construction began only three months after the Ussuri River battles, and continued through 1970 and 1971 in Dairen, and also at Harbin to the north and at Huhehot in Inner Mongolia, a major urban center near the 4,000-mile-long Sino-Soviet frontier. The networks under Peking, Shanghai, and other cities were being constructed at the same time.

Soviet forces stationed along the Sino-Soviet border are equipped to carry out the most advanced nuclear, chemical, and conventional operations against China. Although China has developed a respectable nuclear force of its own, including proven missile delivery systems, it could inflict only relatively minor damage compared with the far more versatile and accurate Soviet nuclear capability. But once the two sides had expended their nuclear weapons on each other, the nature of their conflict would change radically due to the sheer numbers of Chinese into what Harrison Salisbury has called "battle at a range of two hundred meters."

For these and other reasons, Moscow is not likely to wage war with China along a broad front and bog itself down in the northern steppes or western deserts. The most likely Kremlin strategy, according to a number of Western military analysts, is a sudden attack on northeastern China, focusing on Peking and intended to destroy the anti-Soviet government there quickly and replace it with a pro-Soviet junta that would incorporate a few recognizable Chinese figureheads. Such pro-Soviet substitute juntas have been assembled repeatedly by the Kremlin since it began bickering with Mao Tse-tung over the orientation of the Chinese Communist party in the twenties and thirties.

Pro-Moscow factions have not fared well in China, but it was assumed that this would change after Mao's death. Many analysts believed that the reemergence of Teng Hsiao-ping in the leadership after Mao's death, at the same time that the radical Gang of Four was being purged, meant that China's relations with the Soviet Union would improve. Teng is certainly a pragmatist, and in the past was closely linked in the Chinese Politburo and Secretariat with men who were purged for being too pro-Moscow. But the analysts were wrong. Once in control of China, Teng became the personification of China's independence from Soviet interference. As early as 1977, in fact, Teng told the Japanese that the Sino-Soviet alliance was a dead issue. Sino-Soviet tensions sharply increased through 1979 to 1981.

If the Chinese premier falters or if he is replaced by leaders who are less adept, some analysts believe there could be a sudden and overwhelming Soviet strike on Peking.

Most of China's population is in the northeast. So are most of the roads, rails, inland waterways, fuel and power production centers, major agricultural and mineral regions, and industry. The analysts predict an attack by Soviet armor across Manchuria and Mongolia, accompanied by a blanket of lethal chemical agents. Such an attack would be most effective between October and March, the months of the year when northeastern China is subject to polar outbreaks of cold air masses sweeping down from Siberia. In his book *Tomorrow's Weapons,* published in 1964, Brig. Gen. J. H. Rothschild, one of the successors to Amos Fries as head of the U.S. Army Chemical Corps, theorized that this polar outbreak would be the best moment to hit China with anthrax spores. The basic premise applies even better to a Soviet attack on China with biotoxins, since the winds serve the Soviets better from launch sites in Siberia, and since biotoxins— unlike the microbes that secrete them—cannot reproduce and through contagion spread back to the Soviet Union.

Chinese regional military districts would be prevented from going to the aid of Peking by quick Soviet air-mobile strikes all around the Sino-Soviet perimeter, again accompanied by superpoisons.

For the time being, the Soviets have the upper hand in terms of well-equipped military forces. Nearly one-third of the Red Army is based on the borders of China. There are a total of forty-three Soviet divisions in the Far East, compared with only thirty-one divisions facing NATO in central and Eastern Europe. Sixty-three divisions scattered between the Baltic and the Volga; six divisions in the steppes; twenty-three divisions in the south (including the four in

Afghanistan). This means that the largest force faces China. Of the Soviet units along the Chinese border, two divisions are based in Mongolia, only a short distance by air from Peking.

The number of Soviet divisions threatening China has increased from only eleven in 1968 to nineteen in 1974 and forty-three in 1981, an ominous sign.

China claims that the total number of Soviet troops facing her is more than one million. A more realistic figure may be around 800,000. And the Soviet forces have SS-12 tactical nuclear missiles and roughly 1,400 aircraft, including advanced MIG-23 and MIG-25 jet fighter-bombers.

The Soviet SS-4 intermediate-range ballistic missiles and SS-9 intercontinental ballistic missiles based in Mongolia, Siberia, and central Asia can easily reach all of China's strategic targets. The number of these missiles loaded with chemical warheads is not known, but if upward of 50 percent of Soviet missiles in the Warsaw Pact region are chemical loads, it may be presumed that a similar percentage of the missiles facing China—perhaps even more—contain superpoisons. There are also incalculable numbers of Stalin organ multiple rocket launchers along the border that can produce immense blankets of lethal chemicals in seconds.

It is the size of this force and the sophistication of its equipment that make it, for the time being, so vastly superior to the Chinese forces. The People's Liberation Army weapons and equipment are "obsolescent or obsolete" in Pentagon vernacular. China is, in general, about twenty years behind the Soviet Union in military technology.

On the surface, the PLA seems to be a gigantic standing army. There are fifty-five divisions in the Manchuria and Peking military regions; twenty-five divisions in the Tsinan, Anking, and Foochow regions; twenty-one divisions in the Canton and Wuhan regions; fifteen divisions in the Lanchow region; and twenty-six divisions in the western Sinkiang, Chengtu, and Kunming regions. These figures are impressive, but manpower—which would prove decisive in the long run—is not sufficient to turn the Soviets away in the opening stages. In aircraft the Chinese must make do with underpowered and outdated MIG-19s, MIG-21s, and TU-16s. The Chinese have succeeded in "borrowing" an advanced Soviet MIG-23 from Egypt, following Egypt's split with the Soviet Union, and apparently were successful in cloning it. Recent Chinese efforts to purchase British or American jet engines support the belief that the Chinese will shortly introduce their own version of the MIG-23. A nuclear missile program is in advanced stages, and the Chinese satellite program has had impressive achievements, but the numbers of CSS-1 medium-range nuclear missiles, and CSS-3 and CSS-4 ICBMs, are still insignificant compared to the Soviet arsenal.

This lag means that the Chinese army, despite its size, remains in the first rank of the second rate. A crash program to upgrade the PLA's equipment has years to go before it can balance the sleek, well-oiled Soviet machine. Someday it will, and that obviously worries Moscow, as evidenced by the impact of Caspar Weinberger's threat to arm China with American weapons.

Arming China would reduce the threat of a Soviet invasion while not seriously threatening the Soviets in reverse with a Chinese invasion. It is the reduction of the Soviet threat that bothers Moscow. The situation now is very much in Moscow's favor, and the Kremlin would like to keep it that way while the Chinese sweat through the political perils of the next few years. The elaborate system of tunnels in China may seem to offer a crude yet effective deterrent—but in the end they are only dramatic. They can hardly be decisive in a crisis, when the change of government may be settled before the people in the caves reach the far exits.

The United States, as always uncertain of its policy toward China, and dawdling over the fool's issue of binary weapons, would find itself powerless to interfere.

12.

The Sorcerer's Apprentices

In the early mist of an April morning, the Cleveland Park section of Washington, D.C. sleeps in a fragrant cushion of spring blooms—great yellow clouds of forsythia, white dogwood, pink cherry trees, and fuschia azaleas. The massive stone Gothic towers of the Washington Cathedral rise above the foliage into a clear blue sky. At the foot of the cathedral hill, near the intersection of elegant Woodley Road and upwardly mobile Reno Road, a small mint green brick house stands behind a magnolia and a dogwood. Here, at 3305 Woodley Road, with the cathedral ramparts above it on one side and the wooded estate of the Nationalist Chinese embassy residence only a few hundred feet away on the other, is where Maj. Gen. Amos Fries lived out his final years, surrounded by everything that he believed in. The Chemical Corps that he had fought hard for had gone through World War II virtually unused, but always at hand. Although it was Adolf Hitler's personal revulsion for poison gas, as much as anything else, that kept Germany from using its new nerve gases to save the falling reich, the constant readiness of the British and American chemical corps, and their secret research projects, did much to convince the German general staff and Hitler that the Allies also had nerve gas and were prepared to use it on Germany in retaliation. So although Amos Fries retired from the military before the war began, the Chemical Corps did fulfill much of the role Fries had claimed it would.

In the 1980s the ghost of Amos Fries had returned to haunt Washington again. One decade after President Nixon banned biological weapons and renounced the first use of lethal or incapacitating chemical weapons, America was wondering whether it had made a serious mistake. In the midst of a fit of guilt over the Vietnam War, had the executive branch gone too far and left the nation vulnerable to new advances in chemical warfare by the Soviet Union? Was it time to rescue and revitalize the Chemical Corps and the American arsenal of chemical weapons—time for a fresh infusion of hundreds of millions of dollars to produce the newest chemical munitions—the binaries—and scrap the old, leaky stockpile? Was Amos Fries right all along?

Right or wrong, Congress was preparing to make a decision that would affect the rest of the century.

Senators and representatives were lining up to hold hearings: on the poisoning of the Hmong hill people in Laos; on Russia's chemical war against the Mujahideen in Afghanistan; on appropriations for the destruction of America's old nerve gas stocks and on the manufacture of new U.S. nerve gas munitions; on whether the Soviets had violated international treaties with secret biological poison production at Sverdlovsk in the Urals; and on U.S. and NATO military preparedness to meet and counter any Soviet or Warsaw Pact chemical attack.

Staff members in the congressional office buildings were busy marshaling resources, gathering potential witnesses, and locating scientists to provide expert testimony in favor or against column A and column B—or all of the above.

At the Library of Congress, an acned gnome in a carpeted alcove prepared a briefing paper summarizing the main arguments surrounding the new binary nerve gas munitions, so that members of Congress would know what they were talking about when they voted, without having to do any heavy reading.

At the White House, the new Reagan administration was committed to renovating American defenses and restoring an Early American bellicosity. At the State Department, there was considerable excitement among the political and military analysts. During the four years of the vacillating Carter administration, under the stewardship of Secretary of State Cyrus Vance, a brilliant negotiator, resolving all problems by peaceful negotiation became an ideal that all officers of the State Department were supposed to live by; unpleasant information that contradicted this act of faith was suppressed by Vance's lieutenants through misguided zeal. Analysts who had persuasive reports of poison gas could get nobody to believe them. Under the new Reagan administration, with Alexander Haig as secretary of state, there was a sense of exhilaration that the truth would at last come out, whatever that might be. The main concern at lower levels of the foreign service was that the new Congress and the new administration might overdo it, and commit the nation to an excess as gross as the error it was intended to correct.

At the Pentagon, the binary campaign was being mapped out with the sort of sexual excitement aroused by the sight of an open purse. The offices of the assistant secretary of defense for research and development and the assistant secretary of the army for research and development, which would midwife the new chemical munitions if they got through Congress, were busy planning new gas masks, new antidote kits, new laser chemical detection systems—a *Star Wars* generation of paraphernalia for the well-dressed chemical soldier.

Washington was, in effect, being told that the nation was under new management, that the new management was alarmed at the lead taken in chemical warfare by Moscow since the Nixon unilateral ban of 1969, and that the whole American chemical warfare capacity was going to be rebuilt with new defensive equipment and new offensive binary weapons. The word *binary* hit town like *disco,* and stayed. No longer was America going to use *nerve gas,* it was going to use *binaries.* Binaries were *safe.* Binaries were beautiful. Bumper stickers said so.

But were binaries really the answer to the Soviet threat? Were they really safe—and did it mean anything, really, to make the chemical arsenal "safe"? For example, did making it "safe" also mean that it would be sensible, desirable, useful—after decades of being none of those things? Would binaries be acceptable to the NATO allies for storage in their countries, when they had refused to store America's ordinary nerve gas? And if the NATO allies still did not want chemical weapons even in "safe" binary form, what was the point of making binaries? What use would they be to counter a Soviet threat in Europe if they had to remain in Colorado? America had never needed to use its mustard gas stocks against Japan or Germany even in the worst crunches of the war; why assume that after thirty years of not using nerve gas on the Soviets it would make any difference to Moscow whether that nerve gas was in the old unitary form or the new binary form? It was still basically unthreatening unless it could be deployed. Finally, what use were nerve agents when the Soviets were deploying biological poisons and making tactical use of them in several different parts of the world right under our noses? Could it be that binary nerve gas was a dinosaur? Was Congress simply missing the whole point?

It was not entirely balderdash. In autumn 1980, just before the presidential elections measured the mood of the country, the sober Defense Science Board headed by MIT chemist John Deutch reviewed the prospects for chemical warfare and the capability of the United States to wage it. The panel concluded that there was a serious threat, there was indeed a Soviet offensive ability that America needed to respond to, and that America also needed a chemical retaliatory capability to throw onto the scales if the balance of power was to be tipped in favor of any truly effective arms-control agreement.

The panel decided that the existing American nuclear and conventional warfare capability, staggering as it is, was unsuitable as a direct counter to a chemical attack—a question of matching apples with oranges. To counter a poison gas attack by Soviet and Warsaw Pact troops, the panel concluded, the United States needed sufficient operational chemical weapons to threaten Communist air bases, port facilities, and other support operations, and force the enemy soldiers into their cumbersome protective gear.

In order to carry out this reconstruction of American chemical weapons, the panel recommended that Washington "demilitarize" the existing, geriatric stockpile of wet-loaded (premixed) nerve gas munitions, replace a portion of them with new binary weapons, and introduce immediate improvements in protective measures and troop training. The Deutch panel took exception to critics who feel that binaries would jeopardize years of effort to reach an agreement with Moscow banning all chemical weapons. To the contrary, the panel decided that the threat posed by America arming with binaries might prove just the catalyst necessary to press Moscow into agreeing to such a ban.

Ironically, the proposal to make nerve gas weapons safe to handle by keeping their deadly chemical components separated inside a two-part or "binary" weapon, was first recommended in 1949, before the United States had any significant stocks of nerve gas. The Muscle Shoals plant to produce dichlor was not completed until 1953. The Rocky Mountain Arsenal nerve gas plant was not completed until 1952. The Newport, Indiana, plant to produce VX was not completed until 1961. Therefore, nothing prevented the government from adopting binaries at the very beginning to take advantage of the built-in safety factor, except for the numerous drawbacks inherent to the binary weapons during combat—limitations such as trajectory control—which seemed very serious at the time.

Advanced research on binaries was already under way by 1954 at Edgewood Arsenal. Six years passed, during which twenty thousand tons of nerve agents were produced, seven thousand tons of which were immediately loaded into weapons. None of these filled munitions, unfortunately, were binaries. They were all filled with active, premixed agent. Any leaks, any spills, any accidents, and there would be serious trouble.

The binary technology could have been adopted with only minor additional testing. In 1960, the navy gave the binary program a major boost when the admirals decided that they needed a safer way to store lethal chemical weapons aboard ship. By keeping the chemical components separated until fired or dropped, safety could be achieved. So a binary VX bomb called the BIGEYE was developed —the binary version of the existing premixed bomb called the WETEYE. The BIGEYE went into advanced development in 1966, followed the next year by an army 155-millimeter artillery projectile to contain two components of sarin. But Congress continually refused to provide the funds to take these binary weapons beyond the drawing board.

The binary 155-millimeter artillery projectile worked by mixing its two components during flight. The nose of the round contained a fuse and a burster charge. Behind the burster was a canister containing difluor (methylphosphonyldifluoride). Behind the canister of difluor was a second canister filled with liquid isopropanol, a solution much like rubbing alcohol. When the artillery round was fired, the force of inertia would thrust the liquid difluor backward, bursting through the thin plastic wall of the canisters to mix with the alcohol. The spin imparted by the rifling inside the cannon barrel would cause the round to spin at 15,000 rpm, helping the two liquids mix rapidly (in about ten seconds). When the round struck its target, the burster would explode, spreading the flight-mixed GB nerve agent as a vapor.

A similar eight-inch artillery round designed for oily VX worked in the same fashion but with a canister in front filled with gooey dimethylpolysulfide and a canister at the rear filled with a substance called QL (ethyl 2-[diisopropylamino]ethylmethylphosphonite) to mix in flight.

In a bomb there would be no cannon thrust to mix the binary elements, so for the BIGEYE bomb the two parts of VX were to be mixed by the paddling motion of a stainless steel cylinder with blades mounted inside the bomb. Before the bomb was dropped, the pilot or crew member armed the bomb by starting its mixing process. The VX was stirred by a motor inside the bomb's tail, and in ten seconds was ready to be dropped.

The relative safety of the binary designs came from keeping the two chemical components separate until the weapon was used. So long as each component was handled separately, it was comparatively harmless. That is, difluor was about as harmless as strychnine poison, and the QL component of VX nerve agent caused nausea, difficulty in breathing, and skin rash. But compared to mixed GB and VX nerve agents, they were relatively harmless.

The difluor was to be produced at Pine Bluff Arsenal in Arkansas from commercially available methyl phosphonic dichloro, and the alcohol component would be purchased directly from private industry. The difluor cartridge would then be kept inside the weapon, and moved around with it to storage depot or firing point. The alcohol cartridge would be sent separately to storage or firing point. The trouble then was that Congress was willing to provide research and development funds to study binaries, but no production funds to build them while there were already some 3,000,000 GB and VX nerve gas artillery projectiles, land mines, and aerial bombs of the old-fashioned premixed type in the stockpile.

Before 1969, binaries were so secret that the word does not even appear in sanitized transcripts of closed-door hearings by the congressional armed services committees until that year. So only a few members of Congress—those on the various armed services committees in particular—were in a position to be well informed about the advantages of binaries and the deteriorating condition of the existing arsenal. This small group of senators and representatives understood better than anyone else what was behind the public furor that led to the Nixon ban, and it was this same group of congressional watch-dogs who were responsible to follow through on the ban and make certain that the leaky stocks were disposed of as promised. For reasons best known to them, they did not follow through. The old stocks were not destroyed. And nobody was the wiser. Horror stories continued to come out, with the army eventually admitting to an astonishing 955 nerve gas leaks, which had caused some army personnel to suffer what it chose to describe as "mild symptoms" of poisoning. The army said one reason it was not disposing of the obsolete stocks more rapidly was that having to file environmental impact statements was a burden!

The simple truth is that the old premixed nerve agent weapons were never designed to be demilitarized in the first place. During the late 1950s and early 1960s, there had been such a mad dash to produce nerve agents and fill the munitions that nobody responsible even stopped to consider the possibility that all those millions of bombs, rockets, land mines, and artillery rounds might someday have to be uncorked and emptied out.

One former soldier who was trained to take a dummy M-34 cluster bomb of GB apart described the device as being "built like a Swiss watch." Inside were seventy-six individual bomblets. The main fuse could be removed without much difficulty, but the bomb-lets themselves were held together by a wire that must not be broken or tripped. Since the M-34 bombs were by that time already ten to twenty years old, and filled with highly corrosive nerve agents, the components were not in the very best condition. Furthermore, the bomblets never fit snugly into the bomb casing to start with, so the army filled the gaps with rubber balls. *These* had long since disintegrated, and the M-34s stocked at Rocky Mountain Arsenal were said to rattle like a brown bag of empty beer bottles when they were moved or shaken. It was perhaps understandable that the people of Denver wondered not only why these decrepit weapons were stored at the end of their airport but why in fact they existed at all.

To say that the army suffered serious embarrassment during the public furor over chemical weapons in the late sixties is to drop only one shoe. After the Nixon ban, the Chemical Corps seemed to vanish from sight, as if it had been ordered to go underground. Many people, in fact, thought the corps had ceased to exist.

The other shoe was dropped by the Soviet Union. It is incomprehensible that the Soviets, with the U.S. Chemical Corps seemingly in a cleft stick—in hiding, as it were, after the Nixon ban—would forfeit this advantage by parading the growing Russian superiority in chemical weapons. Such showing off would only provoke a predictable reaction in Washington. Yet the Soviet equipment provided to Egypt on the eve of the 1973 Arab-Israeli War was loaded with the most advanced chemical equipment ever seen. The discovery of this equipment on tanks and other Soviet weapons captured by Israel during that war caused the anticipatable anxieties at the Pentagon.

The Defense Department immediately began pushing for binaries again, harder than ever, as well as for new funds to refurbish America's existing chemical arsenal. Congress was clearly moved by the Pentagon's hand wringing, and the evidence of significant Soviet headway, and voted $25 million to clean up the old stockpile.

Congress also began funding new research and development projects in chemical weapons and defensive systems, at a higher and higher rate each year. For the first time since the ban, the race was on again. This time, the bad publicity of Agent Orange was forgotten, the Dugway sheep kill was ignored. When the deterioration of old nerve gas weapons was mentioned, it was only to demonstrate how much the nation needed binaries.

Spending for chemical warfare research rose to $29 million in 1976, and to $106 million for fiscal 1981. That figure increases to $280 million if you include defensive equipment, training, weapons storage, biological defense research, smoke, flame, and incendiary supplies (traditional elements of the Chemical Corps). Among the acquisitions are new electrochemical poison gas detectors, new protective garments for troops, and improved gas masks. Defense contracts worth $10 million were awarded to suppliers of the new M-51 chemical shelter for use on the battlefield. The army set up a chemical warfare training school at Fort McClellan, Arkansas, and on April 15, 1981, announced that troops brought to Fort McClellan would be given full-dress exposure to live lethal agents to condition them for the seriousness of exposure in combat—a training method long in practice in the Soviet Union but never before attempted in America.

The U.S. Air Force completed its first-phase program in Europe, which included providing protective ensembles for every single one of its personnel on the Continent, at a cost of $12 million, and began phase two, in which second suits will be deployed so pilots can change and get back into the air.

Clearly, there was a perceptible ground swell taking shape.

Nobody puts the argument against binaries better than Dr. Julian Perry Robinson of the University of Sussex near Brighton, on the south coast of England. The modern buildings of the college nestle among the plump green buttocks of hills just a mile or so from the ocean. In a new building that houses SPRU (Science Policy Research Unit), I found Dr. Perry Robinson looking much as he must have as a student at Cambridge and Harvard years ago, as if he had just stepped through a time warp—a boyish, long-limbed fellow in rumpled khakis and white oxford shirt rolled up at the sleeves and open at the throat. He was a bit preoccupied at first because some colleague had apparently made off with his card files—an extraordinary archive of man's folly with chemical potions. But after some hours of discussion in his small, cluttered office about Laos and Afghanistan, as the light outside faded we adjourned to a mellow, nearly empty pub in Brighton for bitter.

"In the historical record of U.S. and Soviet CW programmes since World War II," Perry Robinson argues, "there is clear evidence that the programs of one side have driven, at least in part, those of the other, so that at any given moment one side will perceive actual or incipient superiority in the other's programs. Since 1969, when President Nixon reversed the Eisenhower CW policy, there has been no further U.S. chemical-weapons procurement. This is being contested with increasing vehemence by some sectors of the U.S. military establishment on the grounds that it precludes necessary modernization. This is an argument which tends to create belief that the existing stockpile is becoming useless. It would be highly dangerous if a cycle in the opposite direction were now to be set in motion again. The chemical arms limitation talks in Geneva, which are proceeding in both a U.S.-Soviet working group and within the forty-nation U.N. Committee on Disarmament, provide what is probably the only available channel of communication for resolving such uncertainties. The first priority for the West in its policy making on chemical warfare must therefore be to keep this channel open."

In another small, crowded office, in the rabbit warren of the Arms Control and Disarmament Agency (ACDA) in Washington, Dr. Robert Mikulak puts it this way: "To push ahead with binaries now would not help us to reach an effective chemical weapons agreement. Quite the opposite, in fact; one result might well be to revive pressures for an immediate and poorly verified prohibition."

Effective ways simply have not yet been found to determine whether a nation is secretly producing organophosphorous nerve agents. Most countries consider adequate verification to be imperative before a treaty could work. Various methods have been proposed, including economic monitoring of phosphorous purchases, for example, or satellite observation, or analysis of atmospheric effluents and liquid and solid waste samples downstream from suspicious factories, and so forth. Not one has yet seemed reliable, and the Soviet Union adamantly opposes on-site inspection, while paying lip service to the idea of it.

Advocates of a treaty insist that the fact that the Soviets have been engaged in chemical negotiations since July 1977 proves their sincerity. Just the opposite, say others.

Amoretta Hoeber, a defense analyst and the deputy assistant secretary of the army for research and development, believes that Soviet participation in the talks is a ruse designed to keep American hopes up and thereby block any new weapons build-up. "Allowing a potential treaty which is merely under discussion to determine the U.S. posture at this stage makes a travesty of the arms-control negotiation process," she argues.

Even if a treaty banning chemical weapons was magically negotiated overnight, the Pentagon claims, it would take years to conclude the details, and after its entry into force another ten years would be needed to destroy existing stockpiles. So it would be the late 1990s before the chemical arsenals of the signatory states would be eliminated and cease to pose a threat.

In the opinion of the Deutch panel, the United States urgently needs to do something to protect itself and its allies against chemical attack because the Soviet advantage is a serious offensive threat. And if the Soviets are merely playing America along at the negotiating table, the only thing that would prod them to genuine action on a treaty would be the prospect of America rearming with chemical weapons.

"We have not produced a chemical munition in over a decade," argued one of the chief binary proponents in the House of Representatives, Congressman Richard Ichord, in a Capitol Hill office festooned with the bric-a-brac, memorabilia, guns, and signed photographs from a lifetime spent close to the Pentagon brass. "By 1990 we will no longer possess any militarily usable weapons. Our response to this deplorable state of preparedness has been one of moralistic hand wringing and neglect. The army has for the past five years attempted to obtain the necessary preproduction and facilitization money to establish a binary chemical production facility at Pine Bluff Arsenal. In 1975 the Congress denied their request in a highly emotional response against 'bugs and gas.' Subsequent army efforts have been thwarted in the executive branch. This year [1980] the army again asked for funding in its fiscal year 1981 budget request, and even with the backing of the Department of Defense it was ultimately directed to delete binary preproduction funding from its program. The Defense Department's inability to obtain approval is a result of the misplaced logic of the State Department and the arms-control community that to forgo plans will provide us with some ill-defined but significant psychological advantage over the Soviets."

Congressman Ichord loved to tell, with suitable expressions of horror, amazement, and disgust, about a congresswoman who happened to come into the august chamber while the House of Representatives was discussing whether or not to fund the binary factory at Pine Bluff. Not knowing what binaries were, she asked around and was given a hasty explanation. Then, snorts Ichord, she went about collaring as many of her congressional colleagues as she could, advising them that "a vote for binaries was a vote for nerve gas."

"I suppose that I speak from a common point of view," observed chemist Henry Eyring of the University of Utah, "when I say that we often fail, and are often devious, but there isn't any reason to think that, in a potential war, we are faced by people that are less devious than we are. And if we could establish that they are less devious, I would be overjoyed to get rid of all the weapons nobody likes."

On a similar note, a chemical warfare planner acknowledged: "Most forms of war are loathesome. But if we accept a willingness to fight under some circumstances, we must pick up weapons, and the weapons must be suitable for combating those of our adversary. No ban against chemical warfare will work because poison weapons are too effective, too easy to make and use, too simple to conceal before battle, and too easy to deny after wiping out some tribal village."

The last word, perhaps, belongs to columnist George F. Will, writing from the bullet-peppered woods of central Pennsylvania: "Gettysburg had an ordinance against the discharging of firearms."

It was in the House of Representatives that the ghost of Amos Fries scored its most significant gain—the very scene of combat where he waged gas warfare so effectively in the 1920s. For in the House, Amos Fries surely guided the hand of Congressman Ichord as the Missouri Democrat fought the battle of binaries and won against overwhelming odds. Thanks largely to this one legislator, binaries are on their way.

Ichord's battle began in a way strikingly similar to the debate over binaries in 1973. Then, the army announced plans to spend $200 million to produce binaries at Pine Bluff. The debate raged for nearly a year before the House, unmoved by the army's impassioned pleas, summarily struck the money from the Defense appropriations.

In 1980, the army again requested money for the binary plant. The Carter administration reviewed the request and then, like the House in 1974 and despite dire warnings from Ichord and others, dropped the funds. There it would have remained if 1980 had not also been Ichord's year to retire from Congress.

"He is determined to get this funding through before he retires," one of Ichord's staff members confided to me in the congressman's office in fall 1980. "It would be," he said, "a fitting climax to his career in Congress."

Indeed. Ichord was chairman of the Research and Development Subcommittee of the House Armed Services Committee, the kind of friend on Capitol Hill for whom generals put starch in their uniforms. Just how Ichord went about outmaneuvering Congress is an interesting lesson in democracy at work.

Quietly, and with none of the fanfare that had accompanied his earlier open pitch for binary funding, Ichord offered an amendment to the House Military Construction Appropriations Bill, while it was still in subcommittee. The amendment would provide $3.15 million for construction of the building at Pine Bluff—no production equipment, no chemicals, nothing at all except the building. And merely to *begin* construction of the building. But from small acorns great oak trees grow, as any congressman from Missouri can tell you.

Once the amendment was attached to the construction bill, the bill went before the full House Armed Service Committee, where

Ichord was a longtime dues-paying member. In debating the construction bill, the full committee never once even mentioned the Pine Bluff amendment. The bill was passed and went on to the full House.

The Pine Bluff amendment was only two paragraphs long, and it was buried amid such topics as the MX-missile-and-shell-game boondoggle and such other hot issues as the matter of developing U.S. military bases in the Middle East. Nobody on the floor of the House of Representatives even noticed a mere $3.15 million for a building at Pine Bluff.

It was approved without once being mentioned in debate. The date was June 27, 1980.

Over in the Senate, Virginia's redoubtable Senator Harry F. Byrd did not do half as well. Byrd offered a similar miniamendment to the Senate Military Construction Authorization Bill, and then later agreed to withdraw it in the face of heavy opposition. For the next three months, Byrd furiously rallied support.

In the House, meanwhile, Ichord was also busy. Was it not simply reasonable, he argued, that now that the House had agreed to build a building at Pine Bluff, to allow the army to purchase some equipment for that building, so it could serve a useful purpose? Specifically, $19 million worth of equipment. Not to produce binaries, mind you, because everybody knew that binaries could not be produced unless the president of the United States decided that they were in the national interest.

On September 16, 1980, the House—demonstrating either a lack of attention or that it had gone through a significant change of mood in recent months—approved the $19 million. In the Senate, its version of the Military Construction Authorization Bill approved earlier by the House came up for action the same day—and there, tucked in a corner, was Harry Byrd's minuscule Pine Bluff building amendment. After four hours of heated debate, the Senate approved the Pine Bluff factory by a vote of fifty-two to thirty-eight.

Ichord could retire satisfied.

He had succeeded where others had failed in setting the stage for binaries. The allocation included $10.6 million for the purchase of industrial plant equipment and $6.8 million to install it, half a million for other necessary gear and engineering support services, and $1.2 million for start-up and run-in costs. Plus the original $3.15 million for the building, and binaries were on their way.

The money would equip the Pine Bluff building to produce difluor from commercial dichlor, and provide an assembly line to manufacture the binary artillery rounds themselves. It was only the first phase of a four-phase seven-year construction program, beginning in 1981 and running through 1988. Phase two would expand the plant production capacity to 70,000 shells a month, at a price of $42 million yet to be funded. Phase three would add additional factories to make binary bombs like the BIGEYE and artillery rounds for binary filling with the deadlier VX, at a cost of an additional $100 million. Phase four would provide additional factories to produce new binary weapons (multiple-launch rockets, and so on) now in planning stages, probably by then incorporating binary versions of third-generation superpoisons. The cost for the final stage is therefore unpredictable, but estimates for the entire program run up to $4 billion.

Curiously enough, all this happened without anybody ever once field-testing a binary weapon to see if it really did what it was designed on paper to do. Simulation tests have been conducted, but no tests with real binary nerve agent components. Furthermore, according to the Pentagon, these simulation tests have been conducted entirely in a computer—not even with simulated chemicals in the open air. A field test wtih real binary nerve agents would require not only Environmental Protection Agency approval but probably direct presidential authorization as well, because of the disaster caused by the last known nerve agent field test at Dugway Proving Ground, which caused the notorious sheep kill in 1968. Recently there have been a large number of horses killed under suspicious circumstances in the same area at Dugway. This has raised questions about whether the army once again has been carelessly testing lethal agents there. Under the secretive circumstances, it is impossible yet to tell whether a Dugway test was involved, but it does not take a great leap of the imagination to connect the mysterious death of the horses at Dugway to open-air tests, and therefore to wonder whether there might be an association between the horses and the binaries. One would hope that the Pentagon can provide a more convincing denial than it was able to produce with the sheep kill in 1968—and which it was forced to repudiate the next year.

In any case, assuming that there is no connection whatever between binary field tests and the suspicious horse deaths at Dugway, if the binary weapons have not been open-air tested there is no legitimate way to be certain that they work as intended. One previous chemical warfare agent for which the army had great hopes, lewisite, was produced without field tests and proved to be a total failure. It turned out in practice that lewisite was unstable in the presence of moisture.

The lack of adequate open-air testing is contrary to established weapon standardization procedures. But with binary chemical loads, testing becomes a particularly sensitive issue. How liquid chemicals behave at rest is one thing; how they behave under violent inertial forces of artillery fire, high velocity, 15,000 rpm, and commensurate high temperatures, is known only in theory, from the ambiguous results of chemical loads fired in World War I, and by computer projection. It is understood, for example, that a liquid load will affect the ballistics of an artillery shell radically—just how much, we do not know without open-air tests. It is projected that reaction time between the GB binary elements of difluor and alcohol may take roughly ten seconds, dramatically restricting the distance that the round can be fired, because anything less than ten seconds would mean delivering a payload that was not yet completely blended, and anything more than ten seconds would mean that the payload was already decomposing into relatively harmless by-products.

To what extent this chemical mixing is reliable can be determined only by open-air testing. The mixing process is so tricky that volume for volume the binary weapon is nowhere near as potent as the premixed munition it replaces. Binaries, in order to be binaries, carry a necessarily smaller payload because of the space taken up by by-products and accessory chemicals and the incompleteness of the chemical reaction.

The failure to open-air-test before pushing the Pine Bluff funds through Congress indicates that the army has proceeded into political combat without making certain its weapon was loaded and clean.

Ironically, the binaries of GB and VX have properties that give away their presence and reduce the element of surprise so vital to poison attack. Ordinary nerve agents are virtually colorless and odorless, although tabun sometimes has a faint fruity scent, and soman—the principal Soviet nerve agent—has a slightly fruity or camphor scent. The VX binary will produce a strong sulfur smell because of one of the binary components, polysulfide. And GB or sarin in binary form will produce by-products that cause noticeable irritation. These side effects may be just enough to warn enemy troops in time for them to don masks and protective suits.

The newspaper horror stories that surround the painful development of the army's XM-1 supertank, the long-awaited M2 armored infantry vehicle, and the ill-fated Cheyenne attack helicopter can only make taxpayers wince at the prospect of binaries. Compared to all their conspicuous disadvantages, binaries offer only one significant advantage: relative safety. Without safety, the American public has shown an extraordinary fear and loathing for chemical weapons, especially nerve agents. So the public issue resolves itself to a simple equation. Make them safe or get rid of them. But is safety alone sufficient reason to adopt such a doubtful weapon? By making superpoisons safe to handle, do we not also make them easier to use, risk having them become the weapons of terrorists, and make them accessible to second-rate tyrants in countries otherwise unable to afford the complex manufacture of superpoisons?

The safety issue was fundamental to Ichord's campaign for binaries. Realizing that only safety would lower the level of public revulsion, Ichord wrote to Secretary of Defense Harold Brown: "It appears to me that the binaries should be sold on the basis that it is a safety program." Accordingly, Ichord argued that binaries would be safe to produce, safe to store, safe to handle, safe to transport, safe to fire, and safe politically when it came to storing the munitions in areas now denied to conventional premixed lethal chemical weapons.

But by making storage safe, reducing the fear of handling, the risk is increased that security may slacken and binaries may fall into the wrong hands. Terrorists would not have to steal a binary weapon. Once the technology became commonplace, and the chemical precursors began to be produced commercially for government purchase, there would be little to prevent a lunatic or a professional terrorist from assembling a crude version and using it to poison or terrorize whole communities. Even without the exact precursor chemicals, variations could be produced with related chemicals [malathion, parathion] from the pesticide industry. While it might be possible to monitor some suspicious sales of organophosphorous compounds in America, such controls could not easily or reliably be extended to other countries with a modest organophosphorous or pesticide industry. Most small countries already have the means to produce binaries. They are discouraged from doing so only by the assumed high cost and by the fear and apprehension inspired by nerve agents. The proliferation of binaries, like Saturday night specials in the case of firearms, is very real cause for alarm. What makes life easy for the U.S. Army is not necessarily good if it also makes life easy for Black September.

Already, in the case of Vietnam making grisly use of Soviet superpoisons in Laos and Cambodia, we have an example of what can occur in proliferation with nonbinary lethal chemicals. The potential for widespread use of binary nerve agents in local wars and international terrorism makes the prospect of the twenty-first century grim indeed. When you eliminate the need for stringent safety precautions, you put your fate into the hands of the sorcerer's apprentice. The danger posed by chemical weapons is a serious concern—eliminating that danger by making them "safe" is also a serious concern.

It would seem wise to establish beyond doubt that America's European allies—and more than one of them—would be willing to accept binaries on their soil.

"It wouldn't be much of an advantage to have them in Utah," cracked an arms-control expert. If the ground-fire artillery binaries remained in America, they would have to be flown to Europe in the event of a NATO war, precluding any value during the crucial opening hours of battle.

The Europeans are not likely to welcome binaries with open arms. In West Germany, where substantial United States stocks of mustard and nerve agent munitions have been stored for two decades, the Bonn government has repeatedly asked Washington to remove them and not replace them. So far, the Germans have been vocally opposed to playing host to binaries.

Shipping the binaries to Europe in the event of a NATO conflict could pose problems for the Pentagon. It would be interesting to see if one part of the binaries arrived in Germany while the other went to Italy.

As to military value in NATO, there is no doubt that the binaries would force the Soviet and Warsaw Pact troops into cumbersome protective gear. But for many years they have been trained exhaustively to that end—while American troops have not. Julian Perry Robinson observes that Soviet tanks and armored personnel carriers are equipped to roam around the battlefield even in the midst of clouds of GB and VX and do so routinely in training war games. The troops in these Soviet vehicles could therefore be killed or neutralized more efficiently with guided missiles or antitank weapons than with chemicals. In open areas, troops in protective ensembles moving through clouds of nerve agents could be killed easier with fragmentation cluster bombs—each the equivalent of 600 simultaneous mortar rounds.

In the end, making chemical weapons safe for soldiers to handle and fire does not make them any safer for civilians in or near the battlefield. We are no longer dealing with mere chlorine or phosgene but with instantly fatal agents that can cover hundreds of square miles, and can persist for weeks. Doubtless in the long run, if chemical warfare comes of age and becomes commonplace, as it seems destined to be, civilian populations everywhere will envy the farsighted Swedes and Swiss, and agree with the anxious Dutch, that in chemical warfare the best offense is a good defense. From that viewpoint the $4 billion for binaries would be better spent providing NATO civilian populations—to whom the threat of chemical attack is far more real than to Americans an ocean away—with the already-proven high-quality Swedish masks and British protective garments. After squandering $5 billion on the SAFEGUARD ABM program and $7 billion on the B-1 bomber, a mere $4 billion spent on gas masks for threatened allies might do much to endear Congress and the Pentagon to history and America to the world. After such a dramatic gesture, if a chemical attack never takes place, the masks will still be useful—given the rapid saturation of the world with carcinogenic industrial pollution—just to get to the grocery without developing brain cancer.

The proliferation of good, safe binaries helps bring that day even closer.

In summary, the majority of arguments in favor of binaries are vastly outweighed by the arguments against them. If it were not for the sobering threat posed by the new Soviet poison weapons, there would be no sane justification for maintaining a chemical retaliation arsenal in a polluted world, whether binary or unitary. But the Soviet capability is very real, and the casual manner in which these new superpoisons are being brandished, and the cynicism with which they have been used on remote villages, is enough to justify a certain amount of alarm. Relying on Moscow to demonstrate altruism of the highest order, and on Hanoi to exercise humanitarian self-restraint and compassion toward its enemies in Southeast Asia, is utter folly. Any country anxious to rethink its chemical defenses would be well advised to study the Swedish model. Defenses of that magnitude perhaps make great sense for Japan and South Korea as well as Europe. If current industrial and military trends continue, more and more nations are likely to go underground. But because of the formidable obstacle of the Atlantic and Pacific oceans, such precautions appear to be superfluous for the Western Hemisphere, where the only current threat of chemical weapons may originate in Cuba. Under severe pressure, on the order of some future reenactment of the Bay of Pigs invasion, Cuba might feel obliged to retaliate with biotoxins, which are clearly part of its present capability. Fidel Castro has apparently remarked on more than one occasion in recent years that Cuba could inflict various diseases on the United States if not left to its own devices. These would probably be introduced by individual terrorists, making fixed defenses irrelevant.

But over and above defensive needs, should the United States respond to the new Soviet superpoisons by developing the new binary weapons? This question is by no means as simple and straightforward as the cause and effect represented by binary partisans. It is really a conundrum, worse yet a riddle in which the solution is as perilous as the provocation. The only way to arrive at a reasonable answer is to pare away the layers of onion carefully to see what we are left with.

For example, if the question is whether a binary arsenal should come into existence, past history argues emphatically against it. No matter the burden of lies and exaggerations about the existing American chemical weapons stockpile, no matter its true physical condition, it is politically useless and should be totally disposed of without further procrastination and dissembling. And under no circumstances should it be replaced in any form, binaries included. It was a grotesque miscalculation in which the urge to be strong went too far and produced muscle binding. This needs to be stringently avoided with binaries.

But the avoidance of a binary arsenal does not mean that all binary weapons should be ruled out. To be hamstrung is just as bad as to be muscle-bound. The armed forces exist for a sober purpose, and should not be disarmed just because they exhibit human tendencies toward self-indulgence and excess.

The new Soviet superpoisons require some form of response. Until a negotiable solution is reached, and perhaps even for some time thereafter, that response may be largely defensive, but not at the cost of totally crippling a military chemical weapons counterstrike in an unpredictable emergency. Where this issue becomes bogged down is in the matter of degree. Proponents of binaries are so unrestrained that they provoke fatal attacks of nausea and add quickly to the ranks of their opponents. In turn, the opponents feel obliged to respond with equally unrestrained denunciations. In such a quandary, there are only extremists, so the decisions that are made—regardless of the way they go—are always extreme and later require redress.

If we are to avoid creating a new binary chemical arsenal, and yet make an appropriate response to the Soviet superpoisons, this can be achieved by creating an efficient, sophisticated, extremely small and fast-moving binary weapons strike force on the model of existing counterterrorist strike forces. This should be divorced of any defensive role; and the Chemical Corps should be given the defensive responsibility without any offensive role. This may go a long way toward preventing any recurrence of the excessive self-indulgence demonstrated by the corps in the past, when it has existed as something of a special fiefdom in which Amos Fries and his successors were demonstrably answerable only to congressmen with special interests.

If we cannot totally avoid binaries, they should be strictly limited in production to avoid the mindless overproduction that strapped the nation with 400,000 tons of sarin. Careers should be put on the line, and rules of criminal negligence should be applied, to guarantee the close observation of these constraints on production.

A compact, fast-moving binary strike force would offer a far greater deterrence to any casual use of chemical weapons by the Soviet Union or its surrogates than the impotent arsenal in Denver has in the thirty years of its cold-war existence. By keeping such a strike force small, elite, and airmobile, equipped with the most sophisticated and flexible binary compounds and the most advanced hardware, including binary cruise missiles, the armed forces could achieve maximum chemical readiness without raising the highly emotonal issue of creating a new poison arsenal. It is, to a degree, a trade-off. Proponents of chemical weapons would accept the elimination of all standing stocks and the application of severe new guidelines, in return for an abbreviated but highly potent paramilitary binary force. Since nuclear suicide tends to deter any massive Soviet attack on the United States, what needs to be countered is a regional attack by Moscow or its understudies, ranging from the overrunning of Poland, Norway, Yugoslavia, or South Korea to a preemptive strike on China. In none of these cases would the present 400,000 tons of sarin be useful. However, the rapid deployment of a binary strike force to the region at the first sign of impending crisis should have a salutary effect in blocking the introduction of poisons by the aggressor, who would face a quid pro quo reprisal. This is, after all, what it is all about.

Binaries should not be adopted even in the most limited numbers, however, without the greatest public reluctance, and without understanding the immense hazards involved—which are a great deal more subtle at this point than those posed by nuclear weapons. Although the air is filled with false arguments and fraudulent reasons, it is essential to recognize that one of the most important reasons for binary hardware is one that is never advertised.

As a piece of hardware, a binary weapon does not have to be filled with nerve agents. Any superpoison can be loaded in binary form, including biotoxins many times deadlier than the nerve agents —and largely loaded at the discretion of field commanders without public overview.

Nerve agents are the product of technology nearly fifty years old. There have been extraordinary advances in chemistry and biology since then leading to the new generation of biotoxins and to the possibility of new genetic modifiers as weapons, including the so-called "ethnic weapons" tailored to work only on certain genetic groups. Dioxin can also be loaded, with aftereffects lasting more than a century.

What the binary hardware provides is a lunch box into which any variety of sandwiches can be put. The clamor over nerve agent binaries has a tendency to dull the brain to these other uses of the same weapons. Once Congress has approved of binaries in principle, the threshold will have been crossed. To prevent unlimited use of the hardware for other poisons, specific safeguards and restraints need to be applied from the outset. There is no sign whatever that Congress has even considered such a possibility, much less drawn up any guidelines. All the possibilities should be opened for frank public debate, and the fraud of security should not be used to keep the public ignorant. In the matter of poisons, we cannot go wrong if we assume the worst, and if we assume the worst then secrecy becomes pointless. The horror of poisons is half real and half imaginary, so openness can only have a powerful effect on potential adversaries.

It is tragic that the world should find itself at such an impasse in which there is no apparent alternative to the adoption of deadly poisons as part of the struggle for survival. The acceptance of poison weapons, no matter how limited and tightly controlled, is tantamount to an acceptance of psychic rape.

Once there is a breakdown in the public willpower and resistance to binaries, a philosophical and visceral human safety factor will be gone forever. The door will be open to unlimited military development of yet unforeseen poisons, well into the twenty-first century.

A decisive response is definitely needed to the abuse of Soviet chemical weapons and their use on relatively defenseless resistance forces. But to have to respond in kind is to admit a lack of diplomatic cunning and an exhaustion of statesmanship. In an effort to arrive at a reasonable compromise between the extremes, I have found myself grudgingly and bitterly conceding the need for a compact binary strike force. However, having accepted that as the only compromise between two equally unreasonable extremes, I am forced to withdraw myself from the debate and make it clear that I am personally totally opposed to the use of chemical weapons in any form. The net result of my examination of the records has been, first, anger and dismay at what I have found the Soviet Union engaged in, but, second, even greater dismay at what I have discovered about the friendly camp. It is one thing to be objective about the methods of your presumptive enemies. It is entirely another matter to remain objective about the methods of your presumptive friends. The American experience with chemical warfare has been, I contend, one of unrelenting folly compounded with fraud. Just because that turns out to be the case is not sufficient reason to deal with the Soviet threat by anything other than diplomatic wit. The solution is certainly not to hand the Pentagon the key to Pandora's box, or to take that box ourselves, open it, and then dump its contents over our own heads. The cure for a broken leg is not to stick your finger in your eye. In the past decade, Americans have allowed themselves to be thoroughly duped with respect to their own chemical and biological warfare involvements, and have thrown good money after bad. After I examined that sad record with a friend, a Norwegian diplomat, he looked wistfully out the window at the forested hills above the fjord in Bergen, and said to me with a certain regret: "The Americans, they are just like very kind, doting grandfathers when it comes to new weapons—like the binaries. If the spoiled grandchildren are not able to take proper care of the old family Cadillac, the solution is to buy them a Ferrari."

13.

The Pogo Equation

The search that began with a leg bone in Laos ended with the realization that it was not only the Soviet Union that needed to be feared—a point nicely made by the comic strip character Pogo when the possum appeared before his friends looking somewhat startled and announced: "I have seen the enemy, and it is us." But I became aware of that only after I added up everything I had learned:

The Hmong hill people were not lying. More and more skeptics were accepting that as samples of powder left by the yellow rain began at last to come out of Laos for analysis in Western laboratories through the spring and summer of 1981. The Russians had provided the Vietnamese army not only with ordinary toxic chemical agents but with new biotoxins capable of causing agonizing death in minutes. The Vietnamese sprayed the Hmong to eliminate opposition, and the Hmong died. Not just 800–1,000 dead, a number that originated as a clerical error in the Department of State and continues to be cited foolishly in documents, but well over 15,000–20,000 dead among the Hmong alone. The yellow rain killed them with a spastic dance. A red rain caused them to spew blood and then die. More often than not the yellow rain and the red rain came together and hit them like the worst Love Canal had to offer. From small observation planes overhead, the Vietnamese and the Russians watched, and sometimes Cubans watched as well, as the Hmong twitched and died. They continued to be splashed with yellow rain well into 1981 with no sign of a letup.

Soviet generals came to inspect the chemical depots in Laos and Vietnam. Russian junior officers watched over the depots and supervised the selection and distribution of the poisons, which were loaded in rockets, airburst bags, and canisters. They chatted in Russian on their field radios as trucks hauled the poisons off to air bases, and they were overheard and recorded.

The same poisons were used in Afghanistan by the Russians themselves, producing identical medical symptoms thousands of miles from Laos. The Russian army used its deadliest poisons for the most part only in Badakhshan Province in the Hindu Kush, apparently on the assumption that they would draw less attention there. And in autumn 1980, when a lot of people overseas began believing the reports from Badakhshan, the Russians suddenly stopped using the killer poisons there. They should not have stopped so suddenly. If they had let it trickle away with a few random gas reports, perhaps people who had been skeptical all along would have concluded that the whole gas business was trumped up from the start and that the Afghans had just finally grown tired of telling exactly the same lies. But when the Soviets stopped using lethal agents in September 1980, and continued using only Blue-X, they stopped so suddenly that the abrupt cessation of reports was remarkable in itself. You cannot abruptly stop doing something if you have not been doing it all along. After that, the Russians used only Blue-X, which flattened the Mujahideen for eight to ten hours but otherwise left them unharmed.

The most powerful Soviet superpoison, the one that was killing so many people in Laos and Afghanistan, remained to be positively identified, but it appeared to be a compound of T_2 toxin drawn from groups of poisonous fungus that have plagued Russia for centuries. It is one of the grimmest killers that the world has yet seen —a biological poison apparently modified in the laboratory to speed its intake, then combined with related biotoxins to enhance its potency.

Positive evidence of nerve agent in Laos came as this was being written, as blood samples from Hmong victims showed acute depression of cholinesterase enzymes.

Other new Soviet poisons seemed to be in use in Laos and Cambodia as well, including hydrogen cyanide and possibly a modified organoarsenic as lethal as nerve gas but working in a different way on the body. As this book went to press cyanide residue was positively identified in leaves taken from areas in Cambodia where the Vietnamese Army had poisoned the terrain before allowing it to be overrun by the Pol Pot forces.

The Russians had used chemical and biological poisons to assassinate foreign enemies on many occasions before, including the thoroughly documented attacks on Ukrainian emigrés in West Germany and Bulgarian exiles in England and France. The first Russian experiments with these new biotoxins on a massive scale against large numbers of people, rather than one-on-one assassinations, came in the 1960s during the Yemen civil war in the Middle East. In the buried records of that forgotten war the eyewitness accounts and expert on-site investigations establish, as certainly as possible with elusive war poisons, the use of a wide range of deadly chemical warfare agents, including the first appearance of the T_2 toxins.

These biotoxins were evident not from physical residues (few poisons leave residues, which is a major reason why they are used) but from analysis of the medical symptoms of the victims. Yemen was the first time that unnatural bleeding became rampant in medical reports—the same outpouring of blood reported years later in Laos and Afghanistan. Nothing else but T_2 toxin is known to produce such extraordinary hemorrhaging, and also act quickly through the skin.

Only the crudest World War I chemical agents were within the grasp of Egypt during the Yemen war. So the conclusion was inescapable that the Soviet Union, as Egypt's backer in the war, was taking advantage of that remote conflict to field-test its latest chemical and biological poisons. This, in turn, explained why the Egyptians have consistently and convincingly denied using any chemicals themselves in Yemen.

Most of the world failed to notice what was happening in Yemen because of preoccupation with the Vietnam War and the Six-Day War between Egypt and Israel. At nearly the same time, half a world away, the Russians used the same poisons on the Chinese during clashes along the Sino-Soviet border in Siberia. As a result of those attacks, the Chinese hastily dug an extraordinary network of caves beneath their major cities, towns, and villages. But there is reason to doubt whether any precautions China takes could prevent a sudden Soviet preemptive strike on Peking if the Chinese leadership should drop its guard while quarreling. The evidence from China's invasion of Vietnam in 1979 demonstrates that ten years after the Ussuri River incidents, the Chinese army still is not equipped to protect itself from chemical warfare. The Vietnamese drenched Chinese vanguard units with chemicals, causing the loss of at least a battalion and the hasty withdrawal of the Chinese main force.

In Europe, there was serious doubt whether current NATO chemical defenses could cope with a Warsaw Pact surprise attack using war poisons. While Sweden and Switzerland quietly went about making elaborate preparations for chemical defense, the NATO allies bickered with America over the proper approach. It was clear that several NATO partners—particularly the Dutch—preferred the Swedish solution of strong chemical defense, while American officers pushed for a tougher NATO offense.

Despite the danger of a Soviet surprise attack on Peking to resolve the long Sino-Soviet dispute, and the impressive buildup of Soviet military forces along the Chinese border, no similar threat actually seems to exist for NATO. Soviet pressure in Europe may ebb and flow, and there may be more quarrels within the Warsaw Pact, but the general attack long predicted by NATO commanders would invite a joint response escalating quickly to the nuclear threshold. Soviet aggression in Europe, if and when it takes place, will probably be designed to slice off bits and pieces of outlying non-NATO members such as Yugoslavia or NATO partners like Norway. Even then such an attack is farfetched unless it is preceded by destabilizing internal upheaval in those countries. Then Russia's biological poisons are certain to be used heavily in a surprise strike.

Moscow is far more likely to conduct piecemeal aggressions in other parts of the world through proxies, as it has through Vietnam and Cuba. The presence of Soviet war poisons in Vietnam has now been matched in the Caribbean by the extensive training of Cuban army units in chemical combat by Soviet instructors. This is not alarming in itself, since most of these are routine CBW training procedures in the Soviet Union. But along with the training in Cuba has come the recent discovery of a chemical warfare depot on the island, stocked with the same Soviet superpoisons that have been used with dismaying effect in Laos and Afghanistan. The existence of this depot became known only early in 1981, and has yet to be publicly acknowledged by the Pentagon or the CIA, although both have discussed it privately. When it does surface, it could well cause as much uproar as the presence of a Soviet brigade on the island. This stockpile puts Soviet poisons within ninety miles of Key West, which is the sort of discovery that brings out the bellicosity of Americans as do few other concerns. At least one Cuban has died in Havana of symptoms identical to T_2 toxin poisoning, confirming the presence of that most perverse Soviet biological poison in Cuba.

How much of a direct threat this poses to the United States probably depends as much on American provocation as any other factor. In all his years in power, Fidel Castro has yet to carry out any of his threats to spread hoof-and-mouth disease or any other pestilence to America. A repetition of the Bay of Pigs would doubtless provoke Castro to take extreme measures in retaliation. After many years of clumsy CIA attempts to assassinate him with chemical and biological poisons, there is no reason for Castro to be squeamish in his choice of weapons.

Despite propaganda, it would in the end be self-defeating for the Soviet Union to precipitate a general war, as it would be for the United States. Russia ranked among the top five nations of the world in standard of living by 1981. This impressive improvement in the quality of life creates a situation that Russians are not likely to forfeit for the sake of a quarrel.

Short of a major war, however, the prospect of a constantly escalating arms race in chemicals and biotoxins creates serious concern about accidental spills, leaks, or explosions, such as the one at Sverdlovsk in April 1979, and about long-term damage to the earth. The fear of Soviet advances in chemical and biological weapons spurs the Pentagon to demand new and more expensive weapons systems such as binary nerve agent munitions. Binaries may end up being used not for two-part nerve agents as advertised but as packaging for biological poisons, dioxin, and even the ethnic weapons designed to wipe out ethnic groups through genetically targeted chemical agents. Binaries ultimately are just hardware.

Before Americans commit billions of dollars to binaries, and leave the production, disposition, and management of the new weapons entirely up to Congress and the Pentagon as has been the case in the past, it might be wise to examine exactly how Washington has handled chemical and biological warfare matters since the Nixon ban of 1969. It was only when I did precisely that, beginning with the earthquakes in Denver, that some of the most disturbing information came to the surface, and the Pogo Equation became complete. I realized then that the Soviet Union was only part of the threat.

The way in which the truth emerges is often as startling as the truth itself. So I present the final document of this journey in exactly the way it unfolded to me.

I began assembling the chronology simply by going to *The New York Times* files and digging back a bit more than ten years—to March 1968, when the events climaxing in the Nixon ban were occurring. From time to time I added bits and pieces from *Time* magazine and *Science,* the journal of the American Association for the Advancement of Science. But for the most part, the stories that I assembled are merely the daily reporting of the *Times,* without embroidery. All I have done to enhance them in any way has been to extract them from the gray matter of the rest of the news. These are most of the stories that had anything to do with chemical and biological warfare during the past decade. They take on a special impact when they are seen separately from the rest of the daily news, because readers normally see them submerged among PTA meetings, OPEC statements, and stock-market summaries. Once they are lined up like dominoes, the relationship between the stories becomes clear for the first time. Events that occurred six months apart originally did not relate because one story was forgotten before the other one appeared. An admission coming six months after a firm denial does not mean as much as it does when it is put back to back with all the other admissions and denials.

Then something remarkably perverse begins to come into focus. It is called fraud, and I found it popping up like mushrooms after spring rain. In growing fascination, I kept stacking up the dominoes, seeing new frauds appear as I went along. I was reminded of the little "flip" books that circulated when I was a kid, in which the cartoon figures did not move until you flipped the pages quickly, and then you saw them dance or do whatever they were doing in rapid motion like Keystone Cops.

I had read all these stories before, but I had never understood them until now. The experience was shattering. I felt like Pogo, for I had suddenly seen the enemy clearly for the first time. Here is how it unfolded:

1968

MARCH 6: Experts at the National Center for Earthquake Research are blaming a series of tremors in the Denver area over the past six years on a "deep well" drilled by the army in 1962, into which it injected 160 million gallons of waste water from chemical weapons production. Recently the quakes have become more severe. Some scientists fear that if the well is pumped out, worse quakes may result. The Geological Survey is studying the problem and will submit recommendations to the White House in a few weeks.

MARCH 14: Large numbers of sheep are collapsing and dying near Skull Valley, Utah. Veterinarians are working frantically to discover the cause.

MARCH 21: More than five thousand sheep have died. Local residents suspect that the cause may be nerve gas stored at Dugway Proving Grounds twenty miles away. The army, which earlier refused comment, issued a statement today saying that experts are studying the deaths but that "it would be purely speculative to attempt to fix a specific cause of death" until studies are complete. However, Senator Frank Moss announced that he has learned there were three "orientation demonstrations" at Dugway on March 13; 155-millimeter shells containing nerve gas were fired, 160 gallons of a nerve agent were burned in a pit, and 320 gallons of a persistent nerve agent were sprayed from an aircraft. Tom Donelly, information officer at Dugway, said, "No comment."

MARCH 22: Utah Governor Calvin Rampton believes a "toxic substance" released at Dugway killed the sheep. He says the army has agreed to stop nerve gas tests till its investigation is complete. The governor assures ranchers that the federal government will reimburse their losses, estimated at $300,000. The army refused comment. The Agriculture Department says postmortem examinations rule out all known diseases. The Public Health Service is looking into the possibility of poisoning from feed preservative. Senators Moss and Wallace Bennett demand a congressional investigation.

MARCH 23: Dr. D. A. Osguthorpe, heading a state investigation, says nerve gas killed the sheep, adding, "We're very lucky no people were killed." He said state experts narrowed cause of death to "an organophosphate compound," a component of nerve gas. An army spokesman, however, insists that "no definite cause of death" has been established.

MARCH 24: Dr. Mark Fawcett criticizes the army for not admitting they were testing nerve gas; he asserts that antidotes could have saved many sheep. The army insists that results are not conclusive, and insists that previous tests affected neither animals nor people. Dr. Mortimer Rothenberg, the science director at Dugway, claims that the sheep symptoms are "completely atypical from what we would expect from nerve gas."

MARCH 25:   Ranchers have been forced to kill six hundred more sick sheep. Army Brig. Gen. William W. Stone conceded that nerve gas might have killed the animals, but he says there is no evidence "to tell us what the actual chemical compound was or to help us pinpoint the source and how it got to the sheep and not to humans."

MARCH 29:   Senator Moss announces that blood tests of fifty civilians in Skull Valley proved negative.

APRIL 10:   Senator Bennett says doctors found no people in Utah affected.

APRIL 11:   Senator Moss says Agriculture Department evidence proves that gas killed the sheep.

APRIL 12:   The Public Health Service (PHS) announces: "Tests have isolated a compound in the snow, water, sheep blood, sheep liver tissue, and in grass taken from sheep stomachs which is identical to that agent supplied by the army for comparative tests." Meanwhile, Dr. Kelly Gubler says in *Medical World News* that chemical warfare tests could cause "massive human disaster." In an indirect reply, the Pentagon states that the PHS tests show local residents of Skull Valley were not affected.

APRIL 19:   The army tells Senator Moss that it could be "postulated" that a wind shift might have carried a small amount of gas to Skull Valley.

APRIL 20:   Retired Brig. Gen. J. H. Rothschild, former commander of the Research and Development Command, writes to *The New York Times* defending chemical agents, saying they can "save human life and limit human suffering."

JUNE 21:   Popular protest against British research and development of chemical and biological weapons gains ground; the British government, to placate demonstrators, promises to seek an international ban.

JULY 2:   Russia also proposed a ban, and a nine-point program for arms control, accusing the United States of using chemical weapons in its "aggressive war in Vietnam."

JULY 3:   Despite apprehensions, army engineers begin pumping out the deep well at Denver used to dump nerve gas wastes.

AUGUST 17:   Scientists warn that aboveground nerve gas

storage tanks at Rocky Mountain Arsenal in Denver are a threat to the city. While Skull Valley sheep were twenty miles from Dugway, the more than one hundred storage tanks at Rocky Mountain Arsenal are only ten miles from downtown Denver (population 514,678).

AUGUST 21: Army Secretary Stanley Resor recommends paying $281,685 damages to Utah sheep ranchers. Payment requires congressional approval.

AUGUST 22: The army says it will move the Rocky Mountain Arsenal nerve gas stocks out of the Denver area but refuses to say where they will be taken.

SEPTEMBER 2: Pumping out the nerve gas well in Denver has been delayed by mechanical problems with the pump. The poisonous fluids are being pumped into a ninety-acre asphalt-bottomed "evaporation lake" at the arsenal.

SEPTEMBER 7: Utah Congressman Sherman Lloyd says he learned some of the Denver nerve agents will be moved to his state.

SEPTEMBER 28: The Federation of Arab Pharmacists has voted to urge that chemical warfare be taught at Arab pharmacy schools.

OCTOBER 15: It is revealed that Britain is testing LSD on its own soldiers.

OCTOBER 23: American Independence Party presidential candidate Gen. Curtis LeMay tells an audience of Yale students that defoliation has not caused much ecological damage in Vietnam.

NOVEMBER 23: West German scientist Dr. Ehrenfried Petras defects to East Germany, claiming he had been working on chemical and biological warfare projects for the Bonn government. He asks for asylum to work "in the service of peace." Bonn denies the Petras charges, insisting that it studies only defensive problems.

DECEMBER 10: The political committee of the UN General Assembly calls for a study of the chemical and biological warfare threat to humanity.

DECEMBER 20: The army agrees to a panel's recommendations for tighter safety measures in future nerve gas tests at Dugway; attention will henceforth be given to weather forecasts and wind speeds, and to the height at which gas is released, so that no nerve agent will cross nearby Highway 40 for at least three hours after release. The army insists that studies have failed to prove conclusively that nerve gas killed the 6,300 sheep in Skull Valley, but says it has nonetheless paid more than $376,000 in damage claims.

DECEMBER 27:   Australia denies reports that it is conducting joint CBW research with the United States at a secret Australian base. Informants claim that America subsidizes such joint research in foreign countries.

DECEMBER 28:   Geologist Dr. David M. Evans tells an ecological conference that America has 110 deep wells for disposal of chemical warfare agents (up from only 2 in 1950), and warns that they are causing permanent damage to farmlands and urban areas in the Southwest. He said there is "an absolutely beautiful correlation" between the number of gallons poured in and the number of earthquakes produced.

1969

JANUARY 4:   The defection of Dr. Petras and two other West German scientists is causing a furor over West German research in chemical and biological weapons. The director of the institute for which Petras worked says it is experimenting with tabun, sarin, and soman only to develop antidotes.

JANUARY 15:   UN Secretary General U Thant appoints a panel of experts to study the danger of chemical and biological warfare to humanity.

JANUARY 18:   *Pravda* asserts that the United States falsely accuses Russia of making biological weapons to disguise its own chemical weapons program and fool the American people.

FEBRUARY 4:   Former Senator Joseph Clark claims the army is searching for a remote Pacific island to test chemical and biological weapons, under the cover of a Smithsonian Institution $2.8 million bird migration study. There was speculation that the army wanted to find an island where birds did not migrate, so they could not spread germ warfare agents. The army admitted its interest in the study; the Smithsonian said it was not aware of the army link.

MARCH 4:   A congressman has leaked contents of a secret congressional briefing by Brig. Gen. James A. Hebbeler, saying the Pentagon spends $350 million a year to develop and produce CBW weapons, and that 300-gallon containers of nerve agents are regularly shipped by railroad to and from test centers. In recent years the amount the government spends on CBW has been hidden with the collusion of congressional budget committees. Some legislators left the Hebbeler briefing feeling that the army was spending too much on CBW.

MARCH 16: Representatives of the USSR and the United States announced at the Geneva Disarmament Talks that they will work together for a CBW ban.

APRIL 10: Stanford University students demand an end to the school's $2 million secret CBW research program; six hundred occupied a lab in protest.

APRIL 19: The Stanford sit-in ends when the school president is given the power to suspend the demonstrators.

APRIL 29: After a meeting with President Nixon, Representative Gerald Ford attacks politicians who criticize the Pentagon CBW efforts, saying the critics seem to favor "unilateral disarmament."

APRIL 30: Senator J. William Fulbright calls upon Nixon to resubmit the 1925 Geneva Protocol to the Senate for ratification.

MAY 7: Several congressmen protest an army plan to transport 27,000 tons of nerve agents from Rocky Mountain and Edgewood arsenals to the Naval Ammunition Depot at Earle, New Jersey, where they are to be loaded on four liberty ships and sunk 250 miles at sea. Earle is only twenty miles from New York City (population 7,895,563)—the distance of Dugway from Skull Valley. They are worried about accidents on land and threat to marine life. A Pentagon spokesman assures them that similar shipments and dumpings have taken place without difficulty on several occasions, as recently as August, 1968. Representative Richard D. McCarthy says the Department of Transportation has issued a permit and waived even routine safety inspection. A department spokesman replies that inspecting the gas canisters would involve removing the contents—a procedure more dangerous than letting them pass uninspected. Army Maj. Wendell Coats insists that any significant pollution at sea will be "virtually impossible." The containers will sink to the bottom at 7,200 feet, and should any ruptures occur the gas will be absorbed by the water and rendered harmless.

MAY 11: A House subcommittee has reviewed the army disposal plan and finds it satisfactory, but mayors of cities on the New Jersey coast remain opposed.

MAY 13: The army promises not to move the gas till the National Academy of Sciences studies the plan.

MAY 19:   Congressmen are pressing Defense Secretary Melvin Laird to delay the gas shipment and order it neutralized before it begins its journey.

MAY 21:   During a House subcommittee hearing on open-air testing of gas, the army finally and with great reluctance admits that its nerve gas at Dugway killed the Skull Valley sheep one year and two months earlier. Surgeon General Dr. William M. Stewart concedes that even with improved safety measures at Dugway, a life-threatening situation exists and that wind might carry nerve agents to nearby Highway 40. Pressed by congressmen, who spoke of a "pattern of deception with regard to the Skull Valley incident," the Pentagon countered that it has set up a civilian safety review board for Dugway tests. However, later questioning revealed that the board was chaired by a high-ranking official of the E. I. duPont Corporation, one of the largest defense contractors, raising questions of objectivity. Meanwhile, the Pentagon announced that it is unloading 170 railway cars, prepared to transport nerve gas for disposal from Rocky Mountain Arsenal, awaiting completion of the National Academy of Sciences study.

JUNE 11:   In continuing hearings, Brigadier General Hebbeler reveals that eleven ocean dumpings have already been carried out. Representative Cornelius Gallagher wondered why the Pentagon waited until the twelfth shipment before deciding that a review of the program was necessary.

JUNE 17:   President Nixon orders a comprehensive review of U.S. CBW policies.

JUNE 24:   A West German official tells a reporter that millions of fish dying in the Rhine River this week were killed by poison gas leaking from containers sunk in the river at the end of World War II; the storage tanks had apparently rusted out after twenty-five years. Even healthy fish caught elsewhere and put in the Rhine die within minutes. Industrial pollution was ruled out.

JUNE 25:   The National Academy of Sciences completes its study and recommends disposal of poison gases at their storage sites rather than dumping at sea. But sea burial is acceptable as a last resort, NAS says.

JUNE 30:   The army has decided to follow the NAS recommendation and will burn the gas. Utah Governor Rampton asks that this disposal not be done in his state. Utah has already received too much negative publicity over Skull Valley.

JULY 2: UN Secretary General U Thant has received the report of his panel of experts studying the danger of chemical and biological warfare to humanity. The results are not encouraging. The panel concludes that there is no defense against the poisons, and if used widely there is no predicting the duration of their effects on world environment. The potential for development of poison weapons has grown enormously. U Thant appeals to all nations to cease developing and stockpiling war poisons, and to sign the 1925 Geneva Protocol.

JULY 3: The Senate Armed Services Committee has stricken $2 million for chemical and biological offensive weapons from the 1970 defense budget. In House hearings it is revealed that crew members of a Coast Guard station on Peale Island were evacuated in April 1968 after some became ill apparently from leaking containers of chloropicrin gas dumped offshore by Japan at the end of World War II; sixty-eight Guardsmen were hospitalized with eye-ear-throat damage. Chloropicrin is a "nonlethal" agent designed to penetrate gas masks and make soldiers vomit so that they must remove their masks, leaving them vulnerable.

JULY 5: The army now wants to dispose of two thousand tons of nerve gas in four hundred rockets stored at Anniston Depot in Alabama. The rockets were leaking, so they were encased in steel and concrete, complicating disposal since the concrete cannot be cut without detonating the rockets. Experts now fear that the rockets will explode anyway.

JULY 9: A bipartisan group of eighty congressmen wants to reduce by 10 percent the $350 million still in the 1970 defense budget for CBW programs, pending the results of the Nixon review.

JULY 11: The Pentagon announces that it is conducting on-going open-air tests at Dugway, Edgewood, and Fort McClellan in Alabama. In the past three months, tests were conducted with 67 different gas weapons at Dugway, 47 at McClellan. In the next three months, 358 weapons will be tested at Dugway, including tabun, sarin, soman, VX, and mustard in bomblets, mines, rockets, and shells.

JULY 12: New Jersey's Representative Peter W. Rodino announces formation of a legislative group to fight cross-country transport and sea dumping of war poisons.

JULY 15: Representative McCarthy charges that the army is set to develop new binary nerve gas weapons and has advertised for bids. The Pentagon denies the charge. Representative Clarence Long of Maryland has persuaded the army to halt open-air tests at Edgewood (which is in Long's district), pending evaluation by a panel.

JULY 18:   After an accidental discharge of nerve gas at a depot on Okinawa resulting in hospitalization of twenty-five Americans at a U.S. base, it is revealed that the United States has been storing war poisons at some of its major bases overseas since the 1950s. The revelation causes a furor in Japan and Okinawa. The pro-American government in Japan, which is negotiating for the return of Okinawa to its control, is embarrassed. Public outcry on Okinawa mounts. The Pentagon refuses to acknowledge that the illness of the hospitalized Americans is related to gas.

JULY 19:   It is revealed that on Okinawa the United States has several hundred concrete "igloos" to store poisons, with herds of goats for testing. Okinawans now believe that U.S. gas tests are responsible for skin burns suffered by two hundred children swimming near the 137th Ordinance Company's installation in July 1968. The Pentagon refuses to discuss the gas. There are unconfirmed reports that the United States also has gas stocks in South Korea and West Germany, plus other secret foreign locations.

JULY 22:   Assistant Defense Secretary Daniel Henkin refuses to say whether the United States has deployed nerve gas overseas other than at Okinawa. The West German government refuses comment. Henkin blames the Okinawan incident on nerve gas leaking from one weapon during paint removal. Defense Secretary Laird orders a "multiagency review of the entire matter." The Okinawa legislature in special session demands the removal of all war gas stores from the island. Japan is "relieved" when the United States agrees to remove it.

JULY 23:   The German magazine *Der Spiegel* says the United States has four nerve gas depots in West Germany; one is near the East German border. The U.S. Seventh Army refuses comment. An American embassy spokesman says, "We never confirm or deny these things." A Bonn spokesman says the West German government has no knowledge of it.

JULY 25:   The presence of nerve gas in West Germany is becoming a political crisis; the West German political opposition demands an investigation. Meanwhile, in Okinawa, seventy-five students storm a U.S. administration compound and trample the American flag. The United States protests the desecration.

JULY 28: The Pentagon claims it has completely detoxified the nerve gas weapons that were leaking on Okinawa. Defense Secretary Melvin Laird says the Soviets have a much greater CW capability; he says the United States must continue to produce these "deplorable" weapons as a deterrent.

JULY 29: A Bonn government spokesman says West Germany has formally asked for talks with the United States about storage of CBW agents within its borders.

JULY 30: The deletion from President Nixon's message to the Geneva Disarmament Conference of a sentence describing the world's "horror and revulsion" over the specter of chemical and biological warfare is seen as evidence of internal conflict within the Nixon administration. The Pentagon reportedly is ready to block any disarmament accord that would forbid the use of riot agents and defoliants in Vietnam.

JULY 31: The West German government admits that some U.S. nerve agents are present in its territory. The Pentagon confirms this. It is the first time either country admits to storage of war poisons in Germany. Talks are planned on the safe storage of the gas.

AUGUST 1: Jerome Gordon, president of Delphic Systems and Research, tells a Senate subcommittee that all pesticides related to nerve gas should be banned because they are being spread, unchecked, on America's farms and gardens. He says uncounted thousands of migrant farm workers, farmers, and suburban home owners have been fatally overcome or seriously disabled.

AUGUST 3: John O. Rasmussen, chairman of the Federation of American Scientists and a professor at Yale, described the deterrence argument for chemical weapons as being "rather overworked," and warns against opening Pandora's Box. "Even the Nazis with an absolute monopoly on the nerve gases chose not to use them," he said. Instead, the United States should take the constructive step of destroying all stockpiles and production facilities and in so doing recapture world leadership "by decent example."

AUGUST 11: The Senate unanimously approves an amendment restricting the use, transportation, and storage of CBW agents. The Pentagon must give Congress thirty days notice before shipping any poison gas. Congress must specifically authorize all funds spent on CBW weapons, and no "back-door" financing, by which the Pentagon shifts funds from other programs to CBW, will be allowed.

AUGUST 14:   The army is accused of rail-shipping a large quantity of lethal phosgene gas from Rocky Mountain Arsenal to New York State; the fourteen flatcars carrying phosgene containers have just passed through Des Moines, Iowa. The army replies that the gas was sold to Jones Chemical of Caledonia, New York, which has a permit for its shipment. Phosgene is used in making plastics.

AUGUST 25:   The West German magazine *Der Stern* has obtained photocopies of U.S. documents outlining U.S. strategy for nuclear, chemical, and biological warfare in Europe. The magazine did not publish the contents, but revealed that a West German general in NATO was so disturbed by the war plans that he took the photocopies, sent them to *Stern*, and then committed suicide. The Pentagon called the episode a Communist counterintelligence disinformation ploy, intended to make other NATO members distrust the Germans.

AUGUST 29:   The phosgene shipment has created a public furor. Canada has refused to let it cross its borders, forcing rerouting through Indiana and Ohio. Defense Secretary Melvin Laird promises that future shipments will occur only after consultation with the surgeon general and military medical experts. Nobody mentions the ruling by Congress eighteen days earlier that the Pentagon must give thirty days advance notice to Capitol Hill. *The New York Times* finds that there are fifteen train derailments a day, up from nine a day in 1963. Old and faulty equipment is blamed. An official of the Department of Transportation says "one tank car of nitrogen tetroxide could, under the right weather conditions, kill 100,000 persons should a rupture occur. One tank car of nerve gas or phosgene could create a similar catastrophe."

SEPTEMBER 2:   The army announces that it has sold all its phosgene. The last 7,730,000 pounds was sold for $106,695 to Jones Chemical and to Chemical Commodities of Olathe, Kansas.

SEPTEMBER 8:   Representative McCarthy claims that two rail cars of the August phosgene shipment were mistakenly sent to Buffalo and left unattended for twenty-four hours, narrowly avoiding a collision involving freight cars 150 feet away. Two tons of phosgene were present.

SEPTEMBER 9:   The Department of Transportation orders

an end to phosgene shipments from Rocky Mountain Arsenal unless the gas cylinders are first replaced or repaired. The order leaves 1,294 cylinders of phosgene stranded at the arsenal, and the army may have to default on its contract with the two plastic manufacturers.

SEPTEMBER 12: The West German government proposes an international ban on all CBW weapons in an effort to dampen criticism before parliamentary elections three weeks away. In a campaign speech, Foreign Minister Willy Brandt hinted that his government would like the U.S. war gas stocks removed.

OCTOBER 11: The army reveals that it has poison gas stocks at eight sites in the United States and plans to develop two-stage binary munitions. Previously the army denied that it planned to make binaries.

OCTOBER 15: The army reveals that the 1968 Dugway sheep kill cost more than $1 million in investigations and claims.

OCTOBER 17: A civilian panel recommends that open-air testing at Edgewood Arsenal in Maryland be resumed.

NOVEMBER 3: Sixteen Republican congressmen ask Nixon to dispose of all CBW stocks because they undermine national security rather than serve as a deterrent.

NOVEMBER 13: A House committee calls for an end to all open-air tests of war gases and condemns the army for "lack of candor, deception, and disregard of public interest."

NOVEMBER 18: Growing numbers of senators and congressmen are calling on Nixon to submit the Geneva Protocol for ratification.

NOVEMBER 25: Nixon orders a halt to production of biological weapons and pledges no first use of chemical weapons. He promises to submit the 1925 Geneva Protocol to the Senate. He calls his action "an initiative for peace." Administration sources say the use of defoliants and riot agents in Vietnam will continue.

DECEMBER 1: Defense Secretary Melvin Laird admits that the Nixon plan was achieved only over the opposition of high-ranking officers.

DECEMBER 2: Army Secretary Stanley Resor says war poisons removed from Okinawa will be shipped to Umatilla Depot in Oregon. Okinawans are pleased, but fear that there is no way to confirm that the gas is really removed.

DECEMBER 11: The army reveals that a damaged filling plug

caused nerve gas to leak from a one-ton container at Dugway; two hundred people have been evacuated.

DECEMBER 15: The Pentagon and the State Department disagree over whether the Nixon ban includes deadly biotoxins. The army argues that they are chemical agents, not biologicals, although they are secreted by biological organisms. The army reveals that it is producing biotoxins at Pine Bluff Arsenal. Critics say the army is trying to pull an "end run" around the Nixon ban.

DECEMBER 16: The army now denies it is producing biotoxins. A House committee demands army plans for open-air tests at Dugway; the army replies that it is suspending all Dugway tests, so no plans are available.

DECEMBER 29: Residents of Hermiston, Oregon, say they are not opposed to storing nerve gas from Okinawa, despite statewide opposition. The town earns $5 million a year from Umatilla Depot, which employs 17 percent of townfolk. "We grew up with the gas," explains a citizen.

1970

JANUARY 14: A letter to *The New York Times* claims the army is conducting germ and poison warfare tests at Eniwetok Atoll in the Marshall Islands.

JANUARY 24: The army discloses that it has trained 550 officers from thirty-six countries in CBW at Fort McClellan.

JANUARY 25: Nixon is considering whether to include biotoxins in his ban.

FEBRUARY 2: The British government, which is using CS riot-control agent in Northern Ireland, announces that it does not consider CS to be included in the 1925 Geneva Protocol on asphyxiating and other agents.

FEBRUARY 14: Nixon extends his ban to include biotoxins. His aides call his move "another significant step . . . for world peace."

APRIL 7: Canada opposes the shipment of Okinawa nerve gas through the Strait of Juan de Fuca.

APRIL 21: Oregon Governor Tom McCall and Washington Governor Daniel Evans seek an injunction to block shipment of the Okinawa gas to Oregon. The army plan is code-named "Red Hot." Five ships are to bring the gas to Bangor, Washington, and ship it on 744 flatcars in twelve trains over thirty-four days to Umatilla.

APRIL 29: The American Civil Liberties Union and PANG (People Against Nerve Gas) file suit to block the Okinawa shipment. PANG chooses May 4 as the start of "Nerve Gas Week"; 200,000 persons sign petitions against the shipment; radical groups threaten to shoot the nerve gas cars with high-powered rifles.

MAY 15: Nixon will send the Geneva Protocol to the Senate but will exempt riot agents and defoliants, including Agent Orange.

MAY 23: The White House cancels the Umatilla shipment, but the Pentagon may send 13,000 tons of the Okinawa poison gas to Kodiak Island Naval Station instead. Alaska Senator Mike Gravel protests and moves a bill to block transfer of gas to his state.

MAY 24: Cancellation of the removal of gas from Okinawa causes protest rallies. The mayor of Kodiak, Alaska, Pete Resoff, says the army plan to send nerve gas there is like "getting a Christmas present of a sack full of snakes."

JULY 30: The army is going to move two trainloads of nerve gas rockets from Alabama and Kentucky through seven southern states to Charleston, South Carolina, for dumping 282 miles at sea in 16,000 feet of water east of Cape Kennedy. The thirty M-55 rockets containing sixty-six tons of nerve gas are encased in steel reinforced concrete slabs and will cross 1,400 miles of track through twenty-one populated areas including Atlanta. The operation is dubbed CHASE, an acronym for "Cut Holes And Sink 'Em."

AUGUST 3: The army reveals that the rockets were encased in concrete because they were leaking nerve gas. Florida's Governor Claude Kirk seeks an injunction to block the shipment.

AUGUST 6: Several of America's allies protest the CHASE ocean dumping.

AUGUST 7: A House subcommittee concludes hearings on CHASE by blasting the army for "almost unbelievable negligence" in storage of nerve agents. UN Secretary General U Thant declares that the sea dumping violates a UN resolution and the Geneva Convention of 1958.

AUGUST 8: The CHASE trains are loaded in Kentucky and Alabama.

AUGUST 10: The trains pull out. In Washington, Senator Stephen Young says the Pentagon has stocks of nerve gas for use against domestic rioters.

AUGUST 12:   The army will send the Okinawa gas to Johnston Island, seven hundred miles southeast of Hawaii.

AUGUST 13:   The Environmental Defense Fund is suing over CHASE. The trains arrive at Sunny Port, North Carolina, to load on the Liberty ship *Le Baron Russell Briggs*. Judge June Green orders the ship to remain in port till she considers the Defense Fund suit.

AUGUST 14:   Judge Green permits the ship to sail with "serious misgivings" about CHASE, which she calls "a tragedy of errors." A tropical storm delays sailing.

AUGUST 16:   Chief Justice Warren Burger delays sailing until an appeals court can rule on the fund's request for an injunction. The Bahamas holds an emergency cabinet meeting.

AUGUST 17:   The appeals court upholds Judge Green, and the ship sails. Defense Secretary Laird promises that the Pentagon will never do it again. In West Germany, scientists test Baltic Sea water to determine if poison gas canisters dumped after World War II are leaking.

AUGUST 18:   The *Le Baron Russell Briggs* is sunk.

AUGUST 19:   President Nixon submits the 1925 Geneva Protocol to the Senate with two exceptions: that neither riot agents nor defoliants may be used without presidential authorization—after the Vietnam War is over.

AUGUST 23:   The army will burn 584,000 gallons of mustard gas at Rocky Mountain Arsenal and detoxify or burn 463,222 gallons of nerve gas in cluster bombs there.

SEPTEMBER 25:   Luther Carter writes in *Science* that before CHASE began, the army tried to get the Atomic Energy Commission to destroy the sixty-six tons of nerve agent rockets in an underground nuclear test. The AEC refused because of the potential bad publicity. Carter says the army in 1967–68 secretly dumped "more than 21,000 M-55 rockets, each armed with an explosive charge and 10.8 pounds of GB liquid nerve gas, off the New Jersey coast." Although the rockets were first encased in concrete, offshore oil drilling has begun since then not far from the sea burial site.

SEPTEMBER 30:   Nine persons are arrested at a Pentagon demonstration protesting CBW. They were attempting to plant a small pine tree on government property.

OCTOBER 18:   A Pentagon spokesman admits that the military is developing "nonlethal" sprays and gases for civil-disorder use.

NOVEMBER 20: The Senate appropriates $15 million to convert the Fort Detrick biological warfare laboratory at Frederick, Maryland, to do research in disease control.

DECEMBER 5: The army will soon ship 13,000 tons of nerve agents and mustard from Okinawa to Johnston Island, two years after public protests began.

1971

JANUARY 6: Two hundred canisters of VX, part of a surplus stockpile scheduled to be destroyed at Fort Greely, Alaska, sank through thin ice in 1966 and remained on the lake bottom unmissed until the lake was drained in May 1969. Unaware of the disappearance for three years, the army finally heard rumors and investigated until it found the stocks at the bottom of the lake. The army says all the canisters were recovered.

JANUARY 11: Okinawan demonstrators attacked a U.S. chemical station to protest further delays in removal of poison gas; five thousand protestors demonstrated against lack of safety measures being taken for the shipment.

JUNE 3: The Pentagon announces a five-month operation to destroy more than three thousand tons of mustard gas at Rocky Mountain Arsenal.

AUGUST 3: A Navy ship removes 5,300 tons of nerve and mustard gas from Okinawa.

AUGUST 19: President Nixon sends 1925 Geneva Protocol to the Senate for ratification.

SEPTEMBER 21: The army removes the remaining Okinawa stocks.

NOVEMBER 24: The Senate unanimously approves a bill against ocean dumping of poison gas after being warned that the world's seas can no longer be used as the "universal sewer of mankind."

1972

JULY 30: The Alaskan army command vigorously denies that chemical agents caused the death of fifty-three caribou whose carcasses were found four miles south of Fort Greely, a former center for testing CBW weapons. Experts from the state Fish and Game Department rule out natural causes.

AUGUST 19: The air force evacuates all personnel from Johnston Island because of the threat of Hurricane Celeste.

AUGUST 21: Aerial photographs show that Celeste did only slight damage to the poison gas depot on Johnston Island, says an army spokesman.

SEPTEMBER 7: The Geneva Conference concludes its eleventh year unable to report progress toward banning chemical weapons.

1973

JULY 4: Controversy erupts after a Pentagon safety board blocks a plan by city officials to extend Denver's Stapleton International Airport onto six hundred acres of land that used to be part of Rocky Mountain Arsenal. Although the land was deeded to the city in 1969, as late as this year the army prohibited aircraft from flying over it because of "safety factors." In 1968 the army promised to dispose of war poisons stocked at the neighboring arsenal, and later announced it planned to spend $50 million to do so. In 1972 the army gave the Environmental Protection Agency a list of all hazardous materials at the arsenal, but no nerve agents were on the list. The army had assured Representative Donald Brotzman that the obsolete chemical weapons had been destroyed and remaining stockpiles removed. The disposal was supposed to have been completed this year. Various federal, state, and local officials complain of what they call the army's duplicity. *Time* quotes Governor John Love as telling Defense Secretary James Schlesinger that he doubts "the United States needs to maintain a nerve gas stockpile as a deterrent, but if it does, it certainly doesn't have to be maintained at an arsenal which adjoins a large metropolitan area." One Pentagon official privately warns that the arsenal is in poor physical condition. *The New York Times* reports that the arsenal still stores bulk tanks of chemical agents, 750-pound WETEYE bombs (some of which are leaking internally). Also present are 163,000 gallons of sarin in 21,104 M-34 cluster bombs; 5.5 million pounds of mustard gas; 4.2 million pounds of sarin in tanks, and 2.6 million pounds of phosgene.

AUGUST 5: Army Secretary Howard Callaway is considering an army proposal to ship one million gallons of sarin from Rocky

Mountain Arsenal to Tooele Depot in Utah, using three or four trains.

NOVEMBER 23: The army reveals a new plan for destroying its chemical stocks that will cost $1 billion and take twelve years. That is more than it cost to manufacture the poison gas in the first place. Three-quarters of the money would go to build a portable poison gas disposal factory called CAMDS (Chemical Agent Munition Disposal System). CAMDS will dispose of poison gas at one army base, then be detoxified and moved to another base. Twelve years are needed because the poisons must be disposed of slowly to avoid damage to the environment.

DECEMBER 9: The army reveals that it plans to spend more than $200 million for a new binary nerve agent weapons system.

1974

JUNE 26: In the first stage of a reported attempt to take over the world, a group called Aliens for America has mailed to all U.S. Supreme Court Justices postcards alleged to have nerve gas concealed beneath the stamps. The FBI has intercepted the cards and found no traces of gas.

DECEMBER 3: The end of American involvement in Vietnam creates the dilemma of what to do with $80 million worth of Agent Orange. Dow Chemical and other manufacturers say they are not interested in buying it back.

DECEMBER 13: The Senate Foreign Relations Committee votes to send the 1925 Geneva Protocol to the Senate for ratification.

DECEMBER 17: The Senate ratifies the 1925 Geneva Protocol, ending a fifty-year deadlock. The United States is the 104th country to ratify the treaty.

DECEMBER 26: Representative Les Aspin accuses the army of trying to get around the congressional ban on production of new nerve gases, citing advertisements that the military placed for bids on contracts to manufacture the two components of a binary nerve weapon system. The army refuses comment.

1976

JULY 25: Fifty wild horses have been found dead near a spring on the Dugway Proving Ground. Army officials attribute the deaths to "some sort of stress and subsequent shock." Other government investigators suggest that the horses died of "heat exhaustion associated with water intoxification." The American Horse Protection Association, however, noted evidence that the horses may have died from a rare African disease.

1980

MARCH 3:   The army announces that it intends to continue storing chemical weapons at Rocky Mountain Arsenal despite protests from Denver residents.

This is a sorry record. Nothing has changed despite the pledges, promises, investigations, scientific panels, ratifications, negotiations, and congressional hearings. The Nixon ban was in the end just a grandstand play, an empty boast, a hollow fraud.

The nation was deceived. And in time the Skull Valley outrage dwindled, the protests diminished, the demonstrators went home. Shielded behind a barricade of lies, evasions, and false moves, the defense establishment resumed its research and development of war poisons and biologicals. The great shell game continued. The poison gas stocks in West Germany remained where they were, as did those on Johnston Island, and at Rocky Mountain, Dugway/Tooele, Pine Bluff, Edgewood, Blue Grass, Anniston, Pueblo, Umatilla, and Fort Greely.

The place of the Skull Valley sheep was taken by caribou and wild horses. What did it matter if they died of a rare African disease near Dugway's Baker Biological Laboratory in the Utah salt flats seven years after Nixon banned biological weapons? Nixon, himself, was gone. Defrocked.

When the Pentagon dumped a few bad lots of leaking poison gas weapons into the Atlantic, press releases gave the public the impression that the whole chemical and biological warfare program was being abandoned. But military contractors and defense suppliers were assured privately that the CBW program would actually continue and expand once public attention was diverted. Within two years after the Nixon ban, a private consulting firm in the defense industry was able to crow to its highly placed clients that CBW research continues "at funding levels equal to or exceeding those prior to the 'public relations' announcements of the cessation of those efforts." The DMS (Defense Marketing Survey) bulletin went on to state flatly: "Despite public announcements to the contrary, the military agencies are not discontinuing chemical and biological warfare research!" The bulletin, which is provided at high cost to wealthy corporate clients, reassured them that "even though the Nixon Administration has pledged to eliminate and reduce CBR procurement programs, FY72's Procurement of Equipment and Missiles, Army (PEMA) request for CBR has actually more than doubled." It went on:

> Though ostensibly on the way "out" of the military weapons arsenal, CBR (chemical, biological, radiological warfare) is merely being conducted in a different environment and, wherever possible, with less public attention. It remains a technology in which there is considerable interest and money. . . . The relatively small research contracts that come from this CBR research program can lead to follow-on production work that averages $12 to $15 million per year in most conservative evaluations. The field is difficult to crack, but there are opportunities for the chemically competent technical organization, either in the industrial or academic communities.

When seen in the context of Watergate, the Nixon ban fraud becomes just another part of the tapestry of lies by an administration that never outgrew the used-car-dealer mentality. The public was lulled with promises, then duped, and the whole fraud was kept hidden by the ruse of security. As a shrewd Okinawan official remarked on December 2, 1969: "Even after they say they have removed the poison gas, how can we know for certain?"

Part of the fraud was to make it appear that the major chemical and biological warfare centers were being shut down or converted to peaceful, humanitarian purposes—notably cancer research, a noble effort but also a buzzword. Since virtually all deadly poisons are carcinogens, any place that develops war poisons, from chemicals to biotoxins, is simultaneously engaged in "cancer research." Another ruse was the labeling of CBW stations as institutions for the study of "toxic effects"—as in the toxic effects of pesticides (nerve agents), food additives (biotoxins), or drugs (psychochemicals).

The object was to sanitize the CBW centers that were most conspicuous, like Fort Detrick, in Frederick, Maryland. After it was penetrated by investigative reporters such as *The New York Times*'s Seymour M. Hersh, Fort Detrick was obviously too vulnerable. The Senate voted $15 million to transform Fort Detrick into a national center for health research. It sounded promising. But it did not happen, at least not the way it was made to sound. The funds were quietly canceled later in a House-Senate conference. The army then conveniently postponed its widely publicized plan to reduce the staff at Detrick by 295 man-years. A change in status did take place, however. Early in 1971, the core of the biological warfare research staff at Fort Detrick—the hard-core "bug and germ warfare" specialists—were secretly moved to Dugway Proving Ground in Utah. Apparently 440 persons were transferred in all, including some from Fort Detrick and some from the biological warfare laboratories at Pine Bluff, Arkansas. An army center remained at Detrick for the study of defensive requirements, and this was allowed to remain plainly visible and accessible to outsiders, even to the extent of granting interviews. A genial public affairs staff was installed, reporting directly to the Pentagon, where all its activities were supervised at the general-officer level—an indication of the priority assigned to maintaining the appearance of "openness" at Fort Detrick.

Security at the front gate, previously identical to the entrance procedures for the Central Intelligence Agency headquarters at Langley, Virginia, and for the Defense Intelligence Agency's center at Arlington Hall, in Arlington, Virginia, was dismantled. The gates were thrown open wide, literally, and now remain open around the clock, with a solitary military guard in the gatehouse who hardly bothers to look up as cars routinely drive in and out without stopping.

One of the units moved from Detrick to Dugway was the "Threat Assessment Group," which studies the vulnerability of targets to biological agents; another was a unit studying alarm systems and physical defense. The remainder were not identified. But the fact that biological warfare research and development was being relocated to a more secret site instead of being dismantled and canceled in keeping with the "ban" was then confirmed inadvertently in congressional testimony by Gen. W. C. Gribble, chief of army research and development, in 1971. Trying to explain why the army's request for funds for defensive research in biological warfare was reduced by nearly $2 million from fiscal 1971 to fiscal 1972, the general said this did not indicate a plan to shut down the biological warfare laboratory, but was caused by "the turmoil in the program of relocating it and gettting it reestablished."

Similarly, at Pine Bluff Arsenal, the biological warfare center there was to be converted into a Food and Drug Administration National Center for Toxicological Research. The army had previously admitted (December 15, 1969) that the biological warfare center at Pine Bluff was producing a variety of biological super-poisons—that is to say, extracting biotoxins from organisms or synthesizing them chemically, and manufacturing substantial quantities. The Pentagon tried hastily to retract this admission the following day by denying that it was doing what it had just said it was doing.

Then, after announcing that this biotoxin production plant was going to be transformed into an FDA Toxicology Research Center, the army proceeded to spend $1.6 million to buy automated chemical-packaging equipment for the plant. An FDA research center would have no reason to mass-produce packs of chemicals on an automated production line, but the biotoxin plant certainly would. In fact, the equipment was capable of packaging the biotoxins in plastic canisters of the sort that would be inserted into the new binary weapons—suggesting that Pine Bluff was able to produce its biotoxins in relatively safe two-part or binary form for combination in the weapon. If so, Pine Bluff was getting the jump on Congress, which did not begin funding development of the binary munitions hardware until the end of 1980, seven years after Pine Bluff acquired the packaging equipment.

Nixon refused to include biotoxins in his "ban" until February 14, 1970, allowing sufficient time for the Pine Bluff plant to be disguised as part of the new FDA "health center." Once this cover was secure, Nixon announced that he had a change of heart and would include biotoxins in his ban after all. If Pine Bluff is a health center, it is so only insofar as its products are spectacularly injurious to human health.

The handling of Senate ratification of the 1925 Geneva Protocol was also disturbing. The protocol originally was merely a compromise, but it has come to be imbued with a certain magical significance, as a metaphor of man's determination to rid the world of chemical weapons. Since it had little intrinsic value, the fact that it remained unratified by the U.S. Senate for fifty years was largely irrelevant. It became relevant only when a number of countries chose to invoke the protocol as if it were the sign of the true cross. From then on, lack of U.S. ratification became a way to scourge the U.S. government. People who did not know anything whatever about the protocol assumed that ratification would prove something important. So as pressure mounted on the American government because of the Vietnam War, Agent Orange, and the Dugway sheep kill, the White House was placed in the predicament of having either to turn over the protocol to the Senate for ratification or to bear the stigma of impeding this noble gesture.

Nixon finally sent the protocol to the Senate on August 19, 1971 —a time when he badly needed favorable press. The Senate Foreign Relations Committee, which had repeatedly joined in the righteous chorus demanding a chance to ratify the protocol, proceeded to sit on it until December 13, 1974, a full three years later. Only then, when it was absolutely certain that the American military involvement in Vietnam was over and most U.S. forces had already been withdrawn, leaving Saigon to collapse four months later, did the Senate Foreign Relations Committee finally pass the protocol to the Senate floor, where it was ratified in two days flat. From this it is abundantly clear that there was collusion with the White House and the Pentagon in the long delay, allowing Nixon to get his favorable press for valiantly moving the protocol to the Senate, but preventing the Senate from acting for three years until the coast was clear on Vietnam.

As for Edgewood Arsenal, its involvement in chemical and biological weapons development remains "unchanged," according to the army journal *Ordnance*, and it has subsequently advertised for contractors to "develop, manufacture, load, and handle ammunition, explosives, propellants, pyrotechnics, chemical, biological, and radiological materials."

At Rocky Mountain Arsenal in Denver, even the pretense of disposing of its vast stocks of war poisons has been dropped in favor of simply thumbing its nose at Denver residents and other critics. The 250 acres on which the poisons are stored are still only ten miles from downtown Denver, and provide an extraordinary target for any aircraft that have the misfortune to collide over Stapleton airport or otherwise fall to the earth on take off or landing.

The fraud of the Nixon ban raises disturbing questions about the validity of the Senate ratification of the 1925 Geneva Protocol, making it yet again a hollow document. It also raises questions about whether American negotiators trying to reach an agreement to ban all chemical and biological weapons may have been purposefully misled throughout. Understandably, these questions could derail the Pentagon effort to obtain binary weapons. Even if the Soviet Union is blatantly exterminating opposition with biological poisons, the American public may feel justified in blocking binaries after a decade of arch duplicity. However, when blocking binaries may only result in their secret procurement, it may be vital to give them public approval just to retain some civilian control and accountability. Regardless, neither Asian nor European allies are very likely to allow U.S. binaries on their soil once it is clear that the allies have no way of knowing what poisons are packed into the binaries. The political consequences would be too risky. The hill tribes of Laos and the rebels of Afghanistan, long puzzled why the chemical attacks on them have been generally ignored, may now understand that an investigation of what Russia was up to would have jeopardized matters America would also prefer to keep hidden.

The arrogance of a military high command is rational and acceptable only when it has a record of efficiency, performance, responsibility, and good judgment. Effective and competent armed forces are a proud possession for any country in any age. But the record of the Pentagon since the disastrous Inchon landing during the Korean War has been one of steadily degenerating command, in which the bungling of chemical warfare responsibilities runs parallel to the blunders of the Bay of Pigs, My Lai, the Tonkin Gulf, the *Pueblo*, and the *Mayaguez*, climaxing in the disaster of the Iranian hostage rescue mission.

The "few good men" at the lower levels are sabotaged by incompetence at the top. Instead of a massive housecleaning, each disaster only brings a fresh coating of technological veneer and new demands for more complex weapons systems. The finest weapons on earth are of little use in such circumstances. Because binaries are "safe" in their basic configuration does not mean that they will remain safe in such hands. How can a binary strike force, big or small, be made effective when the recent Pentagon effort to create a Rapid Deployment Force has only resulted in the mutation of another interservice monster?

Advances in chemical agents make poison war no longer something fought between armies in any case. Biotoxins are a direct threat to civilian survival from the first instant of conflict. Therefore, poisons may be a weapon that can no longer be left to the generals. Civilians, as the ultimate target, may have to exercise themselves to take control of these weapons away from the military. If such an effort can seriously be undertaken, in light of the congressional record to date, it may also be a suitable moment to rethink public policy toward industrial poisons as well—across the board, from pesticides to the booming new genetic-engineering field, with its capacity to produce a new spectrum of biotoxins and genetic modifiers.

The American Chemical Society, to its great credit after years of frenetically backing every expansion of industrial chemicals and the Chemical Corps, has lately joined the advocates of caution and restraint. After eighty years of playing with poisons in war and industry, the international chemical corporations from the I.G. Farben cartel to Dow and DuPont have little time left to turn matters around before we pass the point of no return in the poisoning of the planet. Recent revelations about the spread of brain cancer remind us that we are at the brink of a traumatic plunge into a grim new world where it may be impossible to find refuge from yellow rain.

Acknowledgments

There are a number of people whom I wish to thank for their help and encouragement on this book. I am particularly grateful to my children and to my immediate friends who endured, in generally good humor, four years of seemingly obsessive preoccupation. For their considerable help in providing insights, background, and data, I am especially grateful to Dr. Julian Perry Robinson of the University of Sussex, England, and to Dr. John Erickson of the University of Edinburgh, Scotland. The Queen's Coroner, Dr. H. Price, was gracious in allowing me to have access to the inquest in the case of Vladimir Simeonov. During my field trips, I received invaluable assistance and many kindnesses from the staff of SIPRI, the Stockholm International Peace Research Institute, whose multi-volume study of chemical and biological warfare remains the definitive, encyclopedic source on the subject, although it leaves many questions unanswered.

The Swedish Civil Defense Agency was also of great assistance.

In Afghanistan, Pakistan, Laos, Thailand—and several locations in the Middle East—there were occasions when the rules had to be bent to gain access to certain regions for firsthand investigation. I was given immensely valuable aid in these and other respects by a number of people who must remain anonymous.

The same applies in Washington, where some of the most valuable assistance in obtaining information and comprehension was provided by people variously involved in the intelligence community.

For assistance in coming to an elementary understanding of poisons, I must thank a number of individuals, including Dr. Leigh Thompson of Cleveland, Dr. Paul Scheuer of the University of Hawaii, and investigators at Edgewood Arsenal, Ft. Detrick, the Foreign Technology

Information Center in Charlottesville, Virginia, and at both the Defense Intelligence Agency and the Central Intelligence Agency.

At the Arms Control and Disarmament Agency, Dr. Robert Mikulak was a great help, as was Dr. Matthew Meselson at Harvard.

In Congress, Representative Jim Leach of Iowa was a consistent champion of the Hmong from the beginning, and was a driving force in pushing for a serious investigation of the poison reports from Laos against considerable official resistance and lethargy. Those in the Department of State who pushed for answers from the earliest stages, risking their careers in the process, are best unidentified—but they deserve special thanks. They have already been vindicated by the evidence found to date.

Special thanks is also owed to those who helped obtain copies of the original documents on Yemen, China, Laos and Cuba, which were buried for various reasons deep in secrecy or otherwise submerged by the passage of time. Although I found many reasons to be disturbed by what I learned of America's involvement in chemical and biological weapons development, in the end I was reassured to find a large number of enlightened, hard-working and altruistic individuals in Washington and in the field, whose efforts to resolve the mystery of the new chemical warfare were a source of inspiration. In that context, I would like to thank particularly Dr. Charles W. Lewis and Lt. Col. Charles Dennison Lane for having first led me at the Ban Vinai refugee camp to take the reports from Laos seriously.

For their early interest in the fate of the Hmong, I would also thank Gil Grosvenor and Bill Garrett of the National Geographic Society.

In the preparation of the book as a whole, and on the historical chapters in particular, I was aided in countless ways by Tom Lewis of *Time-Life* Books. The book itself would not have been possible without the tenacious and imaginative help of Edward Leslie in pursuing the more elusive research leads, and in bringing coherence to the research during the preparation of the manuscript. For their editorial insight and unstinting encouragement, I am most grateful to Rafael Sagalyn, to Peggy L. Sawyer of *Time-Life,* and to my editor at M. Evans & Company, Fred Graver.

For those who must go unnamed, there will be satisfaction enough in the fact that the book exists at all. For those already dead, let it be an epitaph.

Notes

CHAPTER 1: THE "BUGS AND GAS" ESTABLISHMENT

Since Chapter 1 serves as a general introduction to the topic of chemical warfare in our time, the sources for its information are cited in the following chapters.

CHAPTER 2: MEDICINE FROM THE SKY

Much of the substance of this chapter comes from my own observations in the field and my conversations with the man I call Jack Schramm. I have given him this nom de guerre or, rather, nom de plume, for a variety of reasons, among them the fact that he continues to cross into Laos clandestinely in the hunt for MIA remains, and the search for an elusive prisoner-of-war camp that may still contain American and other prisoners.

The rest of the information herein was drawn from sources in the departments of State and Defense, and from Dr. Charles W. Lewis, the members of his investigation team, and Hmong refugees in northern Thailand.

The description of the chemical attack is from Col. Lewis' "Final Report of DASG Investigating Team: Use of Chemical Agents Against the H'Mong [sic] in Laos." (Within his paper, the interview pages are not numbered, but are organized chronologically by the date of the incident.) The doctor's general observations come from his introduction to the report, p. 2-6.

CHAPTER 3: PILGRIMAGE TO YPRES

The principle sources for the story of Ypres and its aftermath are Victor Lefebure's *Riddle of the Rhine*, and the war diaries of particular units that participated in the battle. There were contemporary accounts of

Ypres published in the British press; other secondary sources include *SIPRI: The Problem of Chemical and Biological Warfare*, Vol. I, and Joseph Borkin, *The Crime and Punishment of I.G. Farben*. The recollections of the grenadier, the French army doctor and some other eyewitnesses are presented in Gen. Richard Thoumin's *First World War*. The "streaming mobs" scene comes from Reginald Pound's *Last Generation of 1914*. The Von Schlieffen Plan is recounted in Robert Cook's "Mist That Rolled Into The Trenches." Joseph Borkin establishes Germany's need for the components of explosives and the efforts to get them, as well as the fascinating history of the I.G. Farben cartel. The life and accomplishments of Fritz Haber are from Goran's biography, from Greenaway in the McGraw-Hill *Encyclopedia of World Biography* and from Scribners' 1981 *Dictionary of Scientific Biography*.

The wording of the Hague Convention comes from Frederic Brown, p. 7. For the British use in the Boer War see Thomas Pakenham's recent book *The Boer War* and Rayne Kruger's older volume *Good-Bye Dolly Gray*. French use is reported in SIPRI Vol. I, which also details the development of gas masks and the committees' search; I took additional details from Dr. L. F. Haber's *Gas Warfare, 1915-45*. Both Lefebure and SIPRI Vol. I describe the Stokes Mortar and the Livens Projector. The pathetic tale of the German prisoner who scorned phosgene is from Lefebure, as is the quotation of the British officer on the blinding of his own men, p. 67. The facts about mustard were gathered from Brown, Lefebure and Gilchrist. Brown is the source for the American lack of preparedness; he quotes from historian E. Gilman's lecture on "Chemical Warfare," p. 25. Brown and Gilchrist describe the resulting American experience.

The quotation on the plant at Edgewood Arsenal being the largest in the world is from Lefebure, p. 176; those by Fries and the unidentified senior CW officer are given in Brown, p. 26-8; that from Winston Churchill labeling the workers at the Ministry of Munitions as "bees of Hell" is from Brown, p. 32.

CHAPTER 4: THE GAS PROTOCOLS

I first heard the story of the American soldiers' reaction to gas rumors on Omaha Beach from Amoretta Hoeber, who was subsequently appointed Assistant Secretary of the Army for Research and Development. She had run across authoritative official accounts of the episode on the beach and used it in a white paper she wrote on chemical warfare. Mrs. Cornelius Ryan was very kind to provide insights and background details from her late husband's substantial library on the D-Day invasion. Other data came from the unit histories in the National Archives. Douglas Botting tells of Omar Bradley's anxiety in *The Second Front*.

Fries' career climb is outlined by Frederick Brown and Lefebure, who quotes his remarks on the change in warfare, p. 179; while those on the requirements of demobilization and funding come from Brown, p. 74-76. Lefebure gives the statistics for 19 months and quotes Fries on the German quitting, p. 183-4. The chief of staff who rebuffed Fries was Gen. Peyton March. Brown covers the debate over the National Defense Act, and he describes the propaganda campaigns; so does SIPRI Vol. I. The endorsement is quoted in Brown, p. 79-81. The observation on the New York recruiting posters is from *Riddle of the Rhine*, pp. 178-9. Borkin tracks Bosch's protection of the I.G. Farben cartel. Frederick Brown provides information on the Washington Naval Conference; the Hughes report ("The Savage Use of Scientific Discoveries") is quoted on p. 65. I used both Brown and SIPRI Vol. I as sources for the Geneva Protocol. Brown quotes the stirring declarations of Senator Wadsworth, the lame-duck chairman of the Military Affairs Committee, on pp. 106-7.

MacArthur's portentious prescription for outlawing war is to be found on p. 146 of William Manchester's *American Caesar*. See Rothschild on the dead-locking of the Disarmament Conference. The Italian campaign is chronicled in SIPRI Vol. I (Selassie's gas-fog attack description is on p. 144) and the same volume also covers the progress of I.G. Farben between the world wars.

Borkin is the source for the amazing Hitler-Bosch confrontation, p. 57, and the Nazi's false assumption about Allied CW capabilities. The German chemical officer was Lieutenant-General Herman Ochsner, who late in the 1940s wrote a history of his nation's chemical warfare development during World War II for the U.S. Chemical Corps. The document remained classified for many years; it is quoted in SIPRI Vol. I, p. 283.

In *Mein Kampf*, Hitler wrote graphically of his own gas experience while carrying dispatches near Ypres in the Great War: "I stumbled back with burning eyes, taking with me my last report of the war. A few hours later, my eyes had turned into burning coals; it had grown dark around me." (See Brown, p. 236). When Hitler's advisers urged him to authorize the use of nerve gas to prevent defeat at Stalingrad (according to Borkin), I.G. Farben's Otto Ambros—assuming wrongly that allied scientists had also developed nerve agents—successfully persuaded Hitler to decide against it. While others choose to believe from this that Hitler was swayed by the logic of Ambros, I suspect that he was really motivated, as in many other matters, by his irrational instincts—in this case his visceral fear of poison gas as it had stricken him.

The MacArthur quote on preparations is from Manchester, p. 89. Oschner's remarks on Russia and Great Britain are from SIPRI Vol. I, p. 308 & p. 296; they have been abridged. Leonard Shapiro explains why the Russians could not use gas in "The Great Purge," anthologized in Liddell-Hart.

CHAPTER 5: BLUE SKIES & RANCH HANDS

The promotional campaign "Operation Blue Skies," is recalled by Elinor Langer in "Research Policy—United States" and by Hersh, who also tells of the Chemical Corps traveling shows, and quotes from the *Wall Street Journal*, p. 55, and the *Washington Star*, p. 56. The Thornwell settlement was reported in the *Washington Star* on August 8, 1979.

For Perry Robinson's argument on escalation, see (3) "Chemical and Biological Warfare: Analysis . . ." (p. 20).

The statistics on the German "war machine" are from D. E. Viney in Rose and from SIPRI Vol. II, which also describes the other German nerve agents.

The French calculation that approximately 13,500 tons of German nerve agents were captured by the Western Allies at the end of WWII came from Perry Robinson. Other figures are from Viney, p. 130. In the official U.S. version of these events, those 13,500 tons do not seem to have existed.

Richard McCarthy describes the sifting of German documents after the war.

Biographical information on Amos Fries came from Frederick Brown's book on restraints, and from the Fries obituary in the *Washington Star*.

The story of the dichlor scheme is told in the Midwest Research Institute's study. The study also gives the history of the Muscle Shoals plant.

Gen. Rothschild's book is an example of the aggressive biological and chemical warfare thinking popular in the Cold War of the 1950s.

The work of Schrader and others is described in SIPRI Vol. I.

Both the Midwest Research Institute study and the *Scientific American* article by Meselson and Perry Robinson offer accounts of the Newport plant.

The story of Operation Ranch Hand is told by SIPRI Vol. I and by Hersh, who quotes the slogan on p. 155. The quotation from *National Review* was from the issue of April 1963. The recollection of the State Department official on the "humaneness" of tear gas appears in SIPRI Vol. I, p. 185.

Horst Faas' discovery and the furor it caused is from Hersh, who also quotes Dean Rusk denying the involvement of anything "wierd," (p. 169), and the *New York Times* editorial (p. 170).

SIPRI Vol. I repeats the Hanoi charges with very little comment; the figures are from the table on p. 176.

Newspapers repeatedly cite 100 million pounds as the total amount of Agent Orange spread on Vietnam, but this is actually a ballpark figure for the total of all herbicides. More than half was Agent Orange, so 50 million pounds is a conservative figure. If 100 million pounds of Agent Orange alone had been spread, my figure for dioxin would have to be increased from 300 pounds to 600 pounds.

Dioxin's effects are listed by W. A. Thomasson in "Deadly Legacy: Dioxin and the Vietnam Veteran," and by Peracchio in "Army May Have Been Informed of Dioxin Risk."

The grim story of Seveso was widely covered by the media at the time of the explosion. I have relied principally on Schloss and articles in the *New York Times*. I am not satisfied that the story of the cause of explosion is entirely as put out by officials; there were reports of NATO troops moving in to the factory to seal off the blast area, which suggests that something more suspicious than cosmetics production may have been underway at the time of the explosion. The Air Force designed the Ranch Hand Study in 1979—see Constance Holden, "Agent Orange Furor Continues to Build." The *Dagens Nyheter* story appears in Verwey, p. 185; Verwey also recounts the charges of biological weapons being stored in Thailand.

I have included more of the military's difficulties with agents on the home front in Chapter 13.

CHAPTER 6: A POLITICAL NON-EVENT

A summary of the origins of the civil war in Yemen is to be found in Dana Adams Schmidt's article "After Years of Civil War, Yemen Seems to be at Peace," cited in the bibliography as Schmidt (1). (There is, however, still no peace in Yemen two decades later, and South Yemen has become a major Soviet military base.)

Golda Meir's charges are mentioned by Hersh.

Col. Smiley's 12-page report is entitled "Chemical Warfare in Yemen"; these observations are from his p. 2.

The el Kawma attack is described in Schmidt (3) *Yemen: The Unknown War*, and in SIPRI Vol. V.

McLean's observation and Beeston's report are quoted in Schmidt (3), p. 257-8. The "no-evidence" conclusion is to be found in SIPRI Vol. V, p. 226; Schmidt also refers to the political maneuvers and the aftermath of the 1963 bombings.

SIPRI Vol. I lists the allegations of the 1963 attacks.

Smiley's reconstruction of the el Kitaf attack is from p. 7 of his report.

Schmidt (3) is the most comprehensive source for el Kitaf, including Bushrod Howard's mission and Borowiec's narrative, pp. 201-2.

SIPRI Vol. I appendix lists basic raw data of the other bombings.

Just as Smiley's fascinating account was obtained through diplomatic channels, I was able to get my hands on copies of original documents of the political maneuvering at the U.N., including correspondence between the Saudi Arabian ambassador and U Thant or Ralph Bunche. Similarly, I got copies of the ICRC's exchanges with Red Cross people in Yemen, and a transcript of the original analysis of Dr. Lauppi. The signed reports of the Saudi chemists that came into my hands were contemporary translations from the Arabic.

Most interesting of all was the original medical report of the Najran Hospital dated January 8, 1967, which had previously been buried in secrecy for reasons that are not entirely clear. It is a great pity that it was not made widely available at the time or, barring that, made available more recently when the puzzling reports from Laos first began to be taken seriously. It is entirely likely that its significance was not understood, so it remained locked in high security classification where nobody was able to glance at it to determine if it was relevant or not.

All these original documents of that forgotten war, now not forgotten anymore, are cited here under the banket title "Exchange of Communications Between the Representative of Saudi Arabia & U.N. Secretary General U Thant." Since the reader might find it as difficult to obtain these documents as I did. I offer the following secondary sources that touch to some degree on the same points:

The Red Cross team's demand for gas masks is mentioned in Schmidt (3); the Geneva cable traffic is reproduced in SIPRI Vol. V, p. 230, which also details British reaction to the attacks and the Egyptian denial, p. 232. U Thant's assertion that facts are in dispute comes in Schmidt (3), p. 263; the doctor's quote is from SIPRI Vol. V, p. 228.

The non-events are drawn from SIPRI Vol. I appendix as well as from SIPRI Vol. V and Schmidt (3). Smiley's pungent comments are to be found on p. 9 of his report.

I relied equally on SIPRI Vol. V and Schmidt (3) for the basic story of the Red Cross-Gahar incidents. Cesaretti is quoted in the latter, p. 235-6, and Rochat in the former, p. 264. Volume V also reproduces the ICRC statement of June 2, 1967, and the summary conclusion of Dr. Lauppi's analysis (p. 232-5) which were published in the June 3, 1967, issue of *U.S. News & World Report* (p. 60). See also SIPRI Vol. V for the Saudi Arabian chemist's findings of high phosphorous levels.

In "Egypt Stored Nerve Gas Before War," Marquis Childs tells of Israeli efforts to buy gas masks and injectors. Childs' reporting of the Edgewood scientists' tests is from the same article.

CHAPTER 7: A VISIT TO THE HINDU KUSH

This chapter is based largely on material collected firsthand along the Afghan border and in neighboring Pakistan, but there were a number of other sources as well. In the summer of 1980, the State Department collected a large and diverse set of reports that it compiled and distributed under the title "Reports of the Use of Chemical Weapons in Afghanistan, Laos and Kampuchea." The published document was difficult to read and poorly organized, so that it made little sense to the uninitiated. Its greatest virtue was that it demonstrated the surprising number of reports then circulating. The problems arose in part because, after the classified intelligence reports had all sensitive details deleted, they were turned over to a bunch of summer interns at State to massage together. The State Department was so sensitive to charges that it was fabricating all these reports that it bent over backwards to not even edit them smoothly—and was denounced for fabricating it by many foreign critics anyway. However, I had an unexpected opportunity to examine many of the original intelligence reports, as they existed prior to any deletions, and concluded that some of them were very reliable indeed. I have used some of the reliable ones here, and otherwise stuck to reports that I could substantiate in the field.

Among the reports in the published compendium that I was able to confirm in one way or another are first- and third-person accounts including the assaults near Feyzabad, Beharak and Sebak, which appear on pp. 6-7 of the State Department document.

The most valuable analyses of the U.S.S.R.'s chemical equipment and troop-training were John Erickson's (1) "Soviet Chemical Warfare Capabilities," and (3) "The Soviet Union's Growing Arsenal of Chemical Weapons"; Julian Perry Robinson's (3) "Chemical and Biological Warfare: Analysis . . ." and (4) "Chemical Warfare Capabilities of the Warsaw Pact and North Atlantic Treaty Organization"; and, finally, John Westerhoff's *CBR Protection of the Soviet Ground Forces,* obtained from the Defense Intelligence Agency. The reader may find the subtle differences in Erickson and Perry Robinson more significant on knowing that they represent opposing schools of thought. Erickson's analyses represent a solid military backgrounding while Perry Robinson's demonstrate a scientific humanism. As I admire both, and respect their viewpoints, I have tried wherever possible to use the source that seemed most appropriate to the immediate circumstance, that is to err in favor of Erickson on purely military matters, and to err toward Perry Robinson on scientific or non-military concerns.

Erickson (1) points out the defensive nature of the Soviet chemical corps. The lack of Soviet preparation for poison gas in WWI is remarked on by Westerhoff.

Trotsky's crushing of the Kronstadt rebels is recorded in most good histories and is recounted again along with the continual upgrading of Soviet chemical capabilities in the decades following the Revolution, by Col. V. Pozdnyakov. His essay, "The Chemical Arm," appears in Sir Basil Liddell-Hart's book, *The Red Army*. Westerhoff is the source for the 1927 civil defense instruction program. The Pozdnyakov quote on the power of CW is to be found in his essay, p. 384; those on all-weather chemical agents and the modern level of Soviet research, p. 286.

Westerhoff evaluates the performance of Soviet soldiers in WWII; for truly comprehensive descriptions of present day Soviet chemical vehicles, equipment, and training, see Erickson (1) and Westerhoff.

CHAPTER 8: EYE OF NEWT, TOE OF FROG

Stashinsky's biography was nicely narrated by John Steele in his *Life* Magazine article, "Assassin Disarmed by Love"; Bandera's biographical notes are from "The Partisan" in *Time,* and "Ukrainian Rebel Dies in Mystery" from the *New York Times.* Steele's account of the Bandera murder (p. 70A & 72) differs slightly from that in "The Partisan" (p. 20), although the *Life* and *Time* staffs had access to the same correspondents' files. Stashinsky's disenchantment, I think, is reasonably explained by Steele, although we are left to wonder how his parents had so deeply offended him, if indeed they had. Stashinsky might very well have informed on them for no reason whatever.

The basic facts on botulin are taken from the article in *Encyclopedia Britannica 3, Micropedia* Vol. III.

The early uses of poisons are described by C. J. Tedeschi in *Forensic Medicine* Vol. III, and in the *McGraw-Hill Encyclopedia* Vol. V.

The more sophisticated French application is related in *Affair of Poisons,* by Frances Mossiker, which makes spellbinding reading. There are any number of accounts of Rasputin's murder—all of them at odds with one another over particulars; one of the best-known is from Robert Massie's *Nicholas and Alexandra.*

Tedeschi is filled with fascinating information on natural poisons, including ricin; it is Tedeschi who quotes the Reese textbook, p. 1456.

I was able to obtain a copy of the list in the East German manual through the U.S. Army's Medical Intelligence Division at Ft. Detrick.

"Of Dart Guns and Poisons" *Time,* provides specifics on Project M. K. Naomi.

Dr. Paul J. Scheuer's study, "Marine Toxins," is especially valuable on the performance of saxitoxin because he is one of the world's foremost experts in the field and participated in the original studies of palytoxin and other marine poisons.

Powers' option to use saxitoxin, and the details of President Nixon's 1970 order, are from "Of Dart Guns . . ." while Morton Halperin's "CIA Denying What's Not in Writing" recounts the Agency's disingenuousness; he quotes the memo explaining the director's contingency option (p. 12); *Time* lists some of the other "exotic" poisons and drugs in the CIA closet.

The story of Markov's life and death is reported in "Bulgarian Defector Found Dead" and James Peipert's "Markov Died of Blood Poisoning," both printed in the *New York Times;* additional details were gleaned from the unpublished lecture notes of Cleveland toxicologist Dr. Leigh Thompson, who has had at least one celebrated ricin poisoning case in his home town when a marital quarrel led a housewife to swallow commercially available castor bean seeds from a seed packet (thanks to his quick action, she survived and recovered).

The provocative details of the Simeonov case came from the official inquest before Her Majesty's Coroner's Court on Queen's Road in Walthamstow.

Further details and insights were provided privately by persons who participated in the investigation.

CHAPTER 9: RAMPAGE OF PESTILENCE

For information on palytoxin and venoms, see J. S. Wiles, "Toxicological Evaluation of Palytoxin in Several Animal Species"; F. E. Russell, *Snake Venom Poisoning;* and the published research papers of Dr. James A. Vick, late of Edgewood Arsenal, who is probably better informed on biological toxins than most other Western investigators.

H. E. Jacob's *Six Thousand Years of Bread* is a comprehensive and fascinating history including ergot and other fungal bread poisons; the quotation, which is abridged, is to be found on p. 122.

Thomas Wyllie describes the Russian harvesting methods in Vol. 3 of his work on mycotoxins.

The unpublished paper on ATA and mycotoxins that I refer to as the Ft. Detrick Report was put together for interagency use by intelligence officers in January 1981, by the U.S. Army Medical Intelligence Division at Ft. Detrick; the quotation is from pp. 3-4.

The effects of arsenic are taken from an *HEW* publication, *Health Effects of Occupational Lead and Arsenic Exposure* and from *Arsenic,* by the National Research Council. Tedeschi Vol. III was also consulted.

Meselson's argument in favor of a modified adamsite was made in one of several lengthy telephone conversations in the winter of 1980-1981.

CHAPTER 10: MYTH AND REALITY

The scenario of British and American troops being attacked with chemicals comes from Sir John Hackett's recent book *The Third World War*, p. 185; the casualties of such an attack are projected on the following page. On p. 204, Hackett suggests that the Americans would retaliate in kind. Messrs. Meselson and Perry Robinson make a valuable contribution to understanding the threat to civilians with their article "Chemical Warfare and Chemical Disarmament" in the April, 1980, issue of *Scientific American*; the quote is from p. 44.

The Meselson/Perry Robinson piece provides extensive information on NATO equipment; the quote on the objective of U.S. policy is from p. 46. Elsewhere, Perry Robinson draws attention to European fears about CW; in this section, I have relied on several of his papers (3) "Chemical and Biological Warfare: Analysis . . ."; (4) "Chemical Warfare Capabilities . . ."; and (5) "Chemical Weapons for NATO?" The excerpts from Healy and the German White Paper are from Perry Robinson (5), p. 38.

Readers interested in a more politically conservative argument for chemical rearmament should obtain Amoretta Hoeber's crisp and lucid essay "The Neglected Threat of Chemical Warfare," which demonstrates that there are excellent arguments on both sides of this issue.

The quotes from Gen. Pikolov come from an article in the Soviet army journal, *Red Star*.

CHAPTER 11: DIG TUNNELS DEEP

One of the sources I used for background on the conflict between Hanoi and Peking was Bruce Larkin's "China and Asia: the Year of the China-Vietnam War." The Kyodo poison gas story is from the FBIS-Daily Record, February 22, 1979, p. 2A. Kyodo stations only its best people in Peking, and in my experience their reports have been unusually reliable. It is also significant that there was no follow-up story whatever, indicating that the Chinese clamped down tight on the story. This would also explain why other journalists inquiring into the rumors were firmly turned away.

Prime Minister Harry Lee's remark was reported by Congressman "Sonny" Montgomery during the course of a House Armed Services Committee "top secret" hearing on Afghanistan on March 3, 1980, p. 31.

Leo Liu, "The Chinese People's Liberation Army," notes the network of tunnels located under major cities in China, and he quotes the exhortation to heighten vigilance.

After President Nixon went to China, quite a few American correspondents were allowed into the country, some of whom were shown tunnels in various locations; among those giving extensive coverage to the system were John Burns ("Westerners See Peking's Tunnels"), Marilyn Burger ("China Notebook") and Michael Chinoy ("The Tunnels of Manchuria"). Mao's quotation is from Chinoy, p. 653. (I have abridged it.)

Phillip Peterson evaluates various potential strategies for a Sino-Soviet conflict in an article for *Military Review.* Harold C. Hinton's "Moscow and Peking Since Mao" offers insights into recent Chinese political struggles. Those wishing to know more about Russian military strategy might read John Erickson (2); he suggests that the Soviet intention is to encircle China, p. 38.

Rothschild expounds his theory on spreading germs over China on p. 82-4 of his book. David L. Shambaugh, "China's Quest For Military Modernization," is a good supplement to Liu on Chinese advances in war technology.

For general insight on China's predicament, see *The Far Eastern Economic Review,* particularly the articles of Richard Nations.

CHAPTER 12: THE SORCERERS' APPRENTICES

Lois Ember summarizes the Defense Science Board findings in an impressive essay, "Chemical Weapons: Build Up or Disarm?" The Midwest Research Institute report describes the Muscle Shoals Project. Statistics on binaries come from "Old Fears . . ." in the November 10, 1980, issue of the *Defense Monitor,* and from Colin Norman in the *Progressive.* The Navy decision and the Big Eye development is from a paper made available to me by Congressman Ichord's office, "Fact Sheet: Subject: Binary Chemical Munitions."

Ember explains the workings of the 155mm artillery projectile and other binary designs; the GB and VX projectile statistics are from "Old Fears . . ."

Malcolm Browne gives the figure of 955 leaks in the *Times.*

Colin Norman describes the intricacies of the M-34 cluster bomb as well as the Army's paper work complaints with the EPA. My recitation of efforts to upgrade the CW capabilities of the U.S. forces is drawn from Malcolm Browne, from Lois Ember, and from George Wilson's article in *The Washington Post,* "Disposal of Poison Chemical Weapons Seen Costing the Pentagon Billions."

Perry Robinson has voiced the same argument several times; perhaps his clearest statement of it is in (3) March 1980 paper analyzing rumors of Russian CW use. The Mikulak quote is from Ember, p. 26.

Verwei gives methods for detecting organophosphorous in his *Science* article. Amoretta Hoeber's remark is quoted in Ember, p. 27.

Ichord made his argument in a "Statement Before the Subcommittee on Defense," p. 5-7; he retells the story of the Pine Bluff critic in his "Letter to the Secretary of the Army," p. 1.

Dr. Eyring made his comment in a presentation ("Advantages of the Two Component Chemicals in Munitions") during an American Chemical Society symposium (1). The quotation on the loathesomeness of most forms of war comes from Malcolm's Browne's article in the *Times*, p. 38.

C. L. Sulzberger documents the tactics used to pass funding for Pine Bluff in "House Action on Bill Revives Fight." The financial particulars come from Ichord's "Statement." Gordon Burck gives details of the Pine Bluff project overall in "Chemical Arms: a Pandora's Box."

In his lecture before the ACS symposium (1) entitled "Binary Chemical Weapons: Details, Difficulties, and Dangers," Robert Rutman raises questions about testing and suggests that the properties of binaries may negate their effectiveness. The selling of these weapons as safety devices is recommended in Ichord's July 30, 1975 letter. In addition to the sources mentioned above, readers interested in the binary controversy might want to look at the *Atlantic* article by John Hanahan.

CHAPTER 13: THE POGO EQUATION

Readers wishing to know more about any of the events described in the time-line should remember when looking them up in the *Times* that the date I have used for any particular event is usually the date that the event occurred, not the date that the article was published; the article usually appeared on the following day.

Bibliography

"ACS Testifies Against Chemical Warfare." *Chemical & Engineering News.* May 13, 1974.

"Affair of Poisons." *Encyclopedia Britannica 3.* Chicago: Encyclopedia Britannica, 1972.

After Action Reports (June 1944): 5th Corps, 1st & 29th Divisions, 16th & 116th Infantry Regiments; 81st, 13th & 31st Chemical Corps. Washington: Department of Defense, 1944.

American Chemical Society [ACS]. (1) "Binary Weapons and the Problem of Chemical Disarmament—A Symposium." Washington: American Chemical Society, 1976.

—————. (2) "Chemical Weapons and U.S. Public Policy—A Symposium." Washington: American Chemical Society, 1974.

"Authority for the Department of Defense to Sell Stocks of the Chemical Carbonylchloride [Phosgene]." *Report No. 94-635, 94th Congress.* Washington: U.S. Government Printing Office, 1975.

Bacon, Kenneth. "Soviet Threat Spurs U.S. Proposal to Make Chemical Weapons Again." *The Wall Street Journal,* June 26, 1980.

Beckett, Brian. "Chemical Warfare is Available to Terrorists." *New Scientist,* October 12, 1978.

—————. "Patently Obvious." *New Scientist,* October 19, 1978.

Berger, Marilyn. "China Notebook (VII)." *The Washington Post,* March 4, 1973.

Bétit, Major Eugene D. "Political Control of the Soviet Armed Forces." DIA Paper #DDB-2600-1279-78. Washington: Defense Intelligence Agency, 1978.

Borkin, Joseph. *The Crime and Punishment of I.G. Farben.* New York: The Free Press, 1978.

297

Botting, Douglas. *The Second Front*. Alexandria, Virginia: Time-Life Books, 1978.

Bove, Frank James. *The Story of Ergot*. New York: S. Karger, 1970.

Bree, Betsy (ed.). *Review of Soviet Ground Forces*. Washington: Defense Intelligence Agency, 1980.

"British Demonstrate Protective Gear for Chemical Warfare Use." *Aviation Week and Space Technology*, May 19, 1980.

Brcphy, Leo P. et al. *United States Army in World War II: Technical Services from Laboratory to Field*. Washington: Department of the Army, 1959.

_____ and George J. B. Fisher. *United States Army in World War II: The Technical Services: The Chemical Warfare Service: Organizing for War*. Washington: Office of the Chief of Military History, 1959.

Brown, Frederick J. *Chemical Warfare: A Study in Restraints*. Princeton: Princeton University Press, 1968.

Browne, Malcolm W. "Military Backing Chemical Warfare." *The New York Times*, February 24, 1980.

"Bulgarian Defector Found Dead." *The New York Times*, October 3, 1978.

Burck, Gordon. "Chemical Arms: a Pandora's Box." *The New York Times*, October 5, 1980.

Burns, John. "Westerners See Peking's Tunnels." *The New York Times*, April 15, 1973.

"CBW—an Unresolved Horror." *Bulletin of Atomic Scientists*, June 1980.

Carnegie Endowment for International Peace. *Chemical Arms Control*. New York: 1978.

_____. *The Control of Chemical and Biological Weapons*. New York: 1971.

Carter, Luther J. "Approval Sought for Nerve Gas Pilot Plant." *Science*, December 7, 1979.

Chaliand, Gerard. "Bargain War." *New York Review of Books*, April 12, 1981.

"Chemical Arms a Sea of Troubles." *Nature*, April 3, 1980.

Chemical Disarmament. New York, The Humanities Press, 1975.

"Chemical Warfare . . ." LIFE, June 19, 1944.

Clarkc, Robin. *The Silent Weapons*. New York: David McKay, 1968.

Childs, Marquis W. "Egypt Stored Nerve Gas Before the War." *St. Louis Post-Dispatch*, June 18, 1967.

Chinoy, Michael. "The Tunnels of Manchuria." *The Nation*, December 17, 1973.

Colbert, Evelyn. "Poison Gas Use in Indochina." Department of State Bulletin. Washington: Government Printing Office, 1980.

Conrad, J. Lyle et al. "Epidemiological Investigation of Marburg Virus Disease." *American Journal of Tropical Disease*, November, 1978.

"Containing Andromeda." *New England Journal of Medicine*, October 13, 1977.

Cook, Robert E. "Mist That Rolled Into the Trenches." *Bulletin of Atomic Scientists*, January, 1971.

Cookson, John & Judith Nottingham. *A Survey of Chemical and Biological Warfare*. London: Sheed & Ward, 1969.

Doak, G. O. et al. "Arsenic Compounds." *Kirk-Othmer Encyclopedia of Chemical Technology*. New York: John Wiley & Sons, 1978.

Ember, Lois R. "Chemical Weapons: Build or Disarm?" *Chemical and Engineering News*, December 15, 1980.

Erickson, John. (1) "Soviet Chemical Warfare Capabilities." Edinburgh: University of Edinburgh, 1979.

——————. (2) "Soviet Military Policy in the 1980s." *Current History*, October, 1978.

——————. (3) "The Soviet Union's Growing Arsenal of Chemical Warfare." *Strategic Review*, Fall, 1979.

"Exchange of Communications Between the Representative of Saudi Arabia, Ambassador Jamil M. Baroody, and U.N. Secretary General U Thant." Unpublished. New York, 1967.

Farber, Eduard. "Haber." *Nobel Prize Winners in Chemistry*. New York, 1953.

"4th Division Denies Report That Gas Killed 30 GIs." *The New York Times*, November 11, 1967.

"GIs in Highlands Battle a Large Enemy Force." *The New York Times*, November 9, 1967.

Gage, Nicholas. "Islamic Zeal and Talent For War Help Afghan Rebels to Hold Out." *The New York Times*, July 20, 1980.

Gilchrist, H. L. *A Comparative Study of the World War Casualties From Gas and Other Weapons*. Washington, 1928.

"Going Public With The VX Formula—Recipe For Trouble?" *Science*, February 7, 1975.

Goran, Morris. *The Story of Fritz Haber*. Norman, Oklahoma: University of Oklahoma, 1967.

Greenaway, Frank. "Haber." *McGraw-Hill Encyclopedia of World Biography*. New York: McGraw-Hill, 1953.

Haber, L. Fritz. *Gas Warfare 1915-1945*. New York: 1979.

Hackett, Sir John, et al. *The Third World War*. New York: Berkley, 1980.

Haldane, J. B. S. *Calinicus: A Defense of Chemical Warfare*. New York: Garland, 1972.

Halperin, Morton H. "CIA: Denying What's Not in Writing." *New Republic*, October 4, 1975.

Halstead, Bruce W. *Poisonous and Venomous Marine Animals of the World*. Princeton: Princeton University Press, 1978.

Handbook of the Chinese Armed Forces. Washington: Defense Intelligence Agency, 1976.

Harris, B. L. et al, "Chemicals in War." *Kirk-Othmer Encyclopedia of Chemical Technology*. New York: John Wiley & Sons, 1978.

Henahan, John F. "The Nerve Gas Controversy." *Atlantic*, September, 1974.

Hersh, Seymour M. *Chemical and Biological Warfare: America's Hidden Arsenal*. New York: Bobbs-Merrill, 1968.

Hinton, Harold C. "Moscow and Peking Since Mao." *Current History*, October, 1978.

Hoeber, Amoretta M. and Joseph D. Douglas Jr. "The Neglected Threat of Chemical Warfare. *International Security*, Summer, 1978.

Holden, Constance. "Agent Orange Furor Continue to Build." *Science*, June 22, 1979.

Hovey, Graham. "Refugees from Laos Tell of Gas Attack." *The New York Times*, November 4, 1979.

"How Nasser Used Poison Gas: Statements and Medical Report." *U.S. News & World Report*, July 3, 1967.

Hurwitz, Elliott and Lois Lembo. "The Looming Chemical Warfare." *The Baltimore Sun*, March 8, 1981.

Ichord, Cong. Richard H. "Deadly Threat of Soviet Chemical Warfare." *Reader's Digest*, September, 1979.

_____. "Fact Sheet: Subject: Binary Modernization."

_____. "Letter to Secretary of the Army." July 30, 1975.

_____. "Statement Before the Subcommitte on Defense, House Committee on Appropriations." July 1, 1980.

Imbeck, Klaus. "With Allah on Our Side." *GEO*, December, 1980.

"In New Detail—Nasser's Gas War." *U.S. News & World Report*, July 10, 1967.

Jacob, H. E. *Six Thousand Years of Bread*. Westport, Connecticut: 1944.

Kenley, Richard. "Chemical Weapons Production." [Letter] *Chemical & Engineering News*, January 26, 1981.

"A Killer's Confession." *Newsweek*, December 4, 1961.

Kleber, Brooks E. and Dale Birdsell. *The Chemical Warfare Service: Chemicals in Combat*. Washington: Office of the Chief of Military History, 1966.

Kruger, Rayne. *Good-Bye Dolly Gray: The Story of the Boer War*. New York: 1960.

Larkin, Bruce D. "China and Asia: The Year of the China-Vietnam War." *Current History*, September, 1979.

"Last Carter Message on Military Urges Updating of Arsenal." *The Washington Post*, February 15, 1981.

Lefebure, Victor. *The Riddle of the Rhine: Chemical Strategy in Peace and War.* New York: Chemical Foundation, 1923.

Lenorovitz, J. M. "USAF Trains Against Chemical Warfare." *Aviation Week and Space Technology*, July 23, 1979.

Lewis, Col. Charles W. et al. *Final Report of DASG Investigating Team: Use of Chemical Agents Against the H'Mong in Laos.*

Liddell-Hart, Sir Basil. *The Red Army.* Gloucester, Massachusetts: Peter Smith, 1968.

Liu, Leo Y. "The Chinese People's Liberation Army." *Current History*, September, 1978.

"London Court Rules Bulgarian Was Poisoned." *The New York Times*, January 3, 1979.

Lundin, S. J. "Chemical Weapons: Too Late for Disarmament?" *Bulletin of Atomic Scientists*, December, 1979.

Manchester, William. *American Caesar.* Boston: Little, Brown, 1978.

Massie, Robert K. *Nicholas and Alexandra.* New York: Atheneum, 1967.

McCarthy, Cong. Richard D. *The Ultimate Folly.* New York: Knopf, 1969.

Meselson, Matthew. "Behind the Nixon Policy for Chemical and Biological Warfare." *Bulletin of Atomic Scientists*, January, 1970.

_____. *Chemical Weapons and Chemical Arms Control.* New York, 1977.

_____. "Gas Warfare and the Geneva Protocol of 1925." *Bulletin of Atomic Scientists*, February, 1972.

_____ and Julian P. Perry Robinson. "Chemical Warfare and Chemical Disarmament." *Scientific American*, April, 1980.

_____ and Stephen Meyer. "Before We Spend Billions on Chemical Weapons." *The New York Times*, November 12, 1980.

Midwest Research Institute. "Studies on the Technical Arms Control Aspects of Chemical and Biological Warfare." Washington: Arms Control and Disarmament Agency, 1972.

Mossiker, Frances. *The Affair of the Poisons.* New York, 1969.

National Research Council. *Arsenic.* Washington, 1977.

National Technical Information Service. *Chemical and Biological Warfare, A Bibliography in 5 Parts,* Springfield, Virginia, 1980.

Neilands, J. B. et al. *Harvest of Death.* New York: Free Press, 1972.

"Nerve Gas Detection is Almost Human." *New Scientist*, August 10, 1978.

Norman, Colin. "Binary Weapons." *Progressive*, December, 1973.

"Of Dart Guns and Poisons." TIME, September 29, 1975.

"Old Fears . . ." *Defense Monitor*, November 10, 1980.

Pakenham, Thomas. *The Boer War.* New York, 1979.

"The Partisan." TIME, November 2, 1959.

Peipert, James R. "Markov Died of Blood Poisoning." *The New York Times,* September 13, 1978.

Peracchio, Adrian. "Army May Have Been Informed of Dioxin Risk." *The Washington Post,* October 16, 1980.

Perry Robinson, Julian P. (1) "Binary Nerve Gas Weapons." *Chemical Weapons: New Weapons for Old.* New York: SIPRI, 1975.

_____(2) *Chemical/Biological Warfare.* Los Angeles, 1974.

_____(3) "Chemical and Biological Warfare: Analyses of Recent Reports Concerning the Soviet Union and Vietnam." ADIU Occasional Paper No. 1. University of Sussex, March, 1980.

_____(4) "Chemical Warfare Capabilities of the Warsaw Pact and North Atlantic Treaty Organizations: An Overview from Open Sources." *Chemical Weapons Destruction & Conversion.* London: SIPRI, 1980.

_____(5) "Some Implications of Binary Nerve Gas Weapons." *Chemical Weapons & U.S. Public Policy.* Washington, 1974.

_____(6) "Special Case of Chemical and Biological Weapons." *Bulletin of Atomic Scienists,* May, 1975.

Petersen, Phillip. A. "Possible Courses of a Military Conflict Between the USSR and the PRC." *Military Review,* March 1977.

"Playing Russian Roulette." TIME, March 13, 1978.

Pryor, Sen. David. "Let's Stay Out of the Nerve Gas Business." *The Washington Post,* September 9, 1980.

"Rep. Tenzer Says GI Reports Enemy Kills 30 With Gas." *The New York Times,* November 10, 1967.

"Reports on the Use of Chemical Weapons in Afghanistan, Laos and Kampuchea." Washington: Department of State, 1980.

Rodricks, Joseph V. et al. *Mycotoxins in Human and Animal Health.* Forest Park South, Illinois, 1977.

Rose, Steven (ed.). *CBW: Chemical and Biological Warfare.* Boston: Beacon Press, 1968.

Rothschild, Brig. Gen. J. H. (Ret.). *Tomorrow's Weapons.* New York: McGraw-Hill, 1964.

Russel, F. E. *Snake Venom Poisoning.* New York, 1979.

SIPRI [Stockholm International Peace Research Institute.] *Chemical Disarmament: New Weapons for Old.* New York, 1975.

_____. *Chemical Weapons: Destruction & Conversion.* London, 1980.

_____. *Delayed Toxic Effects of Chemical Warfare Agents.* New York, 1975.

_____. "Dioxin: A Potential CW Agent." *World Armaments &*

Disarmament: SIPRI YEARBOOK 1977. Cambridge, Massachusetts, 1977.

_____. *Ecological Consequences of the Second Indochina War.* Stockholm, 1976.

_____. *The Problem of Chemical and Biological Warfare.* Vols. I-IV. New York, 1973.

_____. *Warfare in a Fragile World: Military Impact on the Human Environment.* London, 1980.

Scheuer, Paul J. "Marine Toxins." *Accounts of Chemical Research.* February, 1977.

Schloss, Edith. "The Poisoning of Italy." *The Nation,* October 16, 1976.

Schmidt, Dana Adams. (1) "After Years of Civil War, Yemen Seems to be at Peace." *The New York Times,* August 4, 1969.

_____. (2) "Royalists in Yemen Move to Mount New Drive in 6-Year War." *The New York Times,* March 15, 1968.

_____. (3) *Yemen: The Unknown War.* New York, 1968.

Seagrave, Sterling. "Deadly Signs of Medicine from the Sky." *The Washington Star,* May 4, 1980.

Shambaugh, David L. "China's Quest for Military Modernization." *Asian Affairs,* May/June, 1979.

Shawcross, William. *Sideshow: Kissinger, Nixon, and the Destruction of Cambodia.* New York: Simon & Schuster, 1979.

Sim, Van M. "Chemicals Used as Weapons in War." *Drill's Pharmacology in Medicine.* New York, 1971.

Smiley, Col. David deC. "Chemical Warfare in Yemen," Unpublished.

"Somewhat Alarmed." *The Wall Street Journal,* May 20, 1980.

Stohretal, Col. R. *Chemical Warfare Agents and Protection Against Chemical Agents.* East Berlin, 1977.

Steele, John. "Assassin Disarmed by Love." LIFE, September 7, 1962.

"Strategic Implications of Chemical and Biological Warfare." Hearings Before the [House] Subcommittee on International Security and Scientific Affairs, of the Committee on Foreign Affairs. 96th Congress. April 24, 1980.

Sulzberger, C. L. "House Action on Bill Revives Fight." *The New York Times,* August 26, 1980.

Tedeschi, C. G. et al. *Forensic Medicine.* Vol. III. Philadelphia; W. B. Saunders, 1977.

Thomasson, W A. "Deadly Legacy: Dioxin and the Vietnam Veteran." *Bulletin of Atomic Scientists.*

Thoumin, Gen. Richard. *First World War.* New York, 1964.

Trevor-Roper, H. R. *The European Witch-Craze of the 16th and 17th Centuries.* New York: Harper & Row, 1969.

"Ukrainian Exile Chief a Victim of Poison." *The New York Times,* October 20, 1959.

"Ukrainian Rebel Dies in Mystery." *The New York Times*, October 17, 1959.

"Use of Chemical Agents in Southeast Asia Since the Vietnam War." Hearing before the [House] Subcommittee on Asian and Pacific Affairs of the Committee on Foreign Affairs. 96th Congress, December 12, 1979.

"Vapour Chase on Salisbury Plain." *New Scientist*, October 25, 1979.

Verwei, Albert et al. "Chemical Warfare Agents: Verification of Compounds Containing the Phosphorous = Methyl Linkage in Waste Water." *Science*, May 11, 1979.

Verwey, Wil D. *Riot Control Agents and Herbicides in War*. Leyden, 1977.

Vick, James A. "Effects of Actual Snakebite and Venom Injection on Vital Physiological Functions." Paper. Edgewood. n.d.

_____ and Joseph Wiles, "The Mechanism of Action and Treatment of Palytoxin." *Toxicology and Applied Pharmacology*. Vol. 34. November, 1975.

_____ et al. *Pathophysiological Studies of Ten Poisonous Snake Venoms*. Edgewood, 1966.

Westeroff, John H. *CBR Protection of Soviet Ground Forces*. Washington: Defense Intelligence Agency, 1980.

Wiles, J. S. "Toxicological Evaluation of Palytoxin in Several Animal Species." TOXICON, 1974.

Wilson, George C. "Disposal of Poison Chemical Weapons Seen Costing the Pentagon Billions." *The Washington Post*, March 15, 1981.

Wyllie, Thomas D. and Lawrence G. Morehouse. *Mycotoxins and Mycotoxicosis: An Encyclopedic Handbook*. Vols. 1 & 3. New York, 1977.

Wolfe, Martin L. "Containment of Dangerous Contagions." *New England Journal of Medicine*, December 15, 1977.

Index